Poverty and social sec[urity]

KU-516-999

CN 368.4

AN 53686

LIBRARY AND LEARNING RESOURCES CENTRE
Northern College, Barnsley. S75 3ET

Please return this book by the last date stamped below.

30 NOV 1995
13 DEC 1995
09 MAR 1998
19 MAR 1998
20 APR 1998
22 MAY 1998
11.12.98
4/1/98
5/3/99
8/5
26.3.99
19.4.99
10.5.99
21 7 99
19.8.99
2/3/01
3/4/09

...ces –
youth
...essed
...d for
...fined
...pond

..., the
...ions
... on
...nefit
...ems

...cial
...ing
...ent
...nts
...and

...e.

Northern College Library
NC02321

BARNSLEY
CANCELLED

[illegible] and social security

[illegible] experience, but a [illegible] wrapped in blankets who [illegible] cardboard box on the street [illegible] not only between societies [illegible] kinds of [illegible] enable [illegible]

[illegible] explores the disparate [illegible] poverty [illegible] which it can be understood in practice, and the [illegible] those professionals who must deal with [illegible] assistance, Paul Spicker considers [illegible]

Poverty and social security

Concepts and principles

Paul Spicker

London and New York

First published in 1993
by Routledge
11 New Fetter Lane, London EC4P 4EE

Simultaneously published in the USA and Canada by Routledge
a division of Routledge, Chapman and Hall Inc.
29 West 35th Street, New York, NY 10001

© 1993 Paul Spicker

Typeset by NWL Editorial Services, Langport, Somerset

Printed and bound in Great Britain by
Mackays of Chatham PLC, Chatham, Kent

All rights reserved. No part of this book may be reprinted or reproduced or utilized in any form or by any electronic, mechanical, or other means, now known or hereafter invented, including photocopying and recording, or in any information storage or retrieval system, without permission in writing from the publishers.

British Library Cataloguing in Publication Data
A catalogue record for this book is available from the British Library.

Library of Congress Cataloging in Publication Data
Spicker, Paul
Poverty and social security: concepts and principles /
by Paul Spicker.
p. cm.
1. Social security – Great Britain. 2. Poor – Great Britain.
I. Title.
HD7165.S65 1992 92–11699
362.5′8′0941 – dc20 CIP

ISBN 0–415–05935–6 (hbk)
ISBN 0–415–05936–4 (pbk)

Contents

Tables

Preface

This book is concerned with the ways in which poverty can be defined and identified, and the responses which have been made to the problems of poverty in the development of financial assistance for people who are poor. The first part of the book is concerned with the idea of poverty, the way it has been operationalised, and the kinds of responses which might be made to it. The second part is concerned with social security: its connection with poor relief, the way in which benefit systems operate, and the extent to which such systems do effectively relieve poverty.

On the face of it, this seems straightforward enough as a field for a critical study; on closer examination, though, the focus may seem difficult to justify. The definition of the subject matter depends crucially on a set of conventional interpretations about the ideas of 'poverty' and 'social security'. If the idea of 'poverty' was to be examined adequately, it probably ought to be considered in much wider terms than a consideration of financial assistance would imply; equally, any proper consideration of income maintenance would touch on many topics beyond the relief of poverty. The justification for a narrower focus is in large part centred on a particular kind of problem: the discussion of what sort of benefits should be provided for the relief of poverty, and at what level they should be provided. This problem has been dominant historically in the development of services, and continues to be a major concern in the debates about social security today. The debates around this issue have to a large extent affected the way in which the issues of poverty and poor relief are discussed.

The purpose of the book is, then, to discuss a set of problems and responses. It does this principally by considering a range of interrelated concepts. For reasons which I explain in the text, the book does not offer any authoritative definition of the problems, an approach which I know might drive some readers to distraction. The method has more to do with social philosophy than with social science. What it does is to outline options, and ways of thinking about the issues, in the hope that it will help to establish an understanding of the relationship between poverty and social security, and inform discussion in the future.

Part of the focus, too, is comparative. My own experience is from Britain. I have found it useful to draw on that experience for many of the examples, but concentration on Britain alone is not really adequate to understand either the problems of poverty or the methods which are available to respond to them. Many of the arguments made about social security in Britain – like the case for Child Benefit, or arguments against means-testing – rely on a received wisdom based on a restricted range of policies, and the most effective way to put them into perspective is to draw on material from other countries.

The book is intended mainly for an academic audience: it should be of interest to those studying social policy, sociology, politics and public administration, and there are elements which may be useful to students of economics and philosophy. On the principle that a better understanding should make for better policy – though I really ought to know differently by now – it may also be helpful for those who are involved in policy-making and administration for the poor.

Acknowledgements

As always, I have a number of people to thank for their part in bringing the book to completion. The initial spur which set me to work on this book was an ESRC workshop on Social Security in 1986, at which a number of people – including David Piachaud, Peter Townsend, John Veit-Wilson and Jonathan Bradshaw – took different concepts and means of measuring poverty out for a walk. It seemed to me that what people were trying to find was not simply a definition of poverty, but an instrument which would be interpreted in the way that was most favourable to the poor. I was not convinced that any method was likely to achieve that aim in itself, and it brought me to work over again some of the ideas that people had rejected, in order to try to separate out measures which might be valid from the kinds of politics that they were associated with. David Piachaud and John Veit-Wilson shared some thoughts on the ideas at a very early stage. However, I only began work seriously on the book in June 1990.

I have to thank my colleagues Dorothy Bochel, Tony Black and Colin Doherty, and my wife Dominique, who read drafts of the book and offered comments. My son Theo was born in the same month when I started writing, and I have had to learn a new way of working in the minutes between time with him. I would like to think that by the time he is old enough to understand it, the whole project will seem like a quaint historical curiosity; sadly, I doubt it will.

Paul Spicker

Part I

Poverty

1 Introduction

These are examples of the circumstances in which some people live. They are fictional, but they are drawn from life.

Jane is a single parent, aged 25. She married at 18, had two children, who are now aged four and two, but then her husband left her. She now lives in a council flat in a high-rise block on the outskirts of town. The flat has a full range of amenities, including central heating, but she cannot afford the heating and it has become damp. She has few furnishings. There are no shopping facilities nearby; she has no transport and public transport is expensive, so she goes out very little. She receives benefit but it is reduced because her husband is supposed to pay her maintenance. He only pays irregularly; if she is short of money, she manages by skimping on food.

Robert is 47. A skilled boilermaker, he became unemployed two years ago when his shipyard closed and now he finds that his skills are no longer required in the labour market. He has undertaken some retraining but finds at his age that no employer is currently interested in employing him. Elizabeth, his wife, works as a cleaner at a low wage, but her wages are insufficient to maintain the two of them. They are satisfactorily housed and still have a full range of possessions, though their car was sold six months after Robert became unemployed. They have no savings left and are pessimistic about their prospects for the future.

Edith is 81. She lives alone in a large house, where she has lived for most of her life. Her health has been failing, and she is unable to go upstairs, so she has had the bed moved downstairs and lives solely on the ground floor. She has a pension, and although she does not have many of the modern amenities that others have, like a refrigerator or a washing machine, she feels she is quite comfortable. However, the house needs repairs, which she cannot afford to have done. The fire is too difficult for her to light, and she uses a one-bar electric fire, but sparingly because it is expensive. She is concerned about break-ins in the area, and locks her door after 5.30 p.m., using several locks and chains.

Peter, a single man aged 55, has been discharged from mental hospital. Initially, he lived in a private flat, but he was evicted when his landlord wished to sell the property, and subsequently he has been homeless. He receives assistance benefits on a daily basis, for which he has to spend a part of each day queuing in the social security office. He spends some nights sleeping out, and some nights in a private hostel where he has a dormitory bed. He washes at a public convenience each morning, but he has no change of clothes, and cannot wash them effectively. During the day, he prefers to sit in shopping centres for warmth, but he is usually asked to leave, and so he spends much of the day wandering from place to place in the town.

Eileen is 18. She left home at 16 because of the violence of her father. Since then, she has moved from place to place, sometimes staying with acquaintances, sometimes sleeping out, at times renting when she has been in work. The kinds of work she is able to find, however, have generally been temporary – waitress, shop assistant, bar staff – and low paid, because of her age and sex. She has no possessions other than her clothes.

Simon is 43, and suffers from multiple sclerosis. When younger, and for some time after the initial diagnosis, Simon was working as a teacher, earning a respectable salary. His physical capacity has gradually deteriorated to the point where he cannot move around, wash, dress himself or go to the toilet unaided, and Anne, his wife, who was also a teacher, has had to give up her work in order to look after him. They have one child, a girl of 13, who is at an age where she is expensive to maintain. They have a well-equipped household, but their income has dropped substantially and their savings have gradually been exhausted by the requirements of Simon's special needs. They are now finding it difficult to manage.

Unmesh works in a relative's clothing factory for a low wage. His wife, Surinder, does home work. Together they receive more than they would receive in benefit but substantially less than the average wage. Some benefits may be available, but they are immigrants and restricted in their rights to claim. They live in a two-bedroomed house which they bought on a private arrangement and have now paid for; the house is cold, damp and in a state of disrepair.

I am going to refer to people in these kinds of circumstances as 'poor', which some may find too strong a word, but at least it helps to identify the kinds of problem that this book is concerned with. At the risk of compounding confusion, the discussion of poverty has to begin in the middle of a debate. The idea of 'poverty' has been discussed so much in academic and political circles that it has become difficult for any reader to approach the topic without some preconceptions. The first task of anyone who wants to approach the issue from a new perspective is to disentangle some of the different strands.

POVERTY AND IDEOLOGY

Conventionally, definitions of poverty have been categorised into two main forms: absolute and relative poverty. Absolute poverty is a minimum subsistence level based on essentials for survival. It has been characterised in an OECD report as a definition 'in terms of some absolute level of minimum needs, below which people are regarded as being poor, for purpose of social and government concern, and which does not change over time'.[1] The example that the OECD give is the poverty line in the US, which is based on the cost of a minimum diet determined by the Department of Agriculture. The academic examples most usually cited, rightly or wrongly, are the early work of Charles Booth and Seebohm Rowntree. Booth is thought to have specified a minimum standard of living which was necessary for a person to have basic essentials; Rowntree, a standard of poverty calculated from minimal norms for subsistence. (Both characterisations are disputable.)[2]

The alternative is a relative concept, which defines poverty in terms of its relation to the standards which exist elsewhere in society. This used to be understood primarily in terms of inequality: Roach and Roach, for example, define relative poverty as a standard applying to 'the bottom segment of the income distribution',[3] and the Luxembourg Income Study measures poverty as a proportion of average personal disposable income per capita.[4] Townsend, by contrast, uses the term in quite a different way. He refers to poverty as a form of 'relative deprivation', 'the absence or inadequacy of those diets, amenities, standards, services and activities which are common or customary in society'.[5]

One of the most important assumptions made about the 'absolute' and 'relative' models of poverty is that they represent, not only concepts of poverty, but specific political positions. The 'absolute' model is associated with the right wing, the 'relative' model with the left. The 'right wing' tends to see poverty as a fairly limited problem, and the kinds of response demanded by the state will be restricted in scope. The 'left wing' tends to view poverty as widespread; it is attributed to structural problems in society, and state interventions need to be extensive in order to redress the disadvantages of those who are poor.

There are always grounds for suspicion about any attempt to represent politics in two dimensions, and this kind of analysis should prompt immediate scepticism. Neither 'left' nor 'right' wing politics can be seen as monolithic positions – the right wing, for example, includes examples of both liberal individualism and traditionalist authoritarianism, whereas the left wing includes both pro-state collectivism and libertarian opposition to government.[6] In describing these ideas of poverty as related to the 'left' or 'right' wing, I am referring to a commonly occurring constellation of ideas, and it is important to understand how these ideas relate as a package in order to understand the kinds of argument which have been raging about poverty.

The connection between ideological positions and concepts of poverty is derived through two basic models of welfare – the residual and institutional. Residual welfare sees welfare as a safety net, which is only for those people who need it after they have failed to meet their needs through their own or their family's resources. Institutional welfare rests on the view that everyone has needs at some time – everyone is at some time a child, sick, old, possibly unemployed – and that this is a social responsibility. On the face of it, both residual and institutional models begin from very similar precepts – that the provision of welfare is required to respond to the different kinds of need experienced by people in certain kinds of contingency – and it might be argued that there is little direct incompatibility between the two positions; one might believe in institutional welfare in some respects and residual welfare in others. For example, it is common in Britain to find simultaneous support for the institutional health service and opposition to the institutional aspects of social security, like Child Benefit; the services are judged by different criteria. (Conversely, residual benefits like free prescriptions are viewed in a different light to other benefits delivered on similar terms.)[7] Equally, different criteria might also be applied to different aspects of a service area: a person might, for example, advocate simultaneously both a generally available health service to cover institutional needs and supplementary safety-net provisions for exceptional cases not covered in the normal course of medical care, like special injuries to athletes or musicians; or (as is indeed common in social security provision) a general system of income support backed up by residual benefits meeting special contingencies.

The residual model has, however, come to be associated with a particularly restrictive view of welfare – one which Titmuss referred to as the 'residual burden' model of welfare.[8] If welfare is to be seen primarily as a safety net, a distinction might be made between those who 'succeed' – in the sense of not requiring welfare – and those who 'fail', because they do. The implications of requiring welfare are both that people have failed to manage their affairs in society – whether through bad luck, ill health, ignorance, inadequacy, incompetence or laziness – and that they then become a burden on others who have to support them. The residual model is increasingly linked with the idea of 'dependency' and the 'dependency culture', ideas imported from the US which condemn financial dependency as something which undermines individual responsibility and competence.

The absolute model is seen as reinforcing the arguments for residual welfare because a residual model depends on the definition of some cut-off point or level below which a safety net comes into operation and above which it does not. This requires a justification for not committing resources above the line. If the aim of services is specifically to provide for those who are in need because they do not have enough resources, then a definition is required of what is 'enough'; this is provided by a measure of subsistence.

The relative concept of poverty, by contrast, is associated with institutional welfare and left-wing policies. In a relative model, people are defined as poor – a condition which is defined in terms of social expectations, in relation to others in their society who are not poor. Poverty is, then, a product of social organisation, and in particular of the unequal structure of society. The association with an institutional approach to welfare is justified by Titmuss on the basis that conditions of dependency are produced through social processes and must be accepted as social responsibilities.

The connections between these positions are not self-evident; they reflect, rather, the political history of the concepts. It might be argued with equal force that an assessment of subsistence needs can support a radical position: Rowntree's approach was used specifically to demonstrate the inadequacy of state provision and to press for greater benefits. This kind of analysis has been duplicated by Piachaud for children;[9] Townsend himself notes that 'there are many people in the United Kingdom . . . who feel the real pinch of hunger today'.[10] Equally, there is no reason to suppose that an emphasis on relative poverty leads to more generous benefits – the construction placed on the idea by certain right-wing critics (like John Moore, formerly Secretary of State for Social Services) has been that if poverty is only relative, it doesn't really matter.[11] Sen argues, in my view quite correctly, 'a general increase in ill-health due to widespread expansion of economic hardship, which leaves a person's relative position unchanged, must still be seen as intensifying that person's poverty'.[12] A relative assessment might undermine the position of the poor in circumstances where there is a decline in standards throughout a society.

The effect of the political associations of the different models is to create the immediate concern that any advocacy of an absolute model, or a concept based on subsistence, provides a foundation for a minimalist response. For Peter Townsend, this is a major objection to Sen's work on the idea of poverty. Sen had suggested that 'hunger' was a major issue in the relief of poverty, behind which other values might take lower priority. Townsend wrote in response:

> The problem about this reiteration of the virtues of an 'absolutist core' to the meaning of poverty is the underestimation of the importance of needs other than for food. . . . Without operational specification of the range of needs and resources required to satisfy those needs Professor Sen's argument carries the dangerous implication that meagre benefits for the poor in industrial societies are more than enough to meet their (absolute) needs. . . .[13]

Sen's reply was one of bafflement – how could Townsend possibly attribute such a position to him?[14] He took it, not unreasonably, that Townsend had not understood what his argument was. But I think there is more involved than a simple misunderstanding. Townsend has come to think of poverty within the constraints of certain models, which associate absolute and relative concepts with specific ideological views; and, on the basis of those models, he takes it that a theory which exhibits some of the features of these models will be led, willy-nilly, towards their other features. Hence, his comment that Sen's argument 'opens the door to a tough State interpretation of subsistence rations'.[15] In one sense, this may be true; a government of the new right faced with Sen's argument will doubtless draw on those aspects of the argument which appeal to their overall perspective and approach and reject those which do not. The same might, of course, be true of their arguments from a relative position, as Moore's comments indicate. But, whether or not Townsend is right politically, this is not necessarily a basis for the rational analysis of the concept of poverty.

The association of concepts of poverty with different ideological positions presents a set of dilemmas. It may be possible, in theory, to begin with a blank slate and to try to work out a coherent, cohesive set of propositions about the nature of poverty; but the voyage has to be charted through troubled waters and, at any stage, the propositions are likely to be pulled under by the current of associated concepts. It would be naïve to assume that this book will not in the same way be construed as a contribution to a political debate, for in one sense it is; and it may be necessary to demonstrate not only that alternative approaches to the conceptualisation of poverty can be more coherent, but that they do not entail pernicious consequences. This point will be returned to later in the book.

2 The nature of poverty

DEFINING POVERTY

Some people are poor. Recognising what something means in practice is often much easier than defining or analysing it, which is one of the main reasons for beginning my discussion with illustrative examples. When we say that people are poor, deprived, suffering from hardship, or in need, we usually have a fairly good idea of what we mean. But words like this may well mean different things to different people, and it is difficult to take this kind of ordinary language and make it perform the precise functions which are required in social analysis.

Sometimes, when people define topics, they search for a common characteristic – an 'essential' feature which distinguishes the issue clearly from others. It would be possible, if this was true, to define people as 'poor' if they met a particular criterion or set of criteria, and as 'not poor' if they did not. For example, poverty is sometimes related to a 'poverty line', so that everyone whose income is below a certain level is considered to be 'poor', and everyone above the line is not. But this kind of approach leads to obvious problems – because some people do have a low income without being thought of as 'poor'. It might be thought that all it is necessary to do is to add further criteria besides income. This will refine the definition of poverty and improve the tools which are available for identifying it, but it will not settle the issue. The problem is not that poverty is not simply a matter of low income; poverty is not 'simply' a matter of anything. Most complex ideas, used in everyday language, do not have a single essential meaning which is subject to definition. They have variations and shades of meaning; the more widely the idea is used, and the wider the range of conditions to which it refers, the more likely it is that any definition will include some conditions which should not be included, and exclude others which should be. Readers who hope to find an authoritative, 'scientific' definition of poverty in this book will be disappointed. The use of the term varies, the concept is liable to be contested, and the issues cannot be resolved beyond dispute.

'Poverty' does not describe a particular kind of attribute which people do or do not have; the term is used to describe a range or cluster of conditions. A person starving in Ethiopia, a discharged psychiatric patient living in a derelict house because there is nowhere else to go, a Greek hill farmer, a single parent trapped in an isolated council estate, or a pensioner unable to afford heating, might all be said to be 'poor' in some sense; but it is not necessary to suppose that they are all poor in exactly the same sense. The kinds of problems they face, the reasons for those problems, and the sorts of response which have to be made, may well be different. The examples in Chapter 1 may have some features in common, but it is difficult to point to any unifying factor and say 'this is what makes these people poor'. That is not to say that the problems are not interrelated; but they are not all alike, either, and conditions found at one edge of the cluster may appear, on closer examination, to have little directly in common with features found at the other end. In philosophical writing, this kind of connection between clusters of interrelated ideas is referred to, after Wittgenstein, as a kind of 'family resemblance'.

It should not be supposed from this, though, that the idea of 'poverty' is used indiscriminately, or that it does not really mean anything. People may disagree about the nature of poverty, but there are cases in the Third World – cases where people are without food, clothing or shelter – where there is hardly any disagreement, and which in many ways are paradigmatic of poverty. Some commentators would disagree as to whether these cases bear any resemblance to conditions in industrialised countries,[1] but there are nevertheless some widespread uses of the term in developed countries, and there is still a high level of consensus that certain types of problem can be described as 'poverty'. It is not really important whether poverty in one country is the 'same thing' as in another country; poverty is not a 'thing' at all, but a way of describing people's conditions.

Poverty is not only a descriptive category; it is also a moral one. The term 'poverty', Piachaud writes, 'carries with it an implication and moral imperative that something should be done about it. Its definition is a value judgment and should be clearly seen to be so . . .'.[2] Many of those who deny that people in the kinds of circumstances I have outlined are 'poor' object to the term, not just because they have a particular idea of how the word might be used, but because they do not accept the implication that something must be done about these circumstances. This moral element does not mean that poverty is impossible to define; but it does indicate that, whatever the definition given, there is likely to be some room for debate as to the kinds of condition included in it and the kinds of responses which it is appropriate to make.

THE ELEMENTS OF POVERTY

In order to understand a concept, it is necessary to examine how it is used – the kinds of issue which the idea of 'poverty' refers to. Baratz and Grigsby[3] identify a wide range of factors 'closely associated' with poverty – which is not to say that these factors define people as being poor, but only that they are likely to occur in the circumstances where people are poor. They include the following:

Severe lack of physical comfort

- shelter which does not provide adequate protection from elements; is poorly lighted or ventilated, overcrowded or filthy
- hunger
- highly unpleasant neighbourhood (excessive noise, litter, traffic, etc)
- highly unpleasant environment on job (extreme temperatures and odours, limited working space, etc)
- clothing wardrobe which does not provide adequate protection from the elements.

Severe lack of health

- high probability of short life-span
- frequent illness
- chronic illness
- permanent physical or mental disability.

Severe lack of safety and security

- unsafe housing
- unsafe neighbourhood
- lack of protection against major loss of assets
- unsafe working environment
- unsafe air or water
- lack of protection against major decline of real income.

Severe lack of welfare values

- personally unacceptable ratio of earned to total income
- personally stigmatising form of financial dependency
- inability to perform a socially valued function (e.g. paid work)
- lack of good quality education
- non-possession of symbols of medium–high social status

- highly unfavourable self-conception
- low aspirations for, or hopelessness about, potentiality for upward socio-economic mobility
- severe family instability (e.g. 'broken home').

Severe lack of deference values

- severe restrictions on economic and social opportunity and activity (especially discrimination)
- exclusion from participation in the political process
- victim of injustice in the law enforcement process
- non-possession of socially valued skill
- lack of good quality education
- socially stigmatising form of financial dependency
- non-possession of symbols of medium–high status.

If it is right to suggest that poverty refers to a cluster of concepts rather than a single definable problem, it is unlikely that any list of factors could precisely capture the experience of poverty, and I do not want to imply approval or acceptance of the list of factors as it stands. There are some items which are vague (like 'unsafe' housing), and others which seem oddly specific (the references to conditions at work are inappropriate for large numbers of poor people who have no employment); some problems have been substantially left out (like dependent old age), while there are others (like those principally concerned with psychological factors) which I am not sure should be there. The value of Baratz and Grigsby's approach is not that it constitutes an indisputable or authoritative description of poverty, but that it helps to focus on the kinds of area which people are concerned about when discussing the issue.

I suggested earlier that problems like the lack of food, clothing and shelter are paradigmatic cases in the concept of poverty. Baratz and Grigsby's schema of poverty includes these factors, but it extends much more widely; it includes not only problems which are like them, such as problems with air or water, but many which are not at all like them, such as low aspirations or lack of skills. Material and social problems are not wholly distinct, because there is much in the definition of a person's social position which depends on material factors, like the stigmatising nature of certain kinds of income and the importance of certain kinds of goods as status symbols, and equally much in the nature of material goods which has a social meaning, like the relative quality of housing and the environment. There is besides a substantial level of overlap between the categories – not only in those factors which are directly repeated, but also in interrelated problems (like inadequate shelter and unsafe housing). A person who suffers deprivation in relation to housing, income and health would probably suffer from at least half of the problems listed here.

The experience of poverty is not one of constant, unvarying deprivation of a specified kind, but a series of deprivations. Baratz and Grigsby's schema points to a number of issues – like material deprivation, health, security, social problems, status and power – which are closely bound up with the experience of poverty, and which need to be taken into account in any adequate discussion of the issues. All the factors can be seen, to a greater or lesser extent, as potential consequences of being poor, but some might also be seen as factors which lead to poverty, and others – like hunger, lack of clothing and inadequate housing – as factors which are virtually descriptive of poverty; that is, they are the kinds of thing by which poverty is identified. In practice, these may be difficult to separate, and there may be a vicious circle. For example, bad housing is often found in poor neighbourhoods, because this is the housing least likely to be chosen, and those with the resources to choose go elsewhere. These neighbourhoods become, by virtue of their poverty, focuses for certain kinds of social problem, attracting greater attention from the police and welfare agencies, which reinforces the stigma. Individual poverty may lead to an unfavourable self-conception, which in turn reinforces lack of opportunity and helps to keep people in poverty. A thorough analysis of poverty (which is not my aim here) would have to distinguish the causes of poverty, aspects of deprivation and consequences, all of which contribute to the constellation of factors identified with poverty.

ASPECTS OF DEPRIVATION

The idea of deprivation implies that people are lacking welfare – 'welfare' itself being a wide-ranging term, generally referring to people's well-being. Poverty can largely be described in terms of deprivations, although the moral content of poverty implies a degree of seriousness which is not necessarily the case with deprivation alone. It seems quite reasonable to think of people as 'deprived' if they are lacking some material goods or resources – for example, if they do not have access to recreational facilities – but that is not the same as saying that they are 'poor'. The following argument was put to me, during research into deprived areas, by the representative of a community organisation in rural Perthshire:

> Most children have a walk of around half a mile from school to the outskirts . . . their walk thereafter could be an additional mile. There is no school bus provided even for the youngest children whose daily walk

> is partly along a road with no pavement or verge. . . . The youngsters . . . have no leisure facilities. . . . The village hall . . . is poorly heated . . . and . . . requires extensive redecoration. . . . Compared perhaps to some areas, (this) is not a deprived area. . . . However, in terms of facilities it is a deprived area with relatively little money being spent on it compared to similar communities in the city areas.[4]

This is a legitimate use of the term 'deprivation', but it is not normally the kind of deprivation which is thought of when referring to 'poverty'. The difference appears to be, not a difference in kind, but rather a value judgement as to the relative importance of the issues. If any of the people I considered at the outset should not be classified as 'poor', it would not be because they have no problems, but because their problems are not thought to be as serious as those of others. For that reason, my description of them as 'poor' can be disputed. But the debate should really centre on how serious the problems are and what should be done, rather than what word we use to describe them.

People experience many different kinds of deprivation: the kinds of problem which Baratz and Grigsby describe are physical, material, psychological and social. Material deprivation is perhaps the most important in relation to poverty, not because it is the only kind which poor people experience, but because the paradigmatic cases of poverty – like the lack of food, clothing or shelter – are material.

The lack of physical welfare, or ill health, has much in common with material deprivation. The World Health Organisation defines health as 'a state of complete physical, mental and social well-being',[5] which fails to distinguish health from general well-being at all. In so far as lack of health indicates a more general lack of welfare, it could be argued that it can be used in a similar way to poverty. Certainly, aspects of ill health – like malnutrition, infant mortality, early death, or frequent and chronic disability – constitute some of the common factors by which poverty is identified, being at the same time a cause of poverty, an aspect of deprivation and a potential consequence of poverty.

Psychological forms of deprivation include not only mental health (about which the arguments relating to physical health also apply), but also aspects of personality and emotional relationships. Baratz and Grigsby include a number of such factors: the category of 'welfare values' is explicitly related to the self-appraisal of people who are poor. Although such problems may follow from poverty, it seems wrong to include self-conception in any description of what poverty is; a person with a suicidally low self-conception would still not become poor on that account, and a person with poor housing, income and health with a favourable self-conception does not seem to be richer or poorer than someone else with all these problems and an unfavourable one. (The issue is not simply a problem of definition; it is important in determining responses to poverty, because it implies that measures to improve people's self-conception do not in themselves alleviate poverty.) The same is true, I think, of factors concerning personal relationships.

At the same time, there are related forms of social deprivation – particularly of the kind that Baratz and Grigsby refer to as 'deference values' – which have to be considered within an understanding of the problems of poverty. It may be difficult, in practice, to distinguish different kinds of deprivation, because people whose welfare is impaired – for example, people who are disabled, mentally ill, or lacking in education and status – are liable to suffer from disadvantages in society, and because people who lack material welfare are vulnerable to other forms of deprivation. People have needs for relationships, for security or for personal development; such needs are expressed through social structures like family, community, education, the workplace and the structure of opportunities. It seems fairly evident that these kinds of deprivation are very closely associated with the problems of poverty, to the point where poverty has been expressed as an inability to participate fully in society.[6] In the European Community, the idea of 'poverty' is increasingly identified with 'exclusion'.[7]

Some aspects of people's social position are valued in ways which are very similar to the way they regard material goods; they are referred to as 'positional' goods. The deprivation of status, reputation or power can be no less important than the lack of food, clothing or shelter. One of the tests of important positional goods is that people are prepared to devote resources to obtaining them, often in preference to material goods. In Victorian times, one of the greatest fears was entry to the workhouse – in which one would be fed and nourished often far better than one would outside – and a pauper's burial. In modern Britain, people might opt to be homeless rather than to accept accommodation in the worst local authority areas – 'worst' not in the sense of physical condition (which is in the UK principally the preserve of the private sector), but of social reputation. Poverty may be primarily material in its nature, but it cannot be seen solely in material terms.

NEEDS AND RESOURCES

'Needs' are those things which are necessary to avoid deprivation. The interpretation of the things that people 'need' is likely to be contentious, because it is subject to many competing definitions: definitions from the people in need themselves, from experts and professionals, and from wider social norms.[8] It is debatable, too, how far such items should be thought of as 'necessary', and how far they are simply important or desirable. Taking all this into consideration, the idea of need is hardly less complex than that of poverty, but in this context there is one important issue which distinguishes the concept of 'need'; it is that 'needs' are needs for something. If people are hungry, they need food; if they are homeless, they need housing.

The range of potential needs is enormous: examples include food, shelter, medical care, education, social and environmental services, consumer goods, recreational opportunities, neighbourhood amenities, transport facilities, employment opportunities, clothing, fuel or personal disposable income.[9] 'Welfare' might be spoiled irretrievably for want of a particular item – which is probably true of lack of food, shelter, fuel and certain forms of medical care – but it can also be seen as cumulative, and the lack of some items may be compensated for by the presence of others (for example, excellent neighbourhood amenities might make up for inadequate transport facilities; consumer goods might conceivably make up for other recreational opportunities; and a combination of factors like a personal disposable income, consumer goods, recreational facilities and neighbourhood amenities may, for some, be preferred to employment opportunities). Because of this, there cannot be a definitive list of the things people need, even if some needs are generally more important than others.

Relating poverty to 'need' helps to focus attention on a significant issue: its relationship to resources. Poverty is associated with certain kinds of deprivation, but it is not simply identifiable with specific needs, because there are different ways in which the deprivations could be satisfied. People who are poor are not simply deprived; they are unable to meet their needs. This implies that they lack the resources – the goods, benefits and services which a person might have or have access to – necessary to overcome their deprivation. The kinds of problem I began by describing in terms of 'poverty' were principally the problems of people who lacked adequate resources.

Baratz and Grigsby refer to poverty as 'a severe lack of physical and mental well-being, closely associated with inadequate economic resources and consumption'.[10] This suggests, I think rightly, that poverty is not actually defined in terms of inadequate resources and consumption, but with the lack of welfare which results from them. There are two problems with their formulation. One is that the term 'closely associated' is too loose to be helpful: a person whose resources and consumption are adequate would not normally be thought of as poor, even if that person suffers some kind of deprivation. Second, people may have resources which are adequate for some purposes and inadequate for others. An owner-occupier whose mortgage is foreclosed, someone who faces huge damages from a legal action, or a businessman who goes bankrupt, all have inadequate resources and suffer deprivation as a result, but the inadequacy they experience, and the deprivation which results, affects only part of their lives, and (although all become vulnerable to poverty) they may well continue to draw on resources and avoid deprivation in other respects.

If poverty consists of a relationship between resources and the experience of deprivation, the kinds and patterns of deprivation that a person is likely to experience are necessarily indeterminate. It becomes virtually impossible to establish an authoritative list of factors which define people as being poor. It may be possible to establish some agreement about which forms or patterns of deprivation are particularly severe – though there is clearly much scope for disagreement – and to define the kinds of resources which are needed to provide against them, but in any monetary economy, people are able to choose, to some extent, what they will spend their money on. When resources are inadequate, people are unable to pay for some items or some combination of items. The most common pattern of poverty in developed societies is not that a poor person lacks every kind of good in every sense – a test of 'destitution' rather than of poverty – but that people lack some things, in various combinations, for much of the time. If people are short of food, they may skimp on the electricity bill. When the electricity bill has to be paid, they might not pay the rent. When the rent has to be paid, they go short of food. The process consists of a constant juggling with inadequate resources: there are always options, though the options consist of a number of unpalatable choices between different kinds of deprivation which at different times are more or less pressing, more or less serious. Poverty might, then, be linked with inadequate food, fuel, clothing or shelter, in any combination, but equally it might not include any of these; no single factor, and no consistent set of factors, can be held to be 'essential' to poverty. Deprivations are considered as 'poverty' when they are recognised as particularly serious, which is why deprivations of food, clothing or shelter are so often seen as paradigms of poverty. But none defines or exhausts the list of factors which might be included under the term.

When resources are considered in more detail, the position becomes still less determinate. Resources are important because they represent the ability to gain the kind of things which people lack. This ability might be understood in terms of money or capital goods which can be converted into the things one needs; equally, it may refer to other resources a person is able to draw on. Although I have referred to poverty as reflecting 'a lack of resources', it might be more accurate to refer to Titmuss's concept of a 'command' over resources. 'Command' over resources is another way of saying that people use resources, or are able to use them. This is often judged in terms of income or wealth, but what someone possesses is not always as important as the kinds of resource that person is able to draw on.

Ownership does not guarantee use. Many people own rights in pension funds, but cannot draw on them. Conversely, many people use housing that they do not own: a person who rents a house has the use of it, without owning it. 'Command over resources' also includes the potential to use resources. Some people are able to borrow resources – like the use of credit cards, mortgages or their spouse's car. Some people are able to provide for unexpected contingencies by insuring against risks; they are in a more favourable position than others who cannot.

One implication of relating poverty to 'command' over resources is that the idea is again referred to its social context. The command over resources of individuals may differ. This means that, in circumstances where a person is deprived in other ways, that person's ability to use resources to limit the problems arising from deprivation will also be limited, and so social disadvantage may add to the problems of poverty. People in the kinds of circumstance that I introduced in Chapter 1 – people who are unemployed, single parents, disabled people or ex-mental patients – are liable to be socially rejected. Someone from an ethnic minority may not be able to buy adequate housing. A person living on a poor estate may not be able to get a taxi to call, to obtain hire purchase, or to have milk delivered. Status, power and stigma play a part in determining the command over resources that people have. In the allocation of council housing, which nominally does not depend on an economic market, housing officers have graded people according to their 'type' and 'standards', and offered them housing accordingly.[11] In access to health care, middle-class people not only use their doctors more – an issue which might be taken to reflect, among other things, cultural differences, better transport or communications, or better knowledge – but are more likely to receive the care for which doctors are the main gatekeepers.[12] If status leads to people acting differently towards others, it is changing the ability of people of different statuses to affect critical outcomes. This reinforces the view that the nature of poverty is socially defined.

THE SOCIAL DEFINITION OF POVERTY

The concept of deprivation conceals a nest of value judgements. Implicit in the idea of a 'lack' of something is the existence of a condition in which these things are not lacking. The concept of deprivation implies that there is a standard of *sufficiency* – an amount of food, clothing or shelter which is at least 'enough'. To say that someone is 'poor' is to say that that person does not have enough. But the question 'how much is enough?' can scarcely be addressed, let alone answered, without reference to some values, because the idea of sufficiency depends on the standard which is being applied –

enough perhaps to survive, to avoid suffering, to maintain physical efficiency, to be comfortable, to live decently, or whatever.

Much of the debate about the concept of welfare in the UK has focused on the idea of 'subsistence need' – a standard of sufficiency based on the minimum necessary for physical efficiency. The idea of 'subsistence' is evidently more narrowly defined than the needs which support a more general sense of well-being; transport, amenities or personal disposable income may not be requisite to maintain physical efficiency even if life is worse without them. The selection of subsistence as being of particular importance clearly depends on a value judgement. Historically, the selection of a standard of subsistence was based not least on the desire to put certain core issues beyond dispute, which was the approach taken by Rowntree.

The nature of subsistence, however, is socially constructed. This proposition is generally associated with a 'relative' view of poverty; absolute definitions are widely thought to be incapable of accommodating the idea that needs might be socially determined, and this is taken to be fatal to any attempt to establish a fixed standard of subsistence. This is a basic misconception. It may, in theory, be possible to argue for an absolute concept which is independent of social criteria – for example, that the elements of the nutritional value of food are required for subsistence as a fact of human existence, irrespective of social conditions – but there are very few people to whom this position could be attributed (and certainly not Booth or Rowntree, who are most often used as examples). The nearest I know of is George, who writes that, while much of poverty is relative:

> . . . in all times and in all countries . . . there is a core of basic necessities which is irreducible and which must be satisfied if people are not to be in poverty. Thus poverty consists of a core of basic necessities as well as a list of other necessities that change over time and place.[13]

There are few if any 'basic necessities' which are not subject in some sense to social definition. In relation to food, it has to be established which foodstuffs will supply basic requirements, and where they can be obtained. For example, there is some nutritional value in eating dogs, horses and insects, but the option of doing so is not universally available. (Conversely, milk, which is a staple part of the diet in the UK, cannot be digested by many adults in the Third World; when, after the Second World War, the US shipped dried milk to countries to help prevent starvation, it caused sickness.) Clothing has to be assessed, not only by the warmth or protection it offers, but also in terms of decency and convenience. The fuel which is necessary depends on the conditions in which the fuel is used, and the equipment available for burning it. Equally, the definition of what is a 'shelter' is different in different societies – a function not only of climate and materials but also land tenure and the social organisation of housing. In the Third World, squatting is a widespread, and arguably a 'normal', form of tenure. But a person in Britain who is without a home does not have the option of erecting a squatter shack, not so much because of the lack of materials, as because of the limitations of land use and the restrictions of the law. A person with no accommodation is liable not just to be moved on but to be arrested. There is, then, a clearly defined minimum level, which people are not supposed to fall below. But it is a socially defined condition, because the way it is understood, and the circumstances in which it is applied, are social.

This argument owes something to Marx. Marx argued that needs are necessarily defined in social terms; there may be biological needs, but the way in which needs are interpreted, and the forms in which demands are made, are social.[14] This was the basis of the concept of poverty in the former Soviet Union,[15] which defined an absolute level of poverty in social terms; the idea of a socially defined 'poverty line' was in consequence accepted institutionally. It is also, I think, what Sen means to say when he seeks to distinguish 'capabilities' from 'commodities or characteristics'.[16] 'Capabilities' are the basic needs that everyone has; 'commodities' and 'characteristics' are the means through which these basic needs are interpreted or operationalised. Sen does his argument a disservice by describing this as an 'absolute' core within a 'relative' context, because the terms 'absolute' and 'relative' refer to models of poverty rather than the constituent concepts. What he is saying is that even if needs are basic and universal, the processes through which they are recognised and met are necessarily social ones.

'The necessities of life', Townsend writes, 'are not fixed. They are continuously being adapted and augmented as changes take place in a society and in its products.' [17] The proposition that the meaning of poverty changes over time follows from the fact that poverty is defined and identified in terms specific to particular societies. But it is not, in the way that Townsend suggests, primarily a change in expectations and wants. As societies change, so do the nature and type of goods and resources available. If the income of a society increases, 'poverty goods' – that is, goods which are primarily bought by people with limited resources – are less likely to be available, because it is not worth the while of suppliers to provide them. It can be difficult, even illegal, to obtain cheap cuts of meat, peat for burning, or cheap distilled liquor like poteen. Poor people have to pay more for higher quality goods along with the rest of us. (This should not be taken as an argument to lower standards; there are very good reasons why social minima should be raised. But when social standards are higher, poor people evidently need more to meet them.)

It is also true that things which are not essential in some societies become essential in others. Some societies, for example, have few facilities for transport. This means that other basic resources, like food, have to be obtainable without recourse to transport (and where they are not, we would reasonably describe them as 'poor societies'). In a modern industrial society, many basic facilities are not available on these terms, or are available only at a cost which exceeds the cost of the transport itself. This means, for all intents and purposes, that access to transport becomes a necessity. As Marx says, the structure of society creates needs. But these are not necessarily 'false' needs, in the sense of delusions fostered by a materialist ethic; they are part of the facts of life of specific forms of social organisation.

This prompts some reflections on the applicability of the 'absolute' and 'relative' models to the kinds of points that I have considered. The idea of poverty necessarily includes important social elements, both in the understanding of basic needs and in the nature of the resources with which those needs might be met; this is commonly taken as a criticism of the 'absolute' model. If there is a principal deficiency in the idea of an 'absolute minimum', it is the failure of the concept to take into account positional goods. Positional goods are in their very nature determined by a pattern of social relationships, and not by an interpretation of the need for certain types of core commodities. This implies that an adequate definition of a social minimum cannot be solely 'absolute', but must include some criteria which are relative to the society in which it is applied. That is not to say that there are no 'absolute' criteria, in the sense of criteria which relate to a set standard, but only that absolute criteria cannot be enough in themselves.

This does not mean that a simple 'relative' model is any more satisfactory, if by a relative model one means that people are identified as poor strictly by their relationship to others who are not poor. The 'relative' concept is sometimes taken as a form of inequality, and there are clear indications in the argument that some aspects of inequality – particularly positional goods – have also to be considered as aspects of poverty. But there is no standard to judge how the distinction should be made between those who are poor and those who are not, and it is not clear what there is in a 'relative' model that can make it possible to identify certain needs as particularly important or essential. In other words, the weakness of the 'absolute' model is that it fails to take into account issues which can be seen as 'relative', whereas the 'relative' model fails to identify the kinds of issues addressed by the 'absolute' approach.

3 Operationalisation of the concept

An adequate conceptualisation of poverty goes only part of the way towards the identification of the problem. The concept has to be translated into usable terms, or 'operationalised'. Measures have to be selected which will faithfully reflect the concept of poverty which has been outlined.

It is here that philosophical integrity begins to crumble. The task of finding appropriate measures is so difficult, and so frustrating, that academics, researchers, campaigners and politicians have been driven, again and again, to use measures of poverty that they know to be inadequate, misleading and sometimes even contradictory to the positions they adopt. One of the best known examples in the UK is the use of the basic means-tested benefit (currently named Income Support) as a standard of poverty. It has been referred to, particularly by Townsend, as the 'state's standard of poverty', and, because of Townsend's authority, this use has been widely imitated. This has many disadvantages, not least that if one uses the level of benefit to define people as poor, any increase in that benefit increases the number of people defined as poor – and, conversely, that a cut in benefit leaves more people defined as better off. Why, then, is the benefit used in this way? One reason is that it is convenient. If it is possible to define all people on or below the level of income prescribed for benefits as 'poor', then it is possible to identify large numbers of people as poor without having to undertake fundamental research (which has its own flaws). A second reason is that it is conventional, and as such gives a fairly constant reference point – it makes it possible to discuss other issues about poverty, like why people are poor or what sort of people become poor, without having first to go through the agonising process of defining the problem and identifying the people concerned. The families of disabled people are likely to fall into a band of income close to the level at which people claim benefit. This does not tell us exactly how many disabled people are poor, or what the extent of their deprivation is likely to be, but it is quite sufficient to identify disabled people as a particularly vulnerable group. Third, it offers a basis to analyse other issues. If one learns, for example, that housing tenure is strongly differentiated in terms of income, and that people in receipt of the basic means-tested benefit are more than twice as likely to rent property as to own it, one has established an important fact about housing tenure, whatever the defects of the reference point being used.

The same kinds of argument relate to the method used by the Luxembourg Income Study (LIS).[1] This study relies on a series of statistics drawn from sources in different countries, which it attempts to process into a standard format. Often, the figures are not formed on a directly equivalent basis, and there are problems in potential bias in relation to those groups which are left out of the data. There are discrepancies in the way that people who share incomes, like households or families, are recorded. Poverty is defined, within the study, on a strictly comparative basis, in terms of 'economic distance'; a poverty standard is calculated as 50 per cent of median income calculated on an equivalent basis for each individual. Despite the evident limitations of the material, about which the authors are explicit, and despite the theoretical problems in presenting this as a definition of poverty, which I shall return to, the use of this standard provides information of striking analytical power. It is possible, for example, to identify the relative position of different kinds of household in different countries, and the extent to which social security benefits reduce their relative disadvantage. The authors of the LIS wave aside the problems of definition: 'Although the concept of poverty is controversial, most social scientists agree that the group with the lowest income can be defined as poor even in affluent societies.'[2] There are dangers in this position, but there is some reason in it, too. Irrespective of whether the issues being addressed might really be said to be the problems of poverty, for those who are interested in poverty by any definition, attention needs to be focused on the problems and characteristics of people on the lowest incomes – and this is the type of information that the LIS is dedicated to producing.

The level of Income Support, or the relationship to median income, are being used as indicators – not a precise measurement of a problem, but a signpost towards a range of associated problems. The principle of using indicators is widely accepted in social research, out of necessity rather than conviction. If it is not possible precisely to measure a particular problem, it may still be possible at least to get some idea about the shape or size of a problem by using proxies. But this process is fraught with difficulties.

The criteria for indicators

Validity

A valid indicator is one which actually reflects the problem or condition that it is supposed to reflect. There are many difficulties with this, because most indicators are only approximations of a problem at best. Income statistics, for example, are widely used as an indicator of poverty – that is, as a guide as to where poverty is likely to occur – because income stands as a useful proxy for consumption. However, too close an identification of poverty with low income would not be very satisfactory, because there are people with very low incomes who are not poor. The income of business entrepreneurs may be negligible, or even negative, but their consumption may be high; a very high negative income is a sign of affluence rather than of poverty.

Reliability

Indicators are reliable if they consistently report the same thing in the same way. This means that, even if the indicator is not a very accurate reflection of the problem being studied, one can at least get some feeling for whether a problem is serious, and how it is changing.

Unfortunately, many of the figures which are widely used are unreliable. One of the problems with monetary values is that they change, usually through inflation. It is possible to control for inflation to some degree, but the methods which are used to do it – in the UK, the Retail Price Index (RPI) – are concerned with the value of money overall. The RPI reflects, as faithfully as it can, the 'basket of goods' bought by the average consumer. This will include, for example, the cost of housing or petrol for the car. However, although most people in the UK buy housing, many poor people cannot afford to buy, and so are not directly affected by the mortgage rate, and poor people cannot afford cars, so they probably will not buy any petrol. On the other hand, food and fuel constitute a large part of the budget of poor people, because the needs for food and heat do not diminish in proportion with someone's income. The inflation rate calculated from the RPI does not, then, necessarily reflect the increase in costs faced by people who are poor; it is in the nature of poverty that the 'basket of goods' which is bought is likely to be different. (This problem is not, by the way, insuperable. Bradshaw's research[3] on 'budget standards' identifies the items that poor people actually buy at the cost that they pay, which accounts for inflation very neatly. The point of this example is not to say that inflation always makes figures unreliable, but rather that a very widely used figure, which is reliable for many purposes, is not reliable for the purpose of examining poverty.)

Availability

Those indicators which are readily available have usually been designed for a particular purpose, which may or may not be adequate for an assessment of poverty. Wealth statistics rely on the Inland Revenue's definitions of goods – an assessment complicated both by the extent of liability for tax and by the concern of potential taxpayers to evade or avoid liability.

Effectively, any analysis relies on some heroic approximations using available figures as proxies for other facts that one would really wish to have. But even remote proxies may be hard to find. To take one minor example, in attempting to establish the spatial distribution of poverty for some locally based research, I hoped to draw on information about the distribution of the ownership of goods in different areas; but I found no adequate source of local data. Information on telephone ownership is not made available as it is now considered to be 'commercially sensitive'. Information on TV licences, as a very crude approximation of TV ownership, is not held in a form which allows analysis. Information on car ownership is confused by the level of registration in the names of firms. Probably the best indicator is the level of owner-occupation – but that is not particularly accurate, because it depends largely on estimates initially based on the census, which rusts over time, and there is no reliable way to take account of subsequent vacancies or transfers from and to private rented housing. Examinations of poverty at a local level tend, as a result, to rely on data drawn from much larger administrative units, which limits their application to small areas.

Plausibility

It is not essential for their use, but it is at least desirable, that any indicators used should make sense. Much work which has been done on the measurement of poverty has produced some fairly implausible results. Townsend's 1979 work on poverty, for example, which will be considered in more detail shortly, is based on a description of the lifestyles of poor people. He shows that poor people are more likely not to get three meals a day, and poor children cannot have a birthday party. This may be true, but it is difficult to see factors like these as constituting poverty in themselves. The results appeared because Townsend used a statistical analysis to select the items which best indicated poverty, rather than relying on an explanatory model. The effect may be scientifically valid, but it may be repugnant to 'common sense', and as such it is debatable whether it can subsequently provide a sound and secure basis for policy.

Usefulness and application

Last, but not least, any indicators have to be useful – that is, they have to be applied to the problem they are being used to analyse. Research into poverty does not take place in a political or administrative vacuum, and it is often undertaken for specific purposes. For example, a discussion of the distributive implications of policies can comfortably settle for figures based on income distribution, on the basis that the lower end of the income distribution, even if it is not equivalent to poverty, will pick up most cases of poverty on the way. Research into the spatial distribution of resources, which has been important for resources allocation, tends to rely on different sorts of indicators, such as the types of problem associated with poverty, because these are locally available. And research intended to reflect on the benefits system requires some identification of the recipient unit – usually the household, though in some cases (for example, the attempt to identify the poverty of women within households) individuals. The point here is not to claim that some kinds of figure are better than others for these purposes, which may or may not be true, but rather that the types of indicators which are used may be quite different according to the purpose of the research.

IDENTIFYING POVERTY

Poverty can primarily be identified through two main aspects: the presence of deprivation, and the lack of command over resources. It follows from what has been said that, although these factors are both important within the definition of poverty, neither is requisite in order to identify the problem: deprivation can be taken as an indicator of lack of resources, and the lack of resources is likely to generate deprivation.

The identification of deprivation might be undertaken directly or indirectly. Direct identification can be undertaken by classifying certain types of problem as being serious impairments of welfare of the type associated with poverty and measuring those directly. Indirect identification relies on the association of poverty with a range of factors, causes and consequences – like unemployment, ill health, or low educational attainment. This approach has mainly been undertaken in studies of area deprivation,[4] but in principle it could also be extended to studies of individuals or households. (It is also the basis for a distinct strategy in response to poverty, 'indicator targeting', which is outlined in Chapter 7.)

It is difficult to say with confidence that direct identification is superior to indirect. Both rely, of necessity, on the use of indicators rather than precise measures; both point to factors which are important in their own right. The primary justification for using one approach rather than another is that it better serves the purpose for which the research is intended.

Command over resources is perhaps more difficult to identify directly; in its nature, it refers to a potential set of circumstances as well as the actual situation. In practice, actual resources have to stand as an indicator for potential ones. Resources include income, which is a flow of resources, and wealth, which is a stock. Income is widely used as an indicator of poverty – that is, as a guide as to where poverty is likely to occur – but too close an identification of poverty with low income would not be very satisfactory. The French team contributing to the European Poverty Programme made a number of objections. One was that it represented a 'one-dimensional' approach. Poverty is multi-dimensional and cannot be described through low income alone. A second is that the amount of income is less important as an indicator than its regularity and stability. Third, it invites inclusion of many people within the definition who would not be described as poor. Fourth, it is difficult to measure in any accurate, trustworthy way.[5]

Wealth, equally, proves to be not very convincing as a measure of poverty. Wealth is usually measured in monetary terms, but money is important for what it will buy; the clothes a person wears may be almost worthless in monetary terms, because their only marketable value is second-hand, but the lack of a stock of clothing is very important for poor people.

Despite their defects, income statistics are often a better guide to poverty than wealth statistics. Income is important because it marks, for most people, the level of their consumption – that is, what they are able to use. Income statistics may not reflect the consumption of any individual or family, but when people are taken in the aggregate, many of the differences between individuals cancel out.

An alternative to the use of either income or wealth is the use of consumption, as a truer measure of command over resources. Unfortunately, consumption figures are not readily available, because, for individuals or families, they require that a record is kept; this has been the focus of much empirical research. However, they are still vulnerable to many of the objections made to the use of income as a measure.

The apparent impossibility of measuring poverty practically in any objective, reliable, indisputable way might be seen as reason to despair. The French report to the European Community suggested that:

> . . . while it is impossible to quantify poverty in France, it also appears an unnecessary step. The fact that one does not have a total (fictitious) number of the poor does not prevent one from devising policies in favour

of the most deprived, from determining measures to be taken or from working them out carefully.[6]

I have some sympathy with this position. While I was writing this section, a presenter on the radio happened to ask 'how would you feel if you had a six-foot alligator in your garden?' and the question struck a chord. I think I would have difficulty describing it to the appropriate authorities, especially if they did not want to believe me. I doubt if I could tell it apart from a crocodile. It hardly seems important to know whether it is three feet, six feet or nine feet long. But I do know I would want someone to take it away.

Unfortunately, this will not do as an approach to poverty. The first obstacle is that many people do not believe poverty exists, at least not in their country; one of the most basic reasons for social research has been to provide hard evidence about it in order to persuade governments to action. Second, the problems of poverty are varied and diffused throughout society; policies which focus only on the most obvious problems (like poor areas) are likely to miss large numbers of people. Third, governments (and others involved in the subject) want to know what is involved in the effort, how much it will cost, and what they can expect to achieve. Although none of this can be measured precisely, it can be measured; the use of indicators is, at least, a way forward.

OPERATIONAL DEFINITIONS

Research into poverty has come to rely on a range of assumptions and on definitions of issues which are intended to translate the concept of poverty into practice, and to make it manageable. It is difficult to make sense of a discussion of the issues without first introducing some of the substantive work which has been done in this area. Writers and researchers on poverty have not confined themselves to discrete observations about the topic; they have produced packages of material, primarily in order to operationalise the concept of poverty, but often, it has to be said, with the intention of arguing for a particular political outcome.

Booth: the qualitative description of poverty

For most purposes, the modern study of poverty begins with Booth. Booth's mammoth work *Life and Labour of the People in London*, begun in 1886 and finished in 1903, represented at the time the most thorough analysis of poverty ever undertaken. Booth's methods were distinguished from his predecessors' in three main respects. First, he attempted to establish 'the facts'; as a positivist, he attempted to discover as much as he could of the problems of poverty without prejudging. Second, he attempted to use empirical evidence to quantify the extent of the problem. Third, he used a variety of methods by which to identify the problems, believing that this would reinforce the description of poverty.[7]

Despite widespread misconceptions to the contrary, Booth did not attempt to define poverty according to any prescriptive standard. Rather, he sought to describe the condition of poor people; such attempts as there are to define poverty emerge from the description. Booth based his analysis of poverty on a division between eight classes:[8]

A The lowest class of occasional labourers, loafers and semi-criminals
B Casual earnings – 'very poor' } together
C Intermittent earnings } 'the poor'
D Small regular earnings
E Regular standard earnings
F Higher class labour
G Lower middle class
H Upper middle class

The basis of this classification is not immediately clear. It looks, at first sight, as if people are grouped according to their income; this is certainly what distinguishes classes D and E. But Booth includes at least four groups, classes A, F, G and H, which are identified by their status in society rather than by their income. More importantly, classes B, C and D are distinguished by the frequency of their income. This suggests that Booth was trying to distinguish people by their class, in the sense of groups defined by their economic relationships, rather than by their income.

Williams suggests that the classes were identified on three criteria – relationships to the labour market, the domestic economy of households, and their moral character.[9] These elements certainly occur within the discussion of the classes, but it is going too far to conclude, as Williams does, that the classification is a moralistic one. Booth did not attempt to apply either clear discriminating principles or an explicit explanatory model; this was not his purpose. The primary basis for the distinction between classes is observation rather than theory. *Life and Labour* describes a range of social conditions in which it seemed that people are likely to be poor or on the margins of poverty. The classes represent groups which seemed to experience significant differences in their lifestyle.

The aspect of Booth's description of poverty which was to attract most attention was his use of a 'poverty line', which distinguished poor people from others. He set this at 18 to 21 shillings a week. He did not directly justify the selection of this range of income in terms of needs, a point which has been taken to indicate a degree of imprecision in his research.[10] But the poverty line was nothing more than an estimate of the levels of income at which people were likely to become poor. He explained the way in which he identified this range of income in the final volume of the second series:

> I take 21s as the bottom level for male adult labour in London. The employments in which less than 21s a week (or 3s 6d a day) is paid are exceptional in character. When the rate is 18s or 20s the work is not only characterised by great regularity and constancy with no slack seasons or lost days, but is generally such as a quite young or old man could perform – men who preferably have only themselves to keep.[11]

In other words, the poverty line was identified as the lowest part of the range of regular earnings. The Simeys argue that:

> Booth's poverty line must be regarded as being drawn so as to coincide with popular opinion . . . it was not his fault if his endeavour to translate this into shillings and pence for illustrative purposes was regarded by others as the main factor in his evaluation.[12]

Booth made no attempt to explain how people should spend their money, and he was criticised at the time for not doing so. He responded by constructing a number of indicative household budgets, to give some idea of the lifestyle of people on very low incomes. The poverty line was an indication of the sort of incomes over which people are likely to become poor; the household budgets represented the behaviour of people in the condition of poverty.

The idea of the poverty line, reinforced by Rowntree's attempts to identify minimum levels of income, was to take the debate in a different direction. But the attempt to discover poverty by describing conditions, rather than defining them, has recently been revived; a paper by Bradshaw and Holmes[13] considers the experience of unemployed families by identifying their pattern of expenditure, budgets, diets and financial circumstances. This returns, in effect, to the kind of work pioneered by Booth's household budgets. The emphasis is firmly on the qualitative appraisal of the experience of poverty. If Bradshaw and Holmes's work deserves particular mention, it is not so much for its originality as for its fusion of a range of different types of qualitative method. It combines studies of household budgets and expenditure with interview reports, observation and analysis. The results are intended, not to present the characteristics of every poor person in miniature, but to reflect a particular kind of experience in depth. As such, their work provides an insight into poverty which cannot be achieved through quantitative appraisals. In describing the 'circumstances and conditions of life' of unemployed people, Bradshaw and Holmes identify a series of issues. These included a restricted diet; an inadequate stock of clothing; limited stock of consumer durables, with those which were possessed being in poor condition; limited access to transport; and a high proportion of time spent at home watching television. The problems did not, perhaps surprisingly, include bad housing, which may indicate that the families were not as 'poor' as some others, or may reflect the relatively high standard of housing in the UK. The main gap in the research is that there is little account of people's positional status – for example, the impact of stigma or of living in undesirable areas.

Rowntree and the 'biological approach'

Rowntree's definition of a poverty line was certainly strongly influenced by the debates about Booth's work. One of the objections raised against Booth was that he had failed to distinguish the circumstances of people according to their behaviour. C. S. Loch objected to Booth's work

> . . . that poverty is so entirely relative to use and habit and potential ability of all kinds, that it can never serve as a satisfactory basis of social investigations or social reconstruction. It is not the greater or lesser of command of means that makes the material difference in the contentment and efficiency of social life, but the use of means relative to station in life and its possibilities.[14]

Bosanquet, similarly, was prepared to assert that:

> . . . there are comparatively few families in London through whose hands there had not passed in the course of the year sufficient money and money's worth to have made a life free at any rate from hunger and cold, and with much in it of good.[15]

Rowntree's distinction of 'primary' and 'secondary' poverty[16] was a direct refutation of this kind of criticism. People were described as being in primary poverty when they had inadequate income to meet minimum subsistence requirements; secondary poverty arose when, even though the incomes of people were nominally adequate to meet these minimum requirements, their patterns of behaviour or expenditure brought their available resources below the level at which the minimum standards could be met.

The distinction between 'primary' and 'secondary' poverty has been controversial, because of the implication that people in secondary poverty might be condemned for their poverty. But this would be to misinterpret the thrust of Rowntree's argument. The standards he devised for 'primary poverty' were deliberately set at a level so strict as to be beyond controversy; the minimum requirements were calculated on the most restrictive standard that Rowntree could devise. Allowance was made for

53686

food, assessed on the basis of providing a minimally adequate diet with the greatest possible economy; house rent and rates; and household sundries, including clothing, light and fuel. Rowntree made the point quite explicitly that not only was there no room for improvidence or inefficiency, but there was also no allowance for the slightest deviation from the standard.

> . . . let us clearly understand what 'merely physical efficiency' means. A family living on the scale allowed for in this estimate must never spend a penny on railway fare or omnibus. They must never go into the country unless they walk. They must never purchase a halfpenny newspaper or spend a penny to buy a ticket for a popular concert. They must write no letters to absent children, for they cannot afford to pay the postage. They must never contribute anything to their church or chapel, or give any help to a neighbour which costs them money. They cannot save, nor can they join sick club or Trade Union, because they cannot pay the necessary subscriptions. The children must have no pocket money for dolls, marbles or sweets. The father must smoke no tobacco, and must drink no beer. The mother must never buy any pretty clothes for herself or for her children. . . . Should a child fall ill, it must be attended by the parish doctor; should it die, it must be buried by the parish. Finally, the wage-earner must never be absent from his work for a single day. If any of these conditions are broken, the extra expenditure involved is met, *and can only be met*, by limiting the diet. . . .[17]

On this basis, his initial research found that nearly 10 per cent of everyone that he surveyed was in primary poverty, a further 3 per cent were within 2 shillings of the line, and 8.5 per cent more were within 6 shillings of it. Rowntree established, by this process, not only that a substantial number of people were on incomes so low that they must inevitably be poor, but that a high proportion of others were so close to the line that they must be expected to be affected by similar restrictions. These people were described as being in 'secondary poverty'. There is not one 'poverty line' in Rowntree's study: like Booth, he was concerned with a range of income in which people might be considered vulnerable to poverty.

Rowntree might be considered, in the idea of 'secondary poverty', to have offered hostages to fortune. He discussed the influence of drink and gambling on expenditure – for example, concluding that much secondary poverty might be attributed to these vices; and part of *Poverty* is directly concerned with drink and its effects, though Rowntree does suggest that people's lives were so miserable that it is hardly surprising if they sought some social life and entertainments. Equally, though, there are other sections which reflect on the problems of secondary poverty. Rowntree points out that poor people are likely to pay more for their food, that people who spent their money inefficiently invariably went without food to pay for it, and that before condemning their inefficiency it may be appropriate to compare their diets with those of the well-to-do. There is much in Rowntree's work which reflects the dominant attitudes of the epoch in which he was writing, but if he had failed to take account of those attitudes, he could not have hoped for his work to have a major impact.

Rowntree's use of the idea of 'primary' poverty meets several of the important tests for indicators; it has been widely interpreted to refer to a biological minimum necessary for subsistence.[18] Rowntree himself invited the comment by referring to the standard as what was required for 'merely physical efficiency'. He wrote: 'my primary poverty line represented the minimum sum on which physical efficiency could be maintained. It was a bare standard of subsistence . . .'[19] Veit-Wilson has convincingly argued against the view that Rowntree's work excludes social conditions, but the idea of the 'biological approach' has persisted, both in critiques of absolute measures and more recently in an academic reconsideration of the value of defining an absolute minimum. Sen, for example, writes:

> The much maligned biological approach, which deserves substantial reformulation but not rejection, relates to this irreducible core of absolute deprivation, keeping issues of starvation and hunger at the centre of the concept of poverty.[20]

What a biological minimum identifies is a point which people cannot live below, no matter what they do – a level of 'primary poverty'. The basket of goods approach used by Rowntree actually goes somewhat beyond the 'biological' needs represented by a particular calorific intake (as do the determinations of social assistance rates in Germany or the former USSR, which use fairly restrictive normative budgets),[21] because there is generally more in such a basket than is required for biological subsistence alone; but there are measures which use food intake as the central guide, like the US Department of Agriculture, which assumes that food intake constitutes one-third of total expenditure,[22] or the Indian government, which defines the poverty line in terms of the income of those who have a basic minimum calorie intake each day.[23]

There are two main objections to this kind of approach. One is that a measure which is based primarily on people's food intake (and perhaps not even on all aspects of their nutritional requirements) could, in certain circumstances, fall far short of meeting their other needs, and it would be fairly extraordinary to suggest that a family is not poor if it has enough to eat but cannot afford adequate fuel, clothing or shelter. The second is that a measure of biological subsistence does not reflect the way that people actually live, and a standard of 'primary poverty' can be used as a basis to judge the poor for misusing their resources. The purpose of defining the diet necessary for biological subsistence should not be to suggest that poor people must eat according to a particular regime, but at times (e.g. in the menus published by the US Department of Agriculture) it can seem that way. Poor people do not necessarily buy 'healthy' food when they are short of money; they have good reasons for not doing so. Recent research in Britain suggests both that healthy food costs more, and that where there is not enough food, people need to supplement their energy intake with high-calorie foods, such as sweets and biscuits. This is particularly true where there are children.[24]

Although these are strong objections, they should not be taken to invalidate the use of biological measures as an indicator. On this most restrictive basis, one-seventh of the population of the US, which is one of the richest countries in the world, still emerges as poor.[25]

Abel-Smith and Townsend: using benefit levels

Although the description of poverty in *The Poor and the Poorest* is not of the same kind as that undertaken by Booth or Rowntree, it ranks as a major work which has had a significant impact on the conceptualisation and analysis of poverty. The argument is based on a secondary analysis of statistics obtained from the Family Expenditure Survey, a government survey describing in detail the income and consumption patterns of a wide range of families. 'Poverty' was taken to be equivalent to the level of benefit offered by National Assistance. The authors defend this by saying:

> Whatever may be said about the adequacy of the National Assistance Board level of living as a just or publicly approved measure of 'poverty', it has at least the advantage of being in a sense the 'official' operational definition of the minimum level of living at any particular time.[26]

The authors sought to identify not only the numbers of people on the basic rates but also those with 20 or 40 per cent more. The reasons for doing this were partly to take into account extra needs not allowed for in the basic rates, and partly to bring in those on the margins of poverty, whose lifestyle would not necessarily be very different from those with a small amount less. The justification for the title of the paper is that their approach distinguishes different levels at which people might be considered poor.

This work was to prove enormously influential: it is largely credited with the 'rediscovery of poverty' in academic literature in the UK (though it is perhaps important to note that at the same period, 'poverty' was being identified, in the US, within a very different conceptual framework).[27] The measure of poverty as equivalent to National Assistance rates, or 140 per cent of those rates, became widely accepted: it is the basis, for example, of the measurement of poverty in the papers of the Royal Commission on the Distribution of Income and Wealth.[28]

The rates of National Assistance, even at the time of that pamphlet, had little to do with the definition of poverty. The National Assistance rates introduced in 1948 were nominally based on Rowntree's surveys, but Beveridge used lower figures than Rowntree; the figures were based on 1938, and no allowance was made for inflation; and the government made adjustments, because of free school meals, which cut the rates for children. Abel-Smith and Townsend calculated that, at 1953 rates, the benefit levels would fall below Rowntree's poverty line.[29]

Subsequent amendments of the benefit levels have had a still greater impact on the relationship between the benefits and Rowntree's estimates. Through the 1970s, benefits increased in line with increases in prices or wages, whichever was the greater. This led to a ratchet upwards of pensions; by contrast, unemployed people were left behind. Inflation was measured by the general increase in the Retail Price Index, not the items used by Rowntree. No account was taken of the continued availability or non-availability of 'poverty goods' – second-hand items, cheap foodstuffs, etc. The allowances for dependants were altered in 1980, and the rates were substantially restructured again in 1988.

The effect of this is to confound any links which might be made between benefit rates and poverty. Benefit rates are not based on any measure of basic needs. If anything, Income Support is below subsistence levels for large numbers of people. Piachaud has used a technique similar to Rowntree's to show that benefit rates were inadequate to meet the subsistence of a child.[30] Mack and Lansley argue that serious deprivations began, for most people, when incomes fell below 150 per cent of the Supplementary Benefit (SB) level.[31] And research by the Policy Studies Institute shows that more than half of all the families with children on SB were in debt, had had serious anxieties about money while on benefit, and ran out of money most weeks.[32] The Income Support rates are effectively lower than SB was for many households.

Townsend: poverty as 'relative deprivation'

Peter Townsend's *Poverty in the United Kingdom*[33] is certainly the most important study of poverty after Rowntree. Townsend explains his research in terms of a developed conceptual analysis of poverty, which I have already addressed in part and shall consider further in the following chapter. Poverty is described in terms of the normal activities and amenities which are available to others in society. In order to establish who was poor, Townsend consequently contrasted those who underwent a series of deprivations with those who did not, a condition he refers to as 'relative deprivation'.

Townsend's approach relies on the analysis of observed circumstances and behaviour. The importance of this approach is that, unlike studies which concentrate on income or a 'poverty line', Townsend's work has been able to describe in great detail the experience of poverty among a wide range of people, and to offer a quantitative basis for comparison. In many ways, his theoretical analysis, and the detailed consideration of people in various types of circumstances, is of greater interest than the process that he ultimately uses to summarise the primary circumstances of people who are poor, but in so far as this chapter is concerned with the ways in which poverty has been described, it is important to outline it here. Townsend begins with 60 factors which may be associated with poverty, and then uses a statistical analysis to select 12 factors which seem most strongly associated with low income. The selected items are as follows:

1 Has not had week's holiday away from home in last 12 months.
2 *Adults only*. Has not had a relative or friend to the home for a meal or a snack in the last four weeks.
3 *Adults only*. Has not been out in the last four weeks to a relative or friend for a meal or a snack.
4 *Children only*. Has not had a friend to play or to tea in the last four weeks.
5 *Children only*. Did not have a party on last birthday.
6 Has not had an afternoon or evening out for entertainment in the last two weeks.
7 Does not have fresh meat (including meals out) as many as four days a week.
8 Has gone through one or more days in the past fortnight without a cooked meal.
9 Has not had a cooked breakfast most days of the week.
10 Household does not have a refrigerator.
11 Household does not usually have a Sunday joint (three in four times).
12 Household does not have sole use of four amenities indoors (flush WC; sink or wash-basin and cold water tap; fixed bath or shower; and gas or electric cooker).

The index looks odd, because the statistical analysis has some important effects on the form which the index takes. In the first place, the factors which are selected are not necessarily those which are most strongly associated with poverty, but those which best help to identify the issue. The reason for this is that some factors which are strongly associated with poverty are frequently found together with others which are also strongly associated, but the inclusion of both does not do any more to identify who is poor and who is not. Each item in the index, then, stands for a number of other associated factors. Second, the factors which are selected are not necessarily appealing to 'common sense'; items which seem plausibly to be associated with poverty, like overcrowding or shortages of fuel, are eliminated in favour of others which are less apparently important, like whether children had a birthday party. Third, and perhaps most important, associations which are established in this way may be conditional on the circumstances in which the survey was undertaken; it would be dangerous to generalise too far from the index, as Townsend himself would undoubtedly stress. The basic research was done in the late 1960s, when the consumption of meat (which has fallen substantially since) probably meant something different in social terms. The techniques that Townsend used may be generalisable; the precise results are not.

More recently, Townsend has extended the basic principle to consider other factors. In particular, he has sought to distinguish 'subjective' factors, related to public views about essential items, and 'objective' factors, which are indicators of deprivation. Whatever the test, the results indicate that benefit levels are substantially too low.[34]

Bradshaw: budget standards

Jonathan Bradshaw's work has been eclectic, being generally more concerned to identify the problems of poverty than to offer an authoritative definition.[35] The idea of 'budget standards' has been based on insights from a number of writers – including Rowntree, Piachaud and Townsend, and sources from the US – with the aim of establishing the minimum levels of income on which people can reasonably subsist.

The definition of 'budget standards' is not directly equivalent to the definition of a subsistence standard. Rowntree's definitions of subsistence made some fairly sweeping normative assumptions about the kinds of thing that people needed to live on at a minimum. But there are major problems in trying to specify such budgets without imposing standards inappropriately, because people's pattern of expenditure changes as their income increases. Where people are short of resources, they have to spend proportionately more on certain items – like food; they have to balance competing claims on their spending; and they buy different kinds of goods. The use of a normative budget overrides this kind of consideration; it may be useful as an indicator, but it does not give much indication of the way in which poor people live, nor of what kind of income would genuinely be adequate.

The Watts Committee[36] suggested that it should be possible to work out people's actual patterns of expenditure, avoiding many of the normative judgements associated with the method. Bradshaw and his colleagues take this suggestion further, by examining the proportions that people on low incomes actually spend on different types of expenditure. This is judged

Table 3.1 An index of deprivation

Item	*% describing as necessary*		*% lacking*	
	1983	*1990*	*1983*	*1990*
Housing				
Heating	97	97	5	3
Indoor toilet	96	97	2	0
Damp-free home	96	98	7	2
Bath	94	95	2	0
Decent state of home decoration	–	92	–	15
Enough bedrooms for children	77	82	3	7
Self-contained accommodation	79	–	3	–
Food				
Two meals a day for adults	64	90	3	1
Three meals a day for children	82	90	2	0
Fresh fruit and veg. daily	–	88	–	6
Meat, fish or equivalent veg. every other day	63	77	8	4
Clothing				
Warm waterproof coat	87	91	7	4
Two pairs of all-weather shoes	78	74	9	5
Household goods				
Beds for everyone	94	95	1	1
Refrigerator	77	92	2	1
Carpets	70	78	2	2
Washing machine	67	73	6	4
Financial security				
Insurance	–	88	–	10
Savings of £10 per month	–	68	–	30
Quality of life				
Public transport	88	–	3	–
Toys for children	71	84	2	2
Celebrations on special occasions like Xmas	69	74	4	4
Presents once a year	63	69	5	5
Out-of-school activities	–	69	–	10
Hobby or leisure activity	64	67	7	7

Source: From J Mack and S Lansley, 1985, *Poor Britain*, London: Allen and Unwin; and H Frayman, *Breadline Britain 1990s*, London: Domino Films/London Weekend Television.

by comparing budgets for items like food, clothing or fuel, and then working out the cost of a family budget from that.

The authors are modest about the potential of budget standards research, for two main reasons. In the first place, what people spend money on is not everything which goes to make up their material welfare, let alone their quality of life. Second, there is still a normative element in the selection of the commodities which are accounted for. But the approach differs from Rowntree, and from the general tradition of normative budgets, in its careful avoidance of any prescription about what people ought to spend on particular items. The amount people actually spend represents both what it is reasonable to spend and what people might expect to spend. The measure takes account, then, of people's behaviour, the costs of meeting basic needs, and probably of dominant social norms. It differs from Townsend in considering, not what people actually do, but what they can afford to do – defining, therefore, a 'poverty line' based on common patterns of behaviour at different levels of income. If there is a way to identify patterns of deprivation as a matter of fact with levels of income, this seems to be it.

Mack and Lansley: consensual standards

The next major development to consider in the progress of empirical research is the 'consensual' standard of poverty – a piece of research undertaken, remarkably, for a television programme, 'Breadline Britain'. The central problem of most methods which rely on the social definition of poverty is the difficulty in establishing what norms are being applied. The way that people live does not necessarily establish what they believe about lifestyle. Mack and Lansley attempted to establish norms, not by examining behaviour, but by asking people what they consider 'essential'. The replies are outlined in Table 3.1; they include all the items considered necessary by more than two-thirds of those asked.

This work attempts to address the controversy over which standards should be applied by appealing to public opinion; this has the advantage both of identifying dominant social norms and of establishing an external standard which can then be applied to the examination of the circumstances of poor people. The list of factors emphasises the social nature of the definition of poverty. Some preferences are clearly cultural, like the descriptions of carpets and hobbies as 'necessary'. Others reflect changing standards: it is intriguing, for example, to see indoor toilets described as 'essential' when they were not even particularly commonplace 60 years before; I have heard anecdotes from housing officers suggesting that people were initially reluctant to accept houses with inside WCs because they feared they would be unhygienic, which does not seem unreasonable. The differences in results in the course of seven years are remarkable, too; some part of this change is probably explicable in terms of a liberalisation of attitudes to the poor, because what one considers 'necessary' for others depends in part on the circumstances which they are believed to be in.

The importance of Mack and Lansley's work rests in its attempt to frame a standard of poverty which reflects the process of social definition. It is uncertain whether public opinion, as expressed in a social survey, is equivalent to an expression of social norms. What it does express, however, is the way in which people are likely to use words; and this, in the terms of the kind of philosophical analysis I have tried to apply to the concept of poverty, is as good as a description of the word's meaning. Bradshaw's method helps to establish what the relationship is between a lack of resources and deprivation; Mack and Lansley's approach helps to identify whether people in such circumstances can or should be identified as 'poor'.

CONCLUSION

On the face of the matter, the operationalisation of a concept develops as a reflection of a theoretical position. However, the examples I have considered suggest that this is not a very good description of the process which is involved. The differences in theory are important, and they will be examined further in the following chapter. But even where there are theoretical differences, the approaches implied by different methods may be complementary; Booth, Townsend and Bradshaw have used not one method, but several. It is possible to 'triangulate', to use several different methods as a means of identifying the cluster of problems at the centre.

The effect of the overlap between methods means that some important similarities can be identified between the approaches. Some aspects of the concept of poverty seem to be fairly universally incorporated. All of them recognise, to some degree, that poverty is socially defined – not least because all of them have to translate the definition of poverty into terms which are current in the society to which they are applied. The process is not simply, then, one in which conceptualisation defines the possible field of operational applications; it is a two-way process, in which the process of operationalisation shapes the kind of concept which is adopted.

4 Concepts of poverty

The dichotomy between 'absolute' and 'relative' poverty is built on a false, or at least an inadequate, interpretation of the kinds of position which people have adopted. The absolute model is supposed to be fixed over time, and conceived without reference to social circumstances. I have yet to encounter a work which considers 'absolute' poverty in these terms: even the classic texts by Booth and Rowntree, which are most commonly cited as examples of the 'absolute' model, show a clear awareness of the social nature of poverty. Booth is particularly misrepresented; what he actually wrote about poverty was:

> The 'poor' are those whose means may be sufficient, but are barely sufficient, for decent independent life; the 'very poor' those whose means are insufficient for this according to the usual standard of life in this country.[1]

The reference to the 'usual standard of life in this country' is virtually equivalent to Townsend's phrase 'common or customary in society'. Rowntree's model comes nearer to an absolute standard, a standard adopted to prove a case – that poor people did not have enough to live on, even if the most stringent standards are used. However, Rowntree clearly accepted, even within this, that standards altered over time.[2] Ringen suggests: 'There never was such a thing as an absolute concept of poverty and no one has argued that there should be. The absolute concept . . . is a straw man. . . .'[3]

The 'relative' concept of poverty is equally liable to be misinterpreted. It is sometimes taken as a form of inequality – which, if the Roaches' definition is used, it is. But Townsend writes:

> Inequality . . . is not poverty. Even if inequalities in the distribution of resources are successfully identified and measured, those in the lowest 20 per cent or 10 per cent, say, are not necessarily poor. . . . Some criterion of deprivation is required by which a poverty line may be drawn. . . .[4]

There is something wrong here; there seems to be a basic inconsistency between the way the models are initially presented and what the supposed advocates actually say about them. There are real differences in the positions that people hold, but they cannot simply be identified as 'absolute' or 'relative'. For the most part, when authors have addressed poverty in conceptual terms, they have sought, of necessity, to modify or qualify the terms in which the problems are addressed. In effect, there is not one 'absolute' or 'relative' model, but a diversity of different approaches, often with a different theoretical basis.

COMPARATIVE AND NORMATIVE CONCEPTS

Comparative standards

The idea that poverty is relative is rooted in the view that poverty can be identified by comparison with the conditions that other people are living in, either with members of the same society or with others in other societies. This confounds two important, but separable, issues. One is the social definition of poverty; the other is the process by which people are compared to establish who is poor and who is not. The distinction may seem difficult to sustain at first, but it is an important one, and it is worth examining in greater depth.

The reason why the two ideas are so often confused is that they both depend on a form of comparison. However, the comparisons which are made are of different kinds. In one sense, almost all words are defined to some extent by comparison: for example, I know that I am sitting on a chair because I compare it to other objects of a similar type and function which I also call 'chairs'. Poverty is identifiable because it represents a set or cluster of conditions similar to other circumstances which we also refer to as 'poverty' – and that is a crucial point, because it means that new circumstances, or circumstances which come to newly to our attention, can be identified as 'poverty' when the effects they produce are like those we associate with poverty. It may not have been obvious in the early 1900s that the impediments to development suffered by many children should be specifically considered as a form of impoverishment, because the same problems – bad housing, poor standards of hygiene, limited nutrition – were identifiable as aspects of poverty on other grounds. Improvements in many of these circumstances, however, reveal that there are other outstanding impediments to development – like the lack of toys, play space or room to study, when parents are unable to afford them. That is not necessarily a sign that the meaning of poverty has changed, but it does indicate that the application of the concept is likely to alter as social conditions change. Social definitions of poverty depend on a comparison of poverty with the things it is like.

By contrast, when poverty is identified by contrasting the circumstances of poor people with others who are not poor, it is being compared to things that it is not like. When Bradshaw refers to 'comparative need', for example, the comparison which is made is based on a strict inequality between the people being compared. 'Deprivation' is certainly a term which implies a contrast between those who have and those who have not; if poverty is rightly described in terms of deprivation, then poverty is defined primarily in terms of the things that one does not have.

This can in turn be taken to mean that poverty can be identified by a contrast with the condition of others who are not poor, but that is not obvious. Deprivation may involve comparison with those who are not deprived, but equally it may involve comparison with some kind of standard or norm. To justify a comparison with other people who are not deprived, one has to establish on what criteria they might be considered to be different. This would imply that there is some pre-existing condition being applied, or a norm of some kind. If deprivation or poverty is to be identified by a process of comparing people's relative positions, it seems to be based on one of two propositions: either this type of comparison helps to reveal the norms which underlie the distinction, or poverty is to be defined in terms of the differences which are identified by the process.

These are very different kinds of argument, and it might be helpful to give them different names. The definition of poverty in terms of differences in circumstances is a 'comparative standard of poverty'. The *process* of comparing people is a 'comparative method', which can be used to support either an attempt to discover social norms or to contrast differences in circumstances.

Comparative standards are being used with increasing frequency, not least because of their convenience and analytical power. The Roaches, for example, define poverty as the condition of a certain proportion of the population, a use also adopted by the National Children's Bureau.[5] This is particularly crude – it has the effect of always defining a proportion of people as poor, irrespective of any changes made in their circumstances – and little used, except as a convenience (because it is evident that if there are poor people, they are likely to be found in the lowest income groups). Much more common is the relationship of low incomes to the average income in a country – a measure which also treats poverty as a form of inequality, but by which increases or falls in relative income can have a clear effect on someone's status. The Leyden study, for the European Commission, experimented with various definitions of poverty as a relationship to median income and family size.[6] Other work for the European Community has experimented with levels at 40, 50 or 60 per cent of average income.[7] Walker and Lawson refer to a standard of poverty set at 60 per cent of average disposable incomes.[8] UK statistics now refer to 'households below average income', again across a range of levels.[9] The Luxembourg Income Study, which promises because of the quality of its data to provide the standard measure, refers to people as poor when they have incomes of less than 50 per cent of the median equivalent income.[10] Each of these approaches treats poverty in terms of relative disadvantage; there are no supplementary criteria in terms of possession of goods, availability of essential items or social capabilities.

In the review of research outlined in the previous chapter, there were three examples of the use of comparative methods – that is, cases in which poverty was identified in terms of a contrast between the circumstances of those who were poor and those who were not. These are Booth's identification of classes, which seems to me to rely on some implicit normative judgements; Townsend's construction of an index of deprivation; and Bradshaw's attempt to classify 'budget' standards, which seeks to identify dominant norms through concentration on observed behaviour. Comparative methods have some attractions. Because the comparison takes place within a social context, the difficulty of coping with shifting social definitions of poverty is largely removed. The comparative method can be adapted to many different kinds of circumstance and condition, without necessarily understanding the dominant social norms. At the same time, social norms are often defined in the light of prevailing conditions, and a comparative measure provides an indicator of normal behaviour; Townsend's measure comes close to doing so, and Bradshaw's closer still.

The process of comparison is a useful one; whatever the conceptual difficulties of treating a comparison as the basis for a description of poverty, it is still likely to be true that poor people are likely to be found among those who are relatively disadvantaged in a society. But comparative methods are still subject to certain difficulties. As Sen points out, it may happen through social changes that a person may suffer greater hardship and be considered less poor. This point undermines the rationale for provision which might relieve poverty. Equally, it suggests that people may become poorer even though their material circumstances are improving in real terms, which makes it an easy target.

Second, a comparative method limits the kinds of cases in which people might be thought to be poor to cases where they are also in a particular relative position. The implication of a measure based on the lowest 10 or 20 per cent of the population is that the remaining 90 or 80 per cent are not poor. The use of the median as a point of reference in a range of studies means that poverty is necessarily confined in all circumstances to the lowest 50 per cent of the population. Leite, for example, claims that more than half the families in Brazil are poor;[11] but using the median as a measure would mean that this is impossible by definition. There is evidently something seriously wrong with this proposition, particularly when one moves to consideration of the least developed Third World countries; it is suspect even when applied to a country like Portugal.[12] The point does not undermine the usefulness of this kind of measure as an indicator, but it is a helpful reminder that the issue under discussion is not that of 'poverty'.

Third, the process of comparison does not necessarily reflect the way in which many people use the word 'poverty'. This is the substance of Joseph and Sumption's obvious objection: 'A family is poor if it cannot afford to eat. It is not poor if it cannot afford endless smokes and it does not become poor by the mere fact that other people can afford them'.[13] The central problem with a simple comparison of poor people with others is that it cannot identify the kinds of value which determine at what point items are considered to be 'essential'. There is, then, no evident criterion on which to judge that people are poor. This relationship depends on some other kinds of consideration about the relationship between poverty and social norms. The central justification for the use of a comparative standard – as opposed to a comparative method – is that there is something within the process of comparison which reflects the social processes through which people become poor.

Townsend argues for an assessment based on 'relative deprivation', which he attempts to assess by examining the objective conditions of poor people. He identifies poverty in relation to 'ordinary living patterns, customs and activities' – a term which includes both norms and patterns of behaviour – but his process of measurement depends on observation of behaviour, or a comparative standard, rather than establishment of dominant norms. There is nothing within the method to identify what is a norm and what is not, and both Townsend's definition of poverty and his selection of the criteria by which people might be thought poor are based wholly on the differences between the circumstances of the poor and those of others. This is not simply a comparative method; it conceals the use of a comparative standard, albeit a standard which is more complex than others.

A comparison of this sort is related to social norms, but it is not equivalent. Not all comparisons reflect expectations. The use of the kind of definition which identifies poverty in terms of inequality[14] implies that poverty changes directly and immediately in response to changes in social conditions. Social expectations may ultimately reflect such differences over time, but they are unlikely to do so in the short term – and perhaps not even in the medium term. Table 4.1 shows the possession of durable goods by income. If people are judged by what other people have, they might reasonably be identified as poor if they lack a telephone or a deep freeze. Perhaps more surprisingly, the same might be said of a tumble drier – owned by 45 per cent of households, and by 63 per cent of families with

Table 4.1 Possession of durable goods by weekly household income, 1989 (%)

	Usual weekly income					
Durable good	*£0–100*	*£100–200*	*£200–300*	*£300–400*	*Over £400*	*All*
Colour TV	84	92	96	98	98	93
Video	23	47	71	79	85	60
Deep freeze	56	78	85	90	94	80
Washing machine	68	83	90	95	97	86
Tumble drier	21	37	46	53	46	45
Telephone	69	82	88	94	99	87

Source: Adapted from Office of Population Censuses and Surveys, 1991, *General Household Survey 1989*, London: HMSO.

children. This is scarcely something that one 'expects' to find – on the contrary, it is initially a surprising figure in a society where poverty is all too apparent. Similarly, not all comparisons which do meet expectations are enforced as social rules; the widespread ownership of deep freezes, telephones and colour televisions is not (as far as I know) accompanied by any obvious expectations or rule of behaviour. It might, I think, be true to say that these items will become necessary as time goes on – food preservation, communications and leisure are all extremely important in modern life – and it may legitimately be argued that social norms are likely, ultimately, to come into line with social circumstances; but the way that people live is not necessarily immediately reflected in what they believe.

Comparisons do not, then, yield information directly about social norms (although a comparative method might still be used as an indicator of norms). A comparative standard assumes, rather, that poverty is a form of inequality. This identification is made explicitly by O'Higgins and Jenkins:

> Virtually all definitions of the poverty threshold used in developed economies in the last half-century or so have been concerned with establishing the level of income necessary to allow access to the minimum standards of living considered acceptable in that society at that time. In consequence, there is an inescapable connection between poverty and inequality: certain degrees or dimensions of inequality . . . will lead to people being below the minimum standards acceptable in that society. It is this 'economic distance' aspect of inequality that is poverty. This does not mean that there will always be poverty when there is inequality: only if the inequality implies an economic distance beyond the critical level.[15]

Poverty and inequality are clearly closely linked. The term 'inequality' does not refer to 'differences' between people; people are 'unequal' if one of them has a relative advantage over the other. The idea of 'inequality' generally refers to disadvantage in a social context. Command over resources is one of the main ways in which advantage or disadvantage in society may be assessed; if a person is poor, that person is disadvantaged in comparison with someone who is not poor. But a comparative standard goes much further than this, by defining poverty in terms of inequality. This follows from the propositions that poverty is socially defined, and that it is based in a comparative concept. The reference to the social definition of poverty supplies the context; the element of comparison identifies the nature of the disadvantage. The conclusion that poverty is of the same nature as inequality is true by definition.

> *If* poverty is defined as a form of disadvantage in a social context, *and*
> Inequality is the name given to disadvantage in a social context, *then*
> Poverty is defined as a form of inequality.

If the initial propositions are accepted, I do not see how the conclusion can be resisted, although Townsend attempts to do so. If there is some confusion between Townsend's view of poverty and the concept of inequality, it is because he is inconsistent in recognising the importance of social norms while attempting to identify poverty through the use of a comparative standard.

Normative standards

Deprivation may involve comparison with those who are not deprived, but equally it may involve comparison with some kind of standard or norm. The concept of deprivation necessarily implies a concept of sufficiency; and if poverty is a form of deprivation, then equally it demands some consideration of sufficiency. (It does not, I should note, require any concept or definition of riches, although from a concept of sufficiency one may be able to move towards a concept of *luxury* (or superfluity), which may fall short of riches.) To move from this position to the view that the term can be arrived at from a comparison with other people, a supplementary argument is required: that the others with whom the comparison is being made are not deprived. This might seem like a very minor condition, but it is nevertheless important. They may not be deprived, but how can you tell? It implies that there is some pre-existing condition being applied – a norm of some kind.

Deprivation is a comparative term, but there is no intrinsic reason why a standard of deprivation, or its associated concept of sufficiency, should have to be derived from a comparison with *the conditions of other people*. If I discover that a person in Britain is short of food, I may need to know more in order to explain why this happens in an apparently affluent society;

but the norm that I am using for the comparison may be a nutritional norm, rather than a comparison with the dominant social standard. Equally, if I discover a society in which everyone is short of food – by whatever social definition – I can see no difficulty in describing them as members of a poor society. The 'absolute core' of need which Sen refers to is not necessarily an objective measure of poverty, but it is a normative one – that is, a standard which applies a norm.

Normative standards are of two main kinds. There are, first, norms identified by experts, which relate to the capacity of people to function in society. These might be described as prescriptive standards of poverty. Rowntree's or Piachaud's measurement of minimum standards are attempts, not to impose arbitrary personal definitions, but to describe a minimum necessary to social functioning. Their position is complicated by their political purpose. Rowntree's standards were deliberately selected to be more restrictive than dominant social norms, because by doing so the authors were able to demonstrate that people were poor beyond question. The purpose of Rowntree's distinction between primary and secondary poverty was not to impose judgements on the poor, but to demonstrate to those who did impose such judgements that even if one applied the strictest imaginable standard, people would still be poor. As such, Rowntree provided a powerful political argument. Piachaud used a similar approach as a direct, and most effective, criticism of the adequacy of benefit rates.[16]

Second, there are socially established norms, a commonly held set of expectations and values. The derivation of 'consensual' standards is based in such norms. This currently falls within the remit of the 'relative' model, but it is 'relative' in a very different sense to comparative standards. Runciman[17] argues for a concept of 'relative deprivation', not to be confused with Townsend's later use of the term. People determine the standards which are appropriate by a comparison of their circumstances with the circumstances of other people. When they do not have things that they can reasonably expect to have, they may consider themselves deprived. Runciman's arguments seem, at first sight, to be based on subjective impressions, but that is a misleading impression; the views which are formed are *inter-subjective*, formed through an interactive process, rather than by individuals in isolation.[18] The process produces social norms of what constitutes poverty and what does not. Norms are a form of expectation which acquire, through familiarity and usage, the force of a rule. (This implies that a social definition of poverty can also have the force of a rule.) The attempt to define poverty in accordance with public opinion – like Mack and Lansley's work – can be seen in part as an attempt to identify the norms which are effective at a particular time. Appeals to 'common sense' – like Joseph and Sumption's rejection of Townsend – are not simply the reaction of individuals; they appeal to what the authors believe is the dominant social expectation.

In talking about poverty, people do seem to be applying a variety of normative standards – which leads people to talk about hunger, destitution and so on as if these were 'absolute' concepts. The concept of normative standards is more difficult to operationalise, but it probably provides a more accurate description of the way in which poverty is conceived.

ESTABLISHING A MINIMUM: THE POVERTY LINE

On the face of it, a 'poverty line' is a crude concept. Poverty lines define thresholds, in terms of income or wealth, below which people may be considered as 'poor'. The weakness of all the approaches which define one or more 'poverty lines' is that they rest in a view of poverty as a simple function of the relationship between resources and consumption. There are, in practice, many other norms which are also used – norms reflected not only in words like want, need or destitution, but in other concepts like homelessness or hunger. Poverty is associated with income and wealth, but it is not the same thing.

The idea was used first by Charles Booth – the Simeys describe it as 'perhaps his most striking single contribution to the social sciences'.[19] Booth was not, as I have explained, attempting to define a subsistence income, even if it looks that way superficially; he was, rather, stating the range of incomes over which people seemed to become poor; the figure was based on a lengthy series of observations rather than any prescriptive standard. The concept of the poverty line was later substantially changed by Rowntree, to become more a definition of poverty than a descriptive indicator, though it is far from clear that this is what Rowntree intended; his descriptions of 'secondary poverty' are based on a 'feel' for the circumstances in which people are poor, and not on any precise system of measurement.[20] Bowley, writing in 1915, was to comment:

> I have . . . still to be convinced that the scale of diet made familiar by Mr Rowntree has that definiteness which is so often assumed by people who quote his results. I rather regard it as a useful arbitrary measurement of a low scale of living, by the help of which we can compare populations in respect of the adequacy of their wages; it makes a useful and intelligible line, even if it is not possible to accept it as the Poverty Line, which divides the poor from those who have a competence. There is not, and cannot be, any such division except an arbitrary one, for every quantity involved varies continuously from grade to grade.[21]

It is important, then, not to take the original idea of the 'poverty line' as indicating too literal or mechanistic a relationship between needs and income.

The first point of controversy, one which is pointed to by Bowley, is whether there can be said to be a 'line' at all. All poverty lines require a distinction to be made somewhere. Veit-Wilson classifies poverty lines on the basis that whereas some use prescriptive criteria, others try to establish where the line falls empirically. Among the first, he gives examples which include Booth, Rowntree, and the statistical measurement of inequality; among the second, he includes Townsend, and Mack and Lansley.[22]

Whether the concept of poverty is normative or comparative, there are conceptual problems in accepting the idea that poverty affects people according to whether they fall above or below a 'line'. If poverty is normative, and defined in terms of a line, then on the face of it a person either is or is not poor. But this is not the way we use the term. People are not simply said to be 'poor' or 'not poor'; they may be 'hard up', deprived, poor, destitute. Within these categories, there are further gradations – like 'very poor', 'poor', 'fairly poor'. Booth distinguished 'poverty' from terms like 'want' and 'distress',[23] want and distress being, in his view, aggravated forms of poverty. These are not precise terms with a universally agreed meaning, and they may overlap with the other categories; there is no clear distinction, for example, between the circumstances in which one would use 'fairly poor' and those in which one would use 'deprived'.

Within a normative standard of poverty, there are two ways in which gradations of poverty can be accommodated. One could be based on a calculus, in which a person's poverty is graded according to the extent to which it falls below a line or an established norm. This approach has an appealing simplicity, but there is a major conceptual problem arising from it. The very idea of a calculus implies that there is some basis for comparison, on a strictly relative basis. The attempt to grade poverty below the normative level becomes, therefore, a comparative exercise. It is possible, of course, to argue that poverty is a mixture of normative and comparative elements, but it is difficult to see why, if a comparative standard of poverty should be accepted below a normative line, the principle should be rejected in its entirety above the normative line. There is no evident reason to accept that 'poverty' must be seen in normative terms but that 'destitution' or 'want' have to be seen as comparative.

The second way in which the idea could be incorporated, and one that I think better reflects the use of the terms, is not through one, but through several, different norms – the approach favoured by Booth. People in general need food to live, and to be healthy; they may have enough food to preserve life but not health. A person without any food at all is more 'in need' than someone who does not have food which is adequately nutritious, but it makes perfectly good sense to talk about both people as being 'poor'. What is happening here is that at least two standards are being applied; 'poverty' is a general term used to indicate serious deprivation on either basis.

The use of a comparative standard of poverty poses a different set of problems. There is little difficulty in coming to terms with gradations in the concept of poverty. A concept of poverty based on relative principles is necessarily transitive, which means that if A is judged to be poor compared to B, and B is poor when compared to C on the same criteria, then A has the greatest degree of poverty and C the least. (This may seem so obvious that it is not worth mentioning, but it contrasts with a normative approach; A, B and C might all fall into the category of 'people in poverty', with the result that the distinctions between them become irrelevant.) The main difficulty is in using the idea of a line or threshold below which people can be said to be 'poor'. The justification for a 'line' rests in large part on the existence of some discontinuity in the distribution of resources. Booth, who based his description of a poverty line on a division between classes, suggested that the line came at the level of the band of income which distinguished people in regular work from those who were casually or intermittently employed.[24] Desai suggests, on the basis of Mack and Lansley's figures, that there is a threshold beyond which people are likely to become poor in the terms of the consensual measure of poverty,[25] but it is uncertain whether this can be justified in these terms. Piachaud argues that the apparent 'threshold' in these figures is a statistical artefact.[26]

The central problems with poverty lines are not so much that they are liable to be arbitrary – that is virtually inherent in the use of indicators of this sort – as that they are subject to systematic biases in application and interpretation. An illustrative problem is that of equivalence. The concept of poverty depends on a relationship between needs and resources, and if a poverty line is to reflect the relationship in any meaningful way, it seems impossible to avoid some kind of adjustment for needs. The needs of a single person are very different from those of a family with six children, and in turn those of a family with six children are not the same as those of eight single adults each maintaining an independent household. This kind of adjustment is usually referred to in terms of 'equivalence scales' – translating the circumstances of different members of a household into equivalent terms.[27] It is still necessary to generalise to some degree. The usual justification for generalisation is that differences between individuals tend to cancel out; for everyone whose needs are greater than average, there is someone else whose needs are less. But 'poverty' is a diffuse and diverse concept, which covers a wide range of contingencies; the main objection to such generalisations is that they can conceal issues in which systematic disadvantages arise. One example is the position of women within households, who because they may not have a proportionate share of resources may be below the standards of others, particularly when those others are at the margins of poverty.[28] This is not an insuperable obstacle; it implies that descriptions of poverty which ignore the disadvantaged position of women have been liable to set the poverty line too low, and that can be countered with an appropriate equivalence scale. Another example is that of disabled people, who have higher costs than others to face, and so are likely to suffer the deprivations associated with poverty at higher levels of income; this means that the application of a general poverty line will fail to identify their needs adequately,[29] which in turn implies that an adjustment is necessary. The problem which emerges is not that such adjustments are impossible, but that as different circumstances are progressively taken into account – like the needs of single parents, of old people, of positions in the life cycle and so forth – the whole process ultimately becomes so complex as to be almost unworkable.

The objections to the use of a 'poverty line' are considerable. But, as in much of this field, it is necessary to make compromises in order to achieve practical results. The main value of the idea of the 'poverty line' is in its use in relation to policy. If it is possible to show that certain levels of income are clearly related to the conditions of poverty, an increase in income can substantially alleviate many of the problems. The poverty line is a means of operationalising this concept.

Booth set his poverty line well above the level of benefits that he recommended. The principle behind this was, first, to allow for people on benefits to use other resources to supplement their lifestyle; and, second, to develop benefits at a level which might be acceptable politically. If benefits are specifically set at a point much lower than the threshold of poverty, it is difficult for those opposed to benefits to argue that the benefits are too generous, offer disincentives to work or are wasteful in their expenditure.

Conversely, there may be a case for setting a poverty line below the level of benefits. If benefits are intended to offer social protection, or a minimum level of income which allows for relative ease rather than basic sufficiency, then it seems unduly limiting to confine the level of benefits to the level of poverty. This seems to be the current argument of the UK Conservative government, which denies that people who are in receipt of benefit are in 'poverty'. Without being very clear as to what this implies, or where the line of poverty falls, it must mean that if there is a level or range of income associated with poverty, it comes somewhere below the level allowed for in benefits.

The critiques developed of subsistence measures of poverty in the 1960s and 1970s were based on the view that such measures justified a minimal response to the problems of the poor. In the 1980s, when it became clear that benefit rates in the UK were inadequate to meet people's needs, a number of authors began to argue again for the definition of a 'basket of goods' of the type used in Germany.[30] Others (like Mack and Lansley, Bradshaw, and Townsend) developed different techniques for establishing a minimum income. The advantage of such approaches is that it becomes possible to measure the success or failure of benefit transfers in redistributing income against an independent criterion. All of them recognise a risk of some arbitrariness, but the political importance of defining some kind of standard by which poverty can be judged is evident.

There is little immediate risk that the definition of minimum standards will lead to a restrictive allowance on benefit. The indications from all of these methods is that benefit rates in the UK are too low for people to live without experiencing serious deprivations. In the long term, however, it is possible to envisage circumstances in which a standard which has been applied for a number of years might fail to meet developing needs, or to allow for fuller participation in society. The Leyden Group or the Luxembourg Income Study[31] avoid the problem by using a measure – derived from average incomes – which defines poverty fairly directly in terms of inequality.

POVERTY AND INEQUALITY

If poverty is seen as normative rather than comparative, this would imply that one cannot validly infer that poverty is defined in terms of inequality. This is not, I should emphasise, the same as saying that poverty is not caused by inequality or does not result from it. There are many things which could be seen as resulting from social inequality, and others which reinforce inequality, which are not defined in terms of it (in a Marxian analysis, almost all social relationships are treated as arising from inequality). Sen argues, for example, that a person with less money will have less command over resources than someone with more – and command over resources is crucial to the concept of poverty.

It is true that if poverty is socially defined, and poverty is identified by comparison with those who are not poor, then poverty is defined in terms of inequality. It does not follow that if poverty is socially defined and poverty is the result of inequality that poverty has to be defined by comparison with others. If I did sufficient violence to the words, I could probably demonstrate this in terms of purely formal mathematical logic – $[(A \& B) \Rightarrow C]$ does not imply that $[(A \& C) \Rightarrow B]$, because B may be contingent on other factors entirely – but the point should be obvious enough as a matter of common sense. The way in which poverty is defined does not have to depend on inequality at all.

This discussion may all seem rather abstract. But the arguments are not simply concerned with philosophical niceties; these definitions have clear implications for policy. If poverty is defined in terms of comparative rather than normative standards, it is the attack on inequality, rather than poor conditions, which becomes the central focus of policy to alleviate the problems; and the approach to inequality does not demand the same kind of measures that an approach to poverty does.

In his discussion of *Equalities*, Rae outlines a number of strategies for redistribution: raising the minimum that someone might have, reducing the ceiling of incomes, reducing the range of inequality, or changing the ratio between rich and poor.[32] Each amounts to the same when taken to an extreme, but there are crucial practical differences from the point of view of the poor. Raising the minimum has the most direct effect, because it directly increases the resources of those who are poorest. Imposing a ceiling has the least effect, because the resources which are redistributed are not necessarily made available to those who are poorest. Changing the ratio, or reducing the range of inequality, should, in most cases, improve the basic resources available to the poor and have the added advantage of addressing not only the problem of resources but also the relative purchasing power of those resources; as such, these strategies also begin to address the problem of positional goods, which constitutes the main link between poverty and inequality. Poverty can be dealt with, then, at the same time that inequality can be dealt with; however, there are strategies for dealing with inequality, particularly levelling down, which are ineffective for dealing with poverty. This is why replacing the idea of 'poverty' with that of 'inequality' will not do.

The identification of poverty with aspects of inequality means that significant improvements might be made in housing, health, education, and personal resources which are held to have no effect on poverty if the relative position of poor people is not improved in the process; conversely, a society in which resources are desperately short but the range of inequality is limited (like Sri Lanka) is not considered as having a serious problem of poverty. I suggested in Chapter 1 that any concept of poverty was liable to be judged by its political consequences. By that test, there are much greater problems with comparative standards than there are with normative ones. The identification of poverty and inequality serves to undermine much of the rationale for the redistribution of resources to the poor. Whether or not inequality remains, it is better to be disadvantaged in a warm, dry house than a cold, damp one. In attempting to avoid an 'absolutist' concept of poverty, many 'relativists' have lost sight of the kinds of problem which make the persistence of poverty an offence against the values of a civilised society.

The approach I am advocating will not, of course, deal with the root causes of poverty. Hospitals cannot deal with the root causes of car accidents, and there is no question that preventative action should be taken to stop the accidents happening in the first place, but that is no argument for doing nothing when people are injured. A stance based mainly on comparison lacks a sufficient sense of outrage against poverty – at the conditions that people live in. The problems I began by describing are problems which ought to be tackled. People should have enough to eat. They should not have to sleep rough. The conditions can be improved, and they should be. That is a moral position, and it can only be sustained on a normative basis.

INTERNATIONAL COMPARISONS

If poverty is socially defined, there is an evident problem in trying to make comparisons between societies. By definition, different societies will refer to different concepts of poverty. This can make it difficult to draw any meaningful comparison between societies – which is an important limitation in view of the growing number of interventions developed on an international basis. The problem is not insoluble, but any of the potential solutions demands some kind of compromise.

One option is to judge each country by the internal standards accepted within that country. This is usually done between countries of a broadly similar rank and industrial framework – for example, the countries of the European Community – though, even here, there may be large disparities in the criteria applied between the richer and poorer countries. When this method is extended further – for example, between industrialised countries and those of the Third World, or even between Eastern and Western Europe – it implies massive disparities in the criteria which are being applied. Despite these reservations, the method is not without its advantages and its applications, provided it is used with caution. The first main advantage is that the insights gained into the particular distribution of resources, powers and opportunities within a country are often most clearly seen by close observers within that country. In other words, many of the more subtle, intangible elements associated with poverty can more clearly be identified; it makes it possible for those conditions to be researched where they occur, retaining a qualitative element. Second, it enables issues to be adapted to the conditions which obtain within different countries. Third, if the aim of such comparisons is to provide a basis for policies which are decided at a national level, then a comparison of this kind may be more relevant to the particular countries than one which uses international criteria.

There are measures which apply a formula to different countries. The welfare function identified by the Leyden group or the standard used by the Luxembourg Income Study apply definitions which are relative to those countries; this means that a different standard is being applied to each country. This does not have the advantages of close qualitative research, but the results that it yields are still potentially useful; poorer countries tend to have greater numbers of people falling below this level. Poverty is not defined solely in terms of a lack of material goods. It includes positional goods, which can be identified by reference to indicators of class, status and power within the different societies.

The main objection to this method is that it substitutes consideration of inequality for consideration of poverty. Even within the industrialised countries, there are important differences, not only in inequality, but in absolute income, in the amount which those countries spend on social services – which helps to provide the residents of countries with a basic level of resources – and in the minimum levels of benefits which are provided. Irrespective of the distribution of income, one would expect on this basis to find more severe problems of poverty in Italy or Ireland than in Denmark or West Germany, and this seems to be the case.[33] If the principle of comparison is extended outside the OECD, then the startling inequalities of most of the South American countries would yield greater proportions in poverty than many deeply impoverished Third World countries. (The observation is still important as an indication of poverty, because such inequalities are also experienced as a lack of positional goods.)

If, however, the aim is to make it possible to draw comparisons across societies – for example, in order to inform the redistribution of resources between nations – a method based on the standards of each country may lead to inequities. Teekens and Zaidi object that if this approach was to be applied within the European Community (EC), it would favour people in richer countries who would not be classified as poor on a common standard, to the disadvantage of others who would be so classified.[34] To avoid this, it is necessary to find some common standard which can be used across different societies. The first option is to use a normative approach to apply to every country. For example, a minimum level of income, a minimum amount of food (or even foods with basic nutritional values), standards of health, housing and education, all can provide basic criteria against which countries, or parts of countries, can be measured. The World Bank, while recognising the arbitrariness of the definition, treats people as extremely poor if they have a purchasing power of less than $275 a year, and poor if they have less than $370 a year.[35] This is useful as a rule of thumb; they supplement the material with other information about public services, health, education and so forth, because the availability of such services affects the basic standard of living for people who are poorest. Teekins and Zaidi attempt a more ambitious normative comparison across EC countries, by determining the prices of an equivalent basket of food and taking this, on the same principle as the US poverty line, to constitute a proportion of the poverty line.[36] A related but different approach might be justified in terms of 'Engel coefficients'.[37] Engel posited that people generally spend less on food proportionately as their income increases; in that case, the numbers of the poor can be determined as the numbers within each country who spend more than a set percentage of their incomes on food, or perhaps other necessities.[38] Clearly, the more sophisticated the measure, the more likely it is to be sensitive to differences in behaviour, differences in circumstances (like the effect of the provision of basic resources in kind) and the problems of recording information consistently in different countries.

It may be possible to compare each country by reference to standards established in a group of countries (like the EC or the OECD). Atkinson notes a peculiarity of the implications of this approach within the EC: as the composition of the EC changes, the accession of a poorer country brings the poverty line for the bloc down.[39] This is probably best avoided by applying the standards of one country or the other. This means that one can identify the problems of poverty within a rich society, like the US or UK, and then extend the same criteria to poorer countries, like Nepal or Sierra Leone. Conversely, one can apply the standards of Sierra Leone or Nepal to the US or UK; the problem with this is that the problems of poverty in the US and UK seem very limited by comparison. This is not outrageously inappropriate: the appalling prevalence of major problems in the poorer countries tends to dwarf the issues in the richer countries, but equally those problems tend to dominate consideration of other latent problems within the poorer countries themselves. The use of the norms obtaining within the richer country tends to imply a more detailed consideration of various kinds of issue which may be overlooked from the perspective of the poorer country. Equally, a concentration on the standards of richer countries may mislead. If issues relating to water supply, malnutrition or deaths during childbirth rarely feature in consideration of poverty in the richest countries, it is because these problems have largely (though not completely) been overcome. It is only from applying the standards of the poorer country that the importance of these issues may be highlighted. This argues, in many ways, for a combination of several standards – the norms of both richer and poorer countries.

5 Understanding poverty

Describing the circumstances of poor people

Poverty is not one kind of experience, but a whole range of experiences. It is expressed differently, not only between societies, but within societies; the term is used for people in very different kinds of situation. In the UK, the term might be used to describe a pensioner wrapped in blankets who stays in bed because she is unable to afford any heat in the house; a youth sleeping in a cardboard box on the street; an unemployed family with no disposable income, in debt to the landlord and the electricity company; a single parent isolated in a flat on a peripheral estate. It is not only the experience and nature of poverty which vary, but the circumstances and characteristics of the people who experience it. It is difficult to convey much of a sense of what 'poverty' is 'really' like, because these are not circumstances in which people necessarily have anything directly in common other than the lack of resources to meet their needs.

Because poverty is complex, it is not really possible to give a comprehensive account of the circumstances in which people become poor; but certain categories and groups of people are clearly much more vulnerable to poverty than others, in so far as they lack material resources, and – no less important for an understanding of policy – they are commonly identified in these terms. Low income is experienced more by people in particular types of household, but for many – particularly those who are in two-parent families and others in households without dependent children – it may be a temporary experience, because the type of household reflects a stage of the life cycle. This tends to present problems in describing people with low income as 'poor'. If poverty is concerned not only with resources but also with issues like opportunities, powers and lifestyle, there is little reason to suppose that many of the people at the lowest end of the income distribution necessarily suffer from poverty. At the same time, people within these categories are likely to be vulnerable to poverty (because a protracted period on low income implies a limited command over resources), and it is within these groups that poverty is most likely to be identified.

Table 5.1 Post-tax and transfer position of persons relative to average incomes

Country/ income distribution	*Percentage of persons in:*			
	Elderly families	*Single-parent families*	*Two-parent families*	*Other families*
Sweden				
Bottom 5th	24	31	22	14
'Poverty'	–	9	5	7
UK				
Bottom 5th	48	45	15	8
'Poverty'	18	29	7	4
Israel				
Bottom 5th	29	22	15	8
'Poverty'	24	12	15	6
United States				
Bottom 5th	25	56	16	11
'Poverty'	21	52	13	10
West Germany				
Bottom 5th	28	33	22	11
'Poverty'	9	18	4	5

Source: From T Smeeding, M O'Higgins and L Rainwater (eds), 1990, *Poverty, Inequality and Income Distribution in Comparative Perspective*, New York: Harvester Wheatsheaf, p 65.

Although it does not show that people are poor, the proportion of each group who are likely to find themselves in the lowest part of the income distribution helps to illustrate the vulnerability of different categories to poverty. Table 5.1, drawn from the Luxembourg Income Study (LIS),[1] shows how many people in each group are likely to be in the bottom quintile of the income distribution, and how many of those are in 'poverty', or at least on low incomes (understood as 50 per cent of median income). Whatever the reservations one may have about identifying these circumstances too closely with poverty, there are clearly some interesting implications to be drawn from these figures. It is evident, for example, that the level of income that pensioners enjoy in Sweden is relatively far greater than in other countries, whereas single parents in the US have a notably lower relative income; these figures draw attention to features of the benefit systems in those countries. Elderly people in the UK are much more likely than in the other countries to find themselves in the lowest fifth of the population, despite a substantial improvement in the situation of this group in the previous ten years.

The LIS is still in its infancy and, at this stage, the broad figures disguise certain elements of poverty. The UK figures for 'households below average incomes', which are calculated on a different basis, point to some other important factors. The greatest risk of low income is for single parents and unemployed people; and those who are sick and disabled are at greater risk than pensioners.[2] The figures fail, too, to take appropriate account of a number of important groups, including women, ethnic minorities, people in part-time work, people living in institutions, and homeless people.3 The latter categories point to further problems, because there are many groups which are too small or difficult to define for them to be taken into account in such an approach – groups like discharged psychiatric patients, travellers, people who are mentally handicapped, young people discharged from care, or women who have suffered from domestic violence. In this chapter, I discuss only the largest categories, which are enough to draw some general conclusions. It is important to remember, though, that the diversity of problems associated with poverty defies any simple, convenient classification.

GROUPS IN POVERTY

Elderly people

It would be misleading to pretend that all old people are poor, or are likely to be. The central reason why old people tend to have a limited income is their withdrawal from the labour market. Not all old people do retire, although the tendency has increasingly been for people over 65 to do so.

The poorest old people are those whose pensions are insufficient to provide a basic minimum income. This might be because the basic level of the pension is inadequate, which is the case in the UK or Israel, or because the numbers of people covered are limited, which applies more in West Germany. The number of pensioners who receive Income Support as a supplement to their pensions has fallen in recent years, to about 1.3 million;[4] this is not, however, enough to bring them up to 50 per cent of median income. It might be estimated, too, that nearly half as many again are eligible for Income Support but not claiming. Those who do receive National Insurance tend to have incomes which are marginally above the Income Support rates; however, it is a level of income at which relatively small increases can make a large difference in command over resources. Because women tend to live longer than men, most pensioners are women. There may be problems where women are not entitled to full pensions, because they have not worked in the labour market throughout their lifetimes, or where they have to rely on earnings-related pensions, because their earnings have been lower than men's. Clayton suggests, I think with some reason, that 'elderly women are in receipt of a lower level of welfare assistance, commensurate with their needs, than elderly men'.[5]

Many pensioners are deprived. They often live in older housing, because they are likely to have lived in one place for some time; those in private rented housing are particularly likely to live in bad conditions. Savings have been eroded by inflation. They are less likely to possess certain items, like fridges and washing machines, which have become part of the modern household. At the same time, they are probably not as badly off as younger people who are not able to participate in the labour market. Their benefits are more generous in most countries, because they are receiving benefits which reflect previous earnings, but also because of a clear preference given to pensioners relative to other groups of beneficiaries like the unemployed.

Chronically sick and disabled people

The problems of disabled people are very diverse; they include conditions like blindness, inability to walk, deafness, inability to sustain a physical effort, epilepsy, and chronic illness, and the definition of disability can be extended to include mental illness and handicap or alcoholism. The kinds of condition leading to disability can be presented clinically, to include, for example, neurological disorders (like multiple sclerosis), blood disorders (like haemophilia), metabolic disorders (like cystic fibrosis) or sensory handicaps. Problems of this kind are referred to as *impairments. Disability* is the functional restriction which results. A person whose disability causes disadvantage in a particular role or set of social roles is referred to as *handicapped.*[6]

The recent OPCS surveys of disability present, with an unusual degree of authority, a set of problems likely to affect people who are disabled. The problems that they took account of were not clinical categories, but rather categories of functional incapacity. These included locomotion; reaching and stretching; dexterity; continence; hearing; seeing; communication; personal care; behaviour; intellectual functioning; loss of consciousness; problems of eating, drinking and digestion; and disfigurement. These categories overlap with handicap – notably in the cases of locomotion, personal care, behaviour and intellectual functioning.

The majority of those who are disabled – and the vast majority of those who are severely disabled – are old people, who are poor because they are not employed. Among younger disabled people, the issue of participation in the labour market is crucial in determining income. Those who are employed, however, are also likely to earn less. Disabled non-pensioners were found to have incomes which were on average 72 per cent of those of non-pensioners in general.[7] The problem is not only that disabled people lack resources, but also that they may have special needs for expenditure.

Most disabled adults (60 per cent) incur regular extra expenditure because of their disability; this may include items from the chemist, visits to hospitals and home services.[8] Overall, the survey concludes: 'disabled adults are likely to experience some financial problems and to have lower standard of living than the population as a whole as a result of having lower average incomes'.[9]

Unemployed people

Unemployment is not a simple phenomenon. Beveridge attributed unemployment to two main factors: cyclical changes in the demand for labour and what he referred to as the 'disorganisation' of the employment market.[10] Cyclical fluctuations arise because industry relies on demand from consumers to keep going; in a slump, this demand is not there. Primary-producing industries – like heavy engineering or energy – are affected first; consumer industries follow. In *Full Employment in a Free Society*, he extended his understanding of this category to cover structural unemployment – major changes brought about either for technical reasons or because demand is deficient in the economy as a whole.[11]

The specific problems of the labour market are classified by Beveridge as 'frictional'.[12] Frictional unemployment included unemployment as a result of technical change (people become unemployed because their skills are made redundant, or because work is replaced by machines); local variations like those caused by the demand for casual labour (which is less important now than in Beveridge's day – it referred to people who looked for work day by day, like dockers, or week by week); and 'seasonal' (certain trades, like building and hotels, take on people at some times of the year and drop them at others).

This is not an exhaustive categorisation. Other categories of unemployment which Beveridge referred to elsewhere include voluntary unemployment – when a person is unwilling to work at the market wage – and job-changing, which is also a form of frictional employment. Beveridge's description of unemployment is not as clear or precise as it might be, but it is important, not least because his recognition of a wide range of different problems was ultimately reflected in the benefit system. For practical purposes, the main importance of his analysis was the implied distinction of short-term (frictional) and long-term (structural) unemployment, which created different kinds of problem, and called for different responses.

Where unemployment is temporary or short term, the effects of low income are unlikely in themselves to be indicative of poverty. But unemployment is a reverse queue: the longer the time a person has waited, the less likely that person is to be re-employed. In the UK, the average period of unemployment for those who are then re-employed is under three months; the average period for those who are still unemployed is about nine months.

The effect of female unemployment deserves special mention. Although women's wages are notably less than men's, they play a crucial role in lifting the collective incomes of households, and are of particular significance for household poverty when the man's wages are low. In cases where both husband and wife are not working, the income of the household is likely to fall critically – unsurprisingly, near to the basic benefit level.

Single parents

Single parents include unmarried mothers, divorcees (male and female), and widows and widowers (who are usually covered by social insurance). They are identified by their responsibility for child care. A person who has responsibility for child care is often unable to work, which creates major financial problems. In addition, single-parent families are most often headed by a female, and female wages tend to be much lower than male wages.

There are significant differences, however, between different categories of single parent. Unmarried mothers are (by definition) female. Many are young, which means both that their earning capacity is limited, that benefit entitlements may be restricted, and that they are unlikely to have a core stock of capital goods. They are also likely to be on benefit for a longer period than other single parents, and less likely to marry. Widows and widowers are likely to be older. They are more likely to have accumulated capital resources, and, if working, they will benefit from age-related increases in income. They may have some insurance, or receive more generous benefits. Divorced people have the greatest degree of variation: some have a work record and working experience; some have capital resources (or at least a proportion of joint resources), where others do not; some have regular maintenance payments for children, and some do not. Poverty, on this account, is most likely to affect unmarried mothers and certain divorcees, although the problems of child care coupled with the restricted status of women in the labour market mean that few single parents are proof against poverty.[13]

People working on low earnings

Low earnings are most prevalent within certain industries – in the UK, particularly agriculture, shops, catering and (depressingly) the public service.[14] The prevalence of low earnings varies according to the location of these industries. Women are particularly vulnerable to low pay, particularly women involved in manual work.

Low pay does not necessarily lead to poverty in its own right, because there is often more than one income in a household. The households which are most vulnerable to poverty while someone is working are those with only one low-paid earner – usually, because women's wages are lower, a female. This includes many single-parent families, and households with couples where the man is unable to work through unemployment or disability.[15]

Women and poverty

The position of women is of particular importance for an understanding of poverty. The problem is not that people are poor simply by virtue of being women; women are more likely than men to be poor, but most women are not poor. It is, rather, that the disadvantages stemming from the structure of gender are cumulative. Millar and Glendinning point to three main routes through which people gain resources: paid employment, social security systems, and the household or family.[16] The labour market is the most significant factor determining the poverty of women relative to men. Social security systems are often discriminatory, but they do not prevent women from obtaining resources altogether. In relation to household income, it is sometimes argued that women within households which have apparently adequate resources may still be poor, because resources are unequally distributed within the household.[17] There are reasons to question this proposition. At the margins of poverty, the arguments are strong ones, because the woman within the household who is denied resources lacks essential items as a result. However, as the income of the household increases, the lack of certain items – like a personal disposable income or replacement clothing – is experienced within a context in which that person also has access to other items, such as furnishings, consumer durables, transport or holidays. The kinds of problem which are experienced are degrading and important, but they are not equivalent to the problems of 'poverty'; if people in this situation are 'poor', then so are middle-class families who overspend their budget, or households whose commitments leave them with no disposable income. It is much more important that these issues contribute to the general disadvantage of women, and so that in cases where household resources cease to be available – such as in a divorce – a precarious position becomes one of poverty.

Because it is only a limited minority of women who are poor, women cannot be treated as a category of people at special risk in the same sense as pensioners, disabled people or single parents. But among those who are poor, women predominate. The lower earnings of women imply an inadequate command over resources when a woman's income is the sole income in a household – that is, particularly for single women or female single parents. (It is single parents who seem to attract most attention in discussions of poverty in the US.)[18] The 'working poor' are often female. Women are equally vulnerable as pensioners, with their liability to interrupted work records and lower earnings-related benefits. With some justification, poverty has been described as becoming 'feminised'; the main reservation to make about this term is the question whether it has not always been the case.[19]

Race and poverty

The identification of race with poverty is now frequently found in the literature, though more often in an ideological context than in relation to any specific empirical analysis. 'Race' is not a simple characteristic. The term is itself socially constructed, and there is a disturbing tendency to lump together people in very different circumstances as 'non-white' or 'black' – disturbing both because it denies people their distinguishing characteristics and because it encourages primary identification by colour.

The strong identification of racial issues and social policies in the US inclines one to the view that racial distinctions are an important element in the experience of poverty: nearly one-third of the Afro-American population is considered poor on the official standard, compared to 10 per cent of Caucasians.[20] It is argued, in fact, that 'the two best predictors of official poverty status in the United States are sex and race',[21] though it is important to recognise that most poor people in the US are not Afro-American, and the over-identification of race and poverty can be destructive. In the UK, the situation is much less clear. There are certainly problems within European nations which relate to the status of immigrants (which is not always the same thing as race). However, the specific information which is available is fairly scanty, and many of the generalisations which are made are questionable. As one major text on poverty in the UK comments, 'The most notable point . . . is the paucity of information that is available.'[22]

Figures from the Policy Studies Institute show average earnings of racial groups and relative levels of dependency on benefits in the UK (see Table 5.2). The figures indicate some degree of disadvantage. The higher earnings of women from the Caribbean probably reflect different patterns of work and perhaps location. There is evidence that 'people of Asian and West Indian origin . . . are more likely than white people to be unemployed, and those who are in work tend to have jobs with lower pay and lower status than those of white workers'.[23]

The figures conceal as much as they show. In the first place, they refer to a wide range of occupations and age groups. Second, they imply a uniformity of experience within groups which is probably inappropriate. It may be valuable to contrast the figures with those given in Table 5.3, which

Table 5.2 Earnings and support from state benefits of different ethnic groups

	'White'	*West Indian*	*'Asian'*
Median weekly earnings (1982)			
Male	£129.00	£109.20	£110.70
Female	£ 77.50	£ 81.20	£ 73.00
Households receiving			
Unemployment Benefit	7%	17%	16%
Family Income Supplement (for low pay)	1%	5%	2%
Supplementary Benefit	14%	20%	11%
Retirement/widows pension	35%	6%	6%

Source: C Brown, 1984, *Black and White Britain*, London: Heinemann, pp 208, 242.

refer to housing tenure. The figures show something of the diversity of different ethnic groups. The pattern of tenure for the whole of the UK at this time was that 56 per cent of households were owner-occupiers, 31 per cent were in local authority housing and 12 per cent were renting privately. Indians, Pakistanis and East African Asians were much more likely to own, while those from Bangladesh or the West Indies were much less likely to. This has to be interpreted with some caution, because although usually there is a strong association between owner-occupation and higher levels of income, housing conditions are far worse for some minority groups. Indians are currently more likely to have central heating, and Pakistanis and Bangladeshis rather less likely to, than other groups. All the minority groups are vulnerable to overcrowding, though perhaps less than popular stereotypes might suggest; according to the 1989 General Household Survey, 2 per cent of 'whites', 10 per cent of West Indians, 13 per cent of Indians and 28 per cent of Pakistani and Bangladeshi families are overcrowded by the 'bedroom standard'.[24] The poorer conditions result in part from a strategy by many ethnic minority families to attempt to use low-income owner-occupation as the most accessible form of tenure; they also reflect, though, the relative youth and low incomes of many of the families, ignorance about grants and services, and discrimination in access to other forms of tenure and to better property. 'From the point of view of amenities', Smith writes, 'it is better to be a white labourer than an Asian chartered accountant.'[25]

The lifestyles of different minority groups are not equivalent. Birthplace is important as an indicator, not so much because of cultural influences as because it represents a process of immigration, which affects the kinds of circumstance in which people are likely to have come to Britain.

Table 5.3 Tenure of racial minorities (%)

Ethnic group	*Owner-occupied*	*Council*	*Private rented*
West Indian	41	46	6
Bangladesh	30	53	11
India	77	16	5
Pakistan	80	13	5
African Asian	73	19	5

Source: C Brown, 1984, *Black and White Britain*, London: Heinemann, p 96.

Bangladesh, for example, is a poorer country than Pakistan, and Bangladeshis in Britain are poorer as immigrants. Indian immigrants tend to be better off than people from the Caribbean. (These broad categories, of course, conceal further distinctions within and between groups.) The main process of immigration occurred at different periods for the principal groups, and the terms of entry changed; the greater number of people from the Caribbean in council housing is explained partly by the terms of entry (later immigrants were prevented from dependency on 'public funds', which led to a general fear of using public services) and partly by longer establishment in particular areas; Bangladeshis, by contrast, are more concentrated in specific local authorities.

The information which is available does indicate that people in ethnic minorities are relatively disadvantaged, which also means that they are likely to be vulnerable to poverty, and over-represented among the people who are poor. The problems of racial disadvantage are also significant because of the positional elements in poverty. Poverty may, then, be an important issue in the understanding of racial problems. However, the figures do not show either that substantial numbers of people in racial minorities are poor or that race is a major category among people who are poor.

THE SOCIAL CONSTRUCTION OF POVERTY

The issues of poverty among women and racial minorities point to a further dimension in the understanding of poverty. If they were intended to be descriptive categories, their inclusion in this context would have to be questioned; it is clear that, even if people in these categories are more likely to be poor, most of them are not actually poor. They are better considered as analytical rather than descriptive; they are intended not simply to convey a sense of who is affected by poverty, but also to put the experience of poverty in the context of social disadvantage. The process of categorisation is not simply descriptive. The assumption that old people, unemployed people, disabled people or single parents are likely to be poor may be justifiable in many cases, but there are clear exceptions, and there are many for whom the generalisations do not hold good. The kinds of contingency I have been describing are themselves understood and responded to within a social context; the process through which such groups are defined is not neutral, factual and value free, but rather depends on a process of interpretation and political negotiation.

Another way of saying this is that the problems of poverty are 'socially constructed'. This is not the same as saying that the nature of poverty is socially defined, though there is a relationship between the two kinds of statement; it means, rather, that the process through which poverty is recognised as a social issue, and the way it is understood, depends on the society (and, one might say, the political process) of which it is a part. This might affect the definition of poverty, but equally it affects the way the problems are perceived, interpreted and responded to. On the face of the matter, the kinds of category I have been outlining are descriptive; they seem to rely on a balanced, dispassionate assessment of the facts. But there are other categories which might equally have been used, and which are used in some analyses, but which, for one reason or another, are not commonly referred to in the analysis of poverty. These might include, for example, mental handicap, people living in poor areas, and social class. The fact that these categories are not referred to in the same way as they have been illustrates the point that the understanding of poverty is based in convention.

Mental handicap

Mental handicap describes the condition of people who have slow intellectual development. This is associated with a range of other problems, because slow intellectual development might reflect organic problems, because it affects a number of other skills (such as when children learn to walk), and it can create problems in communication. Mentally handicapped people tend more often to come from families in lower social classes,[26] and are likely to be on low incomes in later life, if only because of their limited earning power. On the face of the matter, then, mental handicap might seem to be a legitimate inclusion in the list of categories within which people become vulnerable to poverty.

However, there is also a political history to the treatment of mentally handicapped people which may make it undesirable to classify them independently in this way. At the turn of the century, mentally handicapped people were classified as 'degenerates'. Degeneracy was seen as a problem at the root of pauperism, mental illness and crime. Concern was expressed (notably by the Eugenics Society) to prevent them from breeding, because of the supposed social implications. The philosophy is enshrined in the 1913 Mental Deficiency Act, which identified people as being idiots, imbeciles, feeble minded or 'moral defectives'. After the Second World War, much of this philosophy was discredited – not least because of the association of eugenics with fascism – although the idea of degeneracy did survive in the concept of the 'problem family'.[27]

It is difficult to say whether the way in which the issues of poverty and mental handicap became dissociated reflected a conscious break. There was certainly, in the post-war period, a desire to avoid stigmatising language, and 'social security' was separated from 'welfare'; there was some complacency induced by the idea of the 'welfare state', to the effect that groups like mentally handicapped people were now being catered for. However, if there was any desire to protect the status of mentally handicapped people, it did not filter through to policy, and services for mentally handicapped people were ignored disgracefully until at least the late 1960s. Whatever the process, there has been no return to the kind of identification of mental handicap with poverty which was taken for granted 80 or 90 years ago.

People in poor areas

Poor people tend to live in poor areas. To live in a poor area is, properly speaking, part of the nature of poverty itself, rather than a circumstance in which people are likely to become poor. But the category has been an important one, not least because a close identification of poverty with certain areas has been used to justify a concentration on the problems of the urban environment as a response to the problems of poor people.

The process by which poor people come to live in poor areas is a fairly straightforward one. In the private sector, poor people are brought together through the magic of the market; those least able to exercise choice end up in the places which are least to be chosen. The same has been shown to be true, to some extent, of the public sector. Research in Glasgow shows that where applicants for council housing are allowed a choice, the people most able to exercise that choice are those who have the highest incomes and the best housing previously.[28] They are the ones who can wait for a better offer. Social segregation by housing officers has contributed to this process in the past, but it equally happens in the private sector where there is no grading.

Some areas are likely, as a result, to have greater concentrations of problems than others. A study in Liverpool, for example, found extremely high correlations between a range of problems in different wards of the city, including theft, possession orders, warrants for disconnection of electricity, children being deloused, unemployment, assault, welfare conference cases, burglary, debtors, miscellaneous crimes, mentally ill adults, malicious damage (vandalism), children graded as ESN ('educationally subnormal') and job instability.[29] These relationships do not reflect 'multiple problems' in individuals or families, but clusters of problems in parts of a city. Most of the problems are directly attributable to poverty. Unemployment, job instability and adults being mentally ill are causes of poverty. Theft and burglary, possession orders, disconnections and debt are consequences of it. Most of the other factors can be explained indirectly in similar terms: children who perform badly at school may reflect parents in similar circumstances, who live in these areas because their incomes are low; there is more vandalism because there are inadequate facilities to play at home; there is more attention from the police and welfare agencies.

Although area-based analysis is a powerful tool for discovering some of the problems associated with poverty, there are dangers in identifying poverty too closely with poor areas. Most poor people do not live in poor areas, and most of the people in poor areas are not poor. Holtermann, in a study of the 1971 census, found that concentration on the poorest areas was not likely to reach many of the poorest people.[30] In Tayside, where I undertook some work on the distribution of poverty for the Regional Council, the figures from the 1981 census showed that the worst 13 areas, covering approximately 10 per cent of Tayside's population, contained only 20 per cent of overcrowding, 11 per cent of households lacking amenities, 25 per cent of unemployment, 15 per cent of households without a car and 6 per cent of pensioner households. The vast majority of poor people in the region did not, then, live in the most deprived areas. Carley argues that 'however one uses indicators to define socially deprived areas, unless half of Britain is so designated, more poor will be outside the areas than in them and any special treatment may be inequitable'.[31] No analysis of the poorest areas, no matter how refined it is, is going to identify adequately the distribution of poverty.

Social class

The third category is 'social class', or occupational status. This became, in many ways, the dominant means of identifying people who were disadvantaged in the 1950s and 1960s, particularly in the literature on education. Research in the 1950s by Floud, Halsey and Martin showed that the selective process favoured children from the middle classes, who consistently performed better in IQ tests, as well as other tests of educational attainment. They did not find that the difference was due to discrimination: 'If by "ability" we mean "measured intelligence" and by "opportunity" access to grammar schools, then opportunity may be said to stand in close relationship with ability. . . .'[32] The basis for the concern that this prompted was that differential attainment was reinforcing class inequality, and much of the criticism of the educational system in the 1950s and early 1960s was a response to the perceived bias in the selection system against working-class children. The 'secondary modern' schools were clearly second-class schools; selective schooling was gradually replaced from 1965 onwards by comprehensive education. There was concern, too, about early leaving. A number of reports pointed to the disadvantage to working-class children who were required to leave early in order to start earning. The reports included *Early Leaving* and *15 to 18*,[33] and they argued for the raising of the school leaving age to 16, as provided for in the 1944 Act. Most pupils left with no qualifications at all. The introduction of the CSE followed the 1960 Beloe Report and the Newsom Report, which concentrated on those of below average ability.[34] There was concern, too, about higher education: the expansion of higher education in the late 1950s and early 1960s, with the declaration of new universities and the creation of polytechnics, was intended partly to improve the output of people in scientific and technical education, and partly to improve the opportunities for working-class children. (In practice, the main benefit of this expansion has been reaped by the middle classes; the prospects of higher education in a university or polytechnic for a girl from social class V are virtually negligible.)[35]

If social class became less important after the 1960s in policy terms, it was partly because many of the policies which had been argued for had been implemented; it was also due to the fact that disadvantage was increasingly being related to family circumstances or to the structure of society. Disadvantage, it was argued, arises before school, in social settings, and the school tends to reflect this.[36] Later developments took the emphasis of policy away from schooling and more towards the problems of inequality.

There are still many who see in social class a major analytical tool for the prediction of the incidence of deprivation, patterns of behaviour and social outcomes. In the analysis of health care, for example, social class proves to be a powerful indicator of disadvantage in health.[37] People in lower social classes, including children, are more likely to suffer from infective and parasitic diseases, pneumonia, poisonings and violence. Adults in lower social classes are more likely, in addition, to suffer from cancer, heart disease and respiratory disease. There are also gender-related problems. Men in lower social classes suffer more from malignant neoplasms, accidents and diseases of the nervous system. Women in lower social classes suffer more from circulatory diseases, and endocrine or metabolic disorders.

There are various explanations as to why this kind of disadvantage persists. The Black Report considers the possibility that there is some degree of natural or social selection; that there are cultural and behavioural factors influencing health outcomes; and that the apparent associations are an artefact – the result of the way in which occupational categories and health are defined. Poverty remains an important element in the explanation; poor nutrition, bad housing and unsatisfactory environments may all contribute to ill health.

There are, however, reasons to doubt whether social class itself is the principal factor which explains health outcomes; it is at best an indicator. Despite its evident importance as an analytical category, it has not been treated as a central focus for responses to the problems of poverty in Britain since the 1960s; that probably reflects as much on political fashions as it does on the strength of the argument. The central problem with an emphasis on social class is that it depends on a reference to occupational status, when many of the people who are poorest have none. The kinds of issue which occupational status identifies are the issues of structured inequality at different levels of society; the kinds of response which it demands run across several strata, rather than focusing specifically on the poorest.

INTERPRETING POVERTY

If there is a contrast between categories like mental handicap, poor areas and social class and the kinds of category which were considered previously, it is not a strong one. It is possible, perhaps, to describe the first set of categories as 'descriptive' and the second set as 'analytical'. But descriptive and analytical categories are not easy to separate, because the selection of particular classes of description as especially important – like the problems of ethnic minorities or women – is often based on their importance in terms of a causal analysis, while the use of certain explanatory categories – like 'social class' or 'low income', which are defined in terms of inequality – can be justified in terms of their descriptive power. Ultimately, the selection of certain categories as appropriate ones, and the rejection of others, depends to a large extent on the kinds of analysis on which an understanding of poverty is based.

The ways in which poverty is described are important, not only because they affect the way in which the problems of poverty are conceived, but because they shape the kinds of response which are made. In the US, for example, there is a very strong link made between poverty and racial issues, to such an extent that discussion of poverty sometimes stands for racial issues; in the UK, poverty is more commonly associated with unemployment and family policy; in France, poverty is increasingly being taken to mean social exclusion. The kinds of response which are made to poverty reflect these understandings; so, in the US, the 'War on Poverty' was primarily concerned with the circumstances of the urban Afro-American population; the UK's responses to poverty are often described in terms of benefits for people out of work and Child Benefit;

and in France there has been the introduction of the *Revenu minimum d'insertion* directed at the integration or 'insertion' of poor people into society.

It would be wrong, though, to attribute the pattern of response primarily to the way in which poverty is described. The process of interpretation is at least as important, probably more so; political responses to poverty depend to a large extent on the kinds of explanations which are given for poverty, and the beliefs which people hold about those who are poor. In the next chapter, I consider this relationship in greater detail.

6 Causes and responses

One does not have to understand poverty in order to respond to it. For one thing, the way into a problem is not necessarily the way out of it. For another, social problems have to be addressed whether one understands them or not. I think it would be a brave (or foolish) person who claimed to have an adequate understanding of the causes of racism, for example, but ignorance or imperfect knowledge is not a good reason for inaction. At the same time, the kinds of response which are made to poverty are clearly affected by the kinds of understanding which people have of poverty – the way in which the problems are constructed, the kinds of issue which are identified as being important, and the way in which the issue relates to others. Understanding these issues is important for understanding the kinds of response which might be made.

In some cases, the explanations which are given for poverty prompt a particular kind of response, in a fairly simple and direct relationship. If poverty is held, for example, to be the result of genetic inheritance, then the main way in which it is likely to be addressed is by altering the process – which implies some kind of eugenic policy. If, on the other hand, poverty is the result of exploitation of the poorest by a ruling class, then it will remain for as long as such exploitation persists and some restructuring of power relationships is required. There are grounds for suspicion about any simple explanation – if only because poverty is not one kind of problem, but many – but irrespective of the truth or falsity of the reasons which are given, the impact on policy can be considerable.

PATHOLOGICAL EXPLANATIONS

Pathological explanations are those which attribute poverty in one way or another to the characteristics of people who are poor. These include individualistic, familial and subcultural explanations of poverty.[1]

Individualistic views

Individualistic views of poverty attribute poverty to the characteristics of the people who suffer from it. In a competitive society, those who fail might be those who are in some sense inadequate or incompetent; those who have made the wrong decisions, through ill luck or mistaken judgement; and those who have not tried. These ideas are often lumped together, but they are very different. The first proposition is unfortunately expressed, because words like 'inadequacy' and 'incompetence' have a distinctively judgemental and insulting flavour; the terms imply a moral judgement about people's position in society, when it is very questionable whether the system of rewards reflects competence to any great degree. If, however, one takes the proposition to mean that people have different capacities, and that this is likely to affect their opportunities and incomes, it is much less contentious. People might become poor, for example, as a consequence of mental illness, physical disability or mental handicap. The second proposition is not especially contentious; people do make decisions which put them at a disadvantage, whether it is in their education, their choice of spouse, their children, their economic capacity or how they use the money they have. The third category – those who do not try – is the category most clearly associated with moralistic and right-wing views; poverty is widely attributed to 'laziness', though less so in the UK than used to be the case. (In 1976, 43 per cent of people in the UK thought that poverty was the result of laziness – virtually twice the average of the rest of Europe. By 1989, this figure had fallen to 18 per cent.)[2]

This kind of explanation does not of itself determine the likely policy responses. With respect to people with limited capabilities, the view of individualists on the right wing tends to be that they should be treated as 'deserving', while others are seen as 'undeserving'; the left, by contrast, tend to dismiss the distinction as irrelevant to policy or undesirable (because of its effects in stigmatising all recipients). When it comes to people who have made the wrong decisions, the difference between the left and the right wing lies not in the question of whether people ever make wrong decisions but what should be done: the left tend to argue for mutual support and solidarity as a form of protection for the casualities of social processes, while the individualist right suggest that people must face the consequences of their personal decisions if those decisions are to mean anything. With respect to those who do not try, there are mixed feelings: on both right and left, there is a feeling that people should have to contribute to society, but the individualist right tend to magnify the numbers of potential cases, while the left consider the problem to be insignificant or attribute it to structural factors. On both sides, there is some uncertainty as to whether there is room for moralistic judgements within policy decisions, although some on the right have argued for a reassertion of a distinction between the deserving and undeserving poor.[3]

Familial explanations

Some views of poverty link it to the structure of the family. This may be individualistic, in the sense of attributing responsibility to individuals within the family, but it may also rely on issues relating to genetic make-up or family background. Genetic explanations for poverty suggest that the structure of rewards in society in some way reflects either the capacity or the inherited behaviour of the citizens. If the origins of poverty are genetic, it suggests that some intervention is required in the way that people breed – the argument which was central to the eugenics movement.

During the 1950s, the pattern in social work moved towards addressing the problems of deprivation brought about through the pathology of the family. The reinforcement of links between maternal deprivation and juvenile delinquency was a primary justification for the development of personal social services in their present form. Bowlby's *Maternal Care and Mental Heath*,[4] although it did not invent the idea, became established as the received wisdom on the issue, and for over 25 years policies for children suffering from neglect and abuse were formed simultaneously with policies for young offenders. The development of Social Services Departments in England and Wales was initiated by the Seebohm Committee; the government White Paper which had announced the setting up of the committee was entitled *The Child, the Family and the Young Offender*.[5] The summit of this approach was reached in the 1969 Children and Young Persons' Act, which effectively removed the administrative and many of the practical distinctions between young offenders and abused children, supposedly in the hope that it would remove the stigma of criminality from young offenders. (Arguably, it transferred that stigma to everyone else.) The 1989 Children Act has reversed the trend and reasserted the distinction.

The attribution of poverty to family background is perhaps most strongly linked with the idea of the 'cycle of deprivation' or 'transmitted deprivation'. There is at least a good argument to be made that poor parenting leads to disadvantage in development, but the 'cycle of deprivation' goes further: poor parenting, it is held, generates a cycle of inadequate development and further poor parenting. In the words of Keith Joseph, 'parents who were themselves deprived in one or more ways in childhood become in turn the parents of another generation of deprived children'.[6]

The social services enjoyed a major expansion in the early 1970s, not least because Joseph, as Secretary of State, believed that early intervention in families was important to break the 'cycle of deprivation'. It was Joseph, too, who, to his credit, set up the working party on transmitted deprivation to examine the problems. After ten years, the working party was to report that transmitted deprivation did not work in the way that people had thought.[7] There is little evidence to show that there are continuities particularly preserved in certain families, partly because most poor children are not poor as adults, and partly because people marry spouses who are not from similar family backgrounds.[8]

Subcultural explanations

'Subcultural' explanations are those which imply that the values of poor people are in some sense different from others. The best known expressions of poverty as a 'subculture' have been Oscar Lewis's anthropological studies of poor people in Mexico, Puerto Rico and New York.[9] Lewis summarises some of the major characteristics as follows:

> On the family level, the major traits of the culture of poverty are the absence of childhood as a specially prolonged and protected stage in the life cycle, early initiation into sex, free unions or consensual marriages, a relatively high incidence of the abandonment of wives and children, a trend toward female- or mother-centred families . . . a strong disposition to authoritarianism, lack of privacy, verbal emphasis on family solidarity which is only rarely achieved because of sibling rivalry, and competition for limited goods and maternal affection.
>
> On the level of the individual, the major characteristics are a strong feeling of marginality, of helplessness, of dependence and inferiority. Other traits include a high incidence of maternal deprivation, or orality, or weak ego structure, confusion of sexual identification, a lack of impulse control, a strong present-time orientation with relatively little ability to defer gratification and to plan for the future, a sense of resignation and fatalism, a widespread belief in male superiority, and a high tolerance for psychological pathology of all sorts.[10]

Valentine attacks the characterisation on the basis that it is not really about a 'culture' at all[11] – it has far more to do with the supposed effect of poverty on personality. One of Lewis's principal faults is that he mixes psychological characteristics with social relationships, and then compounds them with other factors (like unemployment, lack of savings and lack of privacy) which are aspects of poverty itself, rather than of any 'culture'.[12] Ultimately, Lewis's description can be seen – like many others in the field – as 'a middle-class rationale for blaming poverty on the poor'.[13]

The 'culture of poverty' seemed to be discredited, but it has recently resurfaced in arguments about an 'underclass'.[14] Auletta associates them with 'violence, arson, hostility and welfare dependency'[15] (he has perhaps forgotten rapine and pillage), and Murray with 'drugs, crime, illegitimacy, homelessness, drop-out from the job market, drop-out from school and casual violence'.[16] This kind of argument is not new – it can be traced back, without much difficulty, to feudal times, with the condemnation of 'sturdy beggars'. The credence which is given to work of this kind reflects not simply a long-standing tradition[17] but a form of rejection which is a deep element of social structures.[18] Its importance rests mainly in the effect it has on the political will to relieve poverty. I do not wish to attempt to deny that there are poor people who are unpleasant, anti-social or morally reprehensible – there are people who are not poor who are like this, and it is difficult to see what there could be about poverty which might invest people with a special kind of moral virtue. But there is no reason to suppose that it is especially relevant or convincing, either. As for the belief that the moral turpitude of the poor should deny them relief, one might with equal justice argue, as the Victorian reformers did, that financial support is a precondition for moral regeneration.

The core of truth which lies behind subcultural analysis is that poor people do live differently – that is part of what 'poverty' means. The problem rests in the idea that they choose to live differently. This might be a tenable position if one also believed that poverty is a consequence of the values one holds; but if not, there would be people who had the values who were not poor, and people who were poor who did not have those values. Empirical evidence does not support the view that poor people think differently. Rokeach and Parker, surveying the values of the poor in the US, found that they tend to reflect – sometimes even to exaggerate – dominant values.[19] Rodman points to the problems of reconciling these values with the circumstances they actually live in; he suggests that poor people have to undertake a 'value stretch' to make it possible to maintain a sense of decency despite the limitations of their lifestyle.[20]

Subcultural explanations suggest that it is necessary to establish a different set of values. In the US 'War on Poverty', concern about the culture of poor families became crossed with concern about the supposedly deviant subculture of Afro-American families, and much of what the 'War on Poverty' was concerned with was the development of opportunities for Afro- Americans. The range of policies included, for example, the Office of Economic Opportunity, designed to develop economic initiatives; Headstart, an educational programme aimed primarily at pre-school children, in order to make early intervention possible; and, significantly, in view of the 'cultural' objectives, the co-option of Afro-American leaders into the political process.[21]

STRUCTURAL EXPLANATIONS

Structural explanations are those which attribute poverty in one sense or another to the structure of society. There are a range of different kinds of explanation. What they have in common is the view that when there are structural inequalities, some people will fall to the bottom. The responsibility rests, then, not with the individual but with the social organisation which produces the effect.

Poverty as diswelfare

One view of poverty is that it is the product of the way in which society is organised. Titmuss, for example, saw people in poverty and need as the casualties of a competitive society.[22] If society is unequal, then (of necessity) some people must fall to the bottom, for whatever reasons. If there is not enough work, or work is available only on restrictive terms, then some people will be unemployed. If people have to be able-bodied in order to be eligible for work, then disabled people will be disadvantaged. Titmuss suggested that this could be seen as a form of 'diswelfare', the converse of a position in which others in society, and indeed society as a whole, produced material goods; there are losers as well as gainers, and it is important if this position is to be justifiable that some mechanism exist through which the losers can be compensated for their diswelfare.

The kind of response to poverty which this implies is one which identifies the different kinds of outcome and responds accordingly. In some views, the failure of welfare agencies to respond can be taken to be a cause of poverty in itself,[23] though as this assumes the existence of conditions of poverty it hardly constitutes an adequate explanation. Responses to different outcomes can be made in many ways – for example, through provision for particular kinds of deprivation, or provision for different contingencies, like old age, unemployment and sickness. These options, and others, are considered further in the next chapter.

Structured disadvantage

The main limitation of the view that poverty is the product of social organisation is that it does not take into account the extent to which patterns of disadvantage recur. The arguments centred on women and racial minorities are important, because they indicate not only that some groups tend to be disadvantaged, but that the disadvantage they suffer is structured and persistent.

The process through which disadvantage is structured is the subject of some controversy. There are three main analytical concepts – power, status and class – commonly used to explain the pattern of disadvantage. The terms are closely related, and they are often used interchangeably, and even after the distinction has been made, it is not necessary to consider that any one explanation excludes the others. For the purposes of analysis, though, it is useful to make the distinctions.

Power

Structural explanations for poverty are sometimes also conceived in terms of power relationships. The argument is that poor people do not simply find themselves at the bottom, but that they are put there and kept there by a repressive social structure. This is taken to support a view of society which is based on the dominance of an élite, or of a class in whose interests rule is made. Explanations which are based on interpreting gender relationships and the feminisation of poverty may base the analysis on the understanding of patriarchy, or male dominance.

In order to understand the relationship between power and poverty, one has to refer to the kinds of model through which power is supposed to be exercised. Lukes refers to three main kinds of power. The first is overt power, used when those who have power wish to force the compliance of those who have not. Second, there are 'non-decisions': people who have power are able to control the agenda for discussion, so that certain issues fail even to reach the point at which they may be tackled. Third, there is the 'hegemony' exercised by or for a ruling class, in which the pattern of values and perceptions is shaped in such a way that decisions will ultimately be made in their interests, even though there may be no need for any direct intervention.[24]

It would be easy to suppose, from what I have said about the social construction of poverty and the structure of disadvantage, that this is evidence of the exercise of power. But it is important to recognise that effects are not proof of intentions. Evidence of inequality or the enforcement of social norms does nothing to demonstrate that disadvantage is the product of power relationships. That argument can only be established by examining the processes through which power is exercised – in other words, showing how the exercise of power leads to disadvantage – which is where most of the commentary on power in the context of social policy fails to deliver.[25] In the case of poverty, the argument has more substance than in other areas of social policy, because poverty can be explained to a large degree in terms of the economic system, and the economic system can be seen as reflecting the power and influence of a number of principal actors. Poverty is not necessarily produced directly or deliberately, but it may still be seen as the product of a system in which the welfare of the poorest person is insufficiently important to merit other kinds of economic policy.

The main implications of an argument based on power for responses to poverty are twofold. The first is that, if poverty is produced as a result of deliberate action, or even of knowing indifference, there is unlikely to be an acceptance of measures to alleviate poverty, and the best which can be hoped for will be minor ameliorative measures which do not conflict too far with other objectives. The second is that this situation can ultimately be addressed only through seeking to redress the structure of power in society, a point which takes us beyond the confines of this book.

Status

People's social relationships are not formed randomly; they develop as a reflection of a person's roles in society. 'Roles' describe both what a person does and what others expect that person to do. They affect, and are affected by, people's behaviours in different social settings, including family, workplace and community. A status is a set of such roles.

Statuses are linked with honour and esteem – and, conversely, with patterns of social rejection or stigma. Poor people have been seen as the people of the lowest status. The relationship between poverty and low status is, however, unclear. Poverty can be seen as a product of low status: if a person has a limited set of roles in society, that person's opportunities to accumulate command over resources are limited. Low status can be seen as a product of poverty: if people lack resources, they become unable to participate in society, so that they are marginalised in relation to many social processes. And poverty is sometimes identified with low status; poverty has been identified with 'exclusion' and marginality.[26] As a description of the condition of many poor people, this is not wildly inappropriate, but it should not be confused with the nature of poverty in itself. Marginality and exclusion are issues which relate to social stratification, rather than needs and resources; as such, the problems apply to many groups, including people with physical and mental differences, people from different cultures, and people who breach social norms, who are not necessarily poor.

The experience of exclusion is itself a significant problem, and one which has been described, in the term of 'stigma', as the central problem in social policy.[27] The social processes which lead to stigmatisation are complex, and poverty plays a part within them; but there are also issues relating to prejudice, social norms and the nature of deviance which go well beyond the scope of this book. (I have, however, examined these issues elsewhere.)[28]

Several different kinds of response to poverty are prompted by a focus on exclusion and stigma. One option is a policy of inclusion – through 'rehabilitation', employment, training or similar approaches. A second option might be to grant status and rights – Lister's prescription for the extension of 'citizenship'.[29] And it may be possible to approach the situation of the poor collectively, through participation or positive discrimination. These approaches are flawed:[30] they fail to address either the structural context of disadvantage or the problems of social rejection, and in consequence they are likely to expose people who are vulnerable to further rejection. There may be a distinct argument for improving the resources of people who are excluded; financial resources will not overcome the problem, but they can help to facilitate fuller participation in society, as well as alleviating some of the worst effects of exclusion.

Class

The poverty of different categories of people is linked by a crucial thread. People's poverty reflects their income; and in most cases, their income is determined by their relationship to the labour market. The first, and most obvious, issue is the question of whether people participate within the labour market. Those who do not – like unemployed people, disabled people, pensioners and single parents – are those most at risk of poverty.

This statement needs, though, to be qualified. The effect of non-participation in the labour market is conditioned by both people's employment history – which affects entitlement to benefits and employment prospects – and the length of time during which they do not participate. The second major issue is that people do not participate within the labour market on equal terms. There are two striking examples of the effect of labour market inequalities in the position of people who are subsequently identifiable as recieving low incomes. These are, first, the receipt of occupational pensions by some pensioners, but not others, and, second, the disadvantaged position of women.

This argues for an analysis of the causes of poverty in terms of class. Classes, in Weber's definition, are 'groups of people who, from the standpoint of specific interests, have the same economic position'.[31] This is not the same as an analysis based on 'social class'. The conventional description of people's 'social class', which defines people in terms of their occupational status, misses the most important thing about people who are vulnerable to poverty – they may not have an occupational status at all. The description of poor people as a class is based, rather, on their economic position – that is, their position in relation to the economic market. The policies which are most directly derived from this are those which are concerned either to change economic resources – like redistribution – or people's economic relationships, through employment or the development of legitimate patterns of dependency.

The underclass

Poor people constitute, in important ways, an 'underclass'. The term 'underclass' has been disapproved – for example, by Ruth Lister and Carey Oppenheim[32] – because of the negative use of the term, and, certainly, I would not wish to be associated with such uses. Historically, references to the poorest section of society have often been negative, but one should seek to distinguish between terms which are intrinsically negative – like 'degenerates', 'problem families' or 'lumpenproletariat' – and those which have been considered negative because they refer to a socially rejected and despised group, like the 'submerged tenth', 'hard to reach', 'the abyss'. Matza makes the point that the reason why terms for describing the poorest section of the people are changed so often is that each, in turn, comes to carry the stigma associated with the reference group.[33] The first uses of the idea of the 'underclass' were made from those on the left, not those on the right.[34]

The term 'underclass' is not intrinsically unreasonable. A 'class' of people is defined, sociologically, as a group identified by virtue of its economic position in society. The 'underclass' is composed of people whose economic position is not simply poor but effectively excluded from the mainstream of economic production.[35] Simmel once argued that 'poor' people should be considered, sociologically, to be those who became dependent as a result of poverty; their position was not, he felt, equivalent to those who were poor as a result of low earnings.[36] I do not share this view, for reasons which I shall detail shortly, but the argument should give pause for thought; effectively, it rests on the premise that people are distinguished, as a group, by the nature and source of their income. A Marxist class analysis defines people's class in terms of their relationship to the means of production; there must, then, be some distinction between the proletariat and those who have no direct relationship to the industrial system. A Weberian approach would reinforce this distinction, although it might also suggest a number of underclasses, rather than one homogeneous group. The registrar-general's classification of occupations starts from the significant premise that status groups are primarily defined in terms of occupational categories, and it follows that those with no occupational category are likely to fall below the levels occupied by those who have. The 'underclass' is an economic grouping which falls beneath the criteria by which other economic groups are classified.

The underclass is sometimes represented as excluded, in the sense of being unable to participate in the normal patterns of social life, but the 'exclusion' of the underclass is only partial. It is possible to distinguish two main economic categories. One group consists of those who are genuinely excluded from the labour market altogether, and so are financially dependent. This group includes pensioners and many disabled people. The second group, which is perhaps more important in the study of poverty, consists of people who are not simply excluded, but who have a marginal position in relation to the labour market. These include single parents, some disabled people and many people with low employment status or skills, who may find themselves employed only casually, intermittently or for limited periods of time. Their work is of low status and earning power; when work is scarce, they are likely to be unemployed. In France, these kinds of condition are generally referred to in terms of 'précarité'; Matza and Miller describe the situation in terms of 'sub-employment'.[37] This kind of group is not, in general, covered by Townsend's definitions of poverty, which are concerned primarily with the ability to participate in society at a particular point in time, and there is a case to say that the underclass consists not of people who are poor but of those who are most vulnerable to poverty through the process of exclusion. The categories of 'poverty' and the 'underclass' are therefore related but discrete.

The underclass needs to be distinguished, too, from Simmel's categorisation of the poor as those who are dependent on benefits. Clearly, sub-employment suggests that poor people are likely to have to depend on benefits at some point. However, many of those who depend on benefits do so only for short periods – there are transitions through unemployment, serious illness or single parenthood – and do not necessarily become poor. Conversely, many of those who are poor may have intermittent periods during which they are not dependent.

The response to poverty is affected by a class analysis of this kind. If it is correct, then those people who fall within an underclass differ from others in two main ways. One is that their earning power, even when work is available, is limited, and their resources are irregular and insecure. Benefits which are tied to the labour market – like National Insurance, which relies on an unbroken contribution record, or benefits for people on low incomes – often disadvantage the claimant whose employment status is marginal. Benefits which presume a stable set of circumstances – like benefits for single parents or pensioners – are claimed if, like the cases of pensioners or people with dependent children, the circumstances can be taken to be stable. However, they may not be claimed in other cases where the situation is not stable, like single parenthood, benefits tied to accommodation, recurrent sickness or unemployment.

Second, the low status of the underclass leads to a pronounced set of social problems. The underclass is not defined by its social status, but it is important to note that classifications of status tend to reflect economic position. Status, Runciman suggests, is a lagged function of class;[38] people who have no occupational role, who have no relation to the industrial or commercial system, or whose role is marginal and inferior, all constitute the lowest status groups. Poor people are stigmatised, suffering problems of powerlessness, prejudice and rejection. It sometimes happens that the elements of stigmatisation and low status become confused with the identification of the features of poor people as a class, but this should be seen as a consequence of their class position, rather than a defining characteristic. Ultimately, the effects of this class position are translated into policies which are restrictive and degrading.

IMPLICATIONS FOR POLICY

The different kinds of explanation for poverty are not mutually exclusive. At a school sports day, there will be a number of prizes for a range of events. People can choose which events to enter, and according to their abilities and performance they will receive prizes. The reasons why someone comes first may well be attributable to merit, skill or perseverance; the person who comes last may well be less skilful, less willing to participate. The explanation of who is last would be, in such a case, individualistic. But the explanation of why someone has to come last, why there are not prizes for everyone, or why children are asked to compete is structural – it is determined by the organisation of the event – and this explanation can coexist with the individualistic one, without any contradiction. (It leaves open the question of whether society should be run like a school sports day.)

If people can hold a number of explanatory positions simultaneously, it becomes difficult to associate the kinds of policy which are advocated simply to the pattern of causation implied in particular explanations for poverty. Attempts to link the relief of poverty to a causal analysis substantially reflect a set of moral positions which have been taken about the condition of people who are poor. Those who attribute poverty to the fault, laziness or immorality of the poor are likely to argue that they deserve their fate and that attempts to improve their situation without addressing the root problems are doomed to failure. Those who view poverty as the product of an unequal society in which people are disadvantaged in economic, political and social terms suggest that, since no amount of individual effort can redress the balance, it is inappropriate to structure the relief of poverty through a system which requires them to lift themselves by their own bootstraps. But neither of these positions is set and immutable. Even if poverty is seen as the result of individual fault, it is possible to argue that in a well-ordered society individuals, and their dependants, must be protected from the consequences of individual failure. Equally, it can be argued that even if there are structural problems, people can overcome the disadvantages imposed on them.

Structural explanations for poverty imply that some change in social structure is desirable. The problem with this proposition is not that it is self-evidently wrong or unreasonable, but that it is difficult to translate into operational terms. The Community Development Projects (CDPs), in the UK, were given a remarkable brief by the government: to experiment in deprived areas in order to see what could be done.[39] The CDPs published a series of reports linking deprivation in particular places with the economic structure, and concluded that they were fairly powerless to do anything. When central government abolished the CDPs, the organisations protested vociferously; but by their own argument, if they could do nothing, they had no further function to perform. Equally, the argument that I have made for considering poverty in relation to the labour market is also a structural one. It is clearly very difficult to seek a transformation of the labour market in order to avoid the main effects, if only because any alteration, even if it is successful, is likely to maintain a distinction between those who are able to work and those who are not.

If this kind of analysis is not to be a counsel of despair, it is important to recognise that the responses to problems do not have to rely on successful analysis of their causes. I have mentioned a number of policies, like redistribution and income maintenance, and attempts to 'rehabilitate' people or include them in social networks; there are others, which focus on different client groups (like old people or disabled people), or those which concentrate on the correlates of poverty (like poor areas, gender and race); in the examination of social security policies which follows, other approaches will be considered. None of these policies directly addresses the kinds of problem that the analysis of the 'underclass' implies. But all can help, in different contexts, to improve the welfare and the relative position of some people who are excluded from participation in the labour market, improving their circumstances in the process. If the worst effects of structural disadvantage are at least mitigated, social policy will have made a positive contribution to welfare, as well as acting to some extent to change the structure of society.[40]

Part II

Social security as a response to poverty

7 Strategies for the relief of poverty

Poverty might be responded to in many ways, including some which would not usually be thought of as 'poor relief'. 'Poor relief' is an old-fashioned term; it has fallen into disuse, partly because it is associated with some undesirably stigmatising practices and partly because it seems limited in its scope. 'Relieving' a problem does not necessarily solve it; it merely lifts a burden. But whether or not relieving poverty is enough, the burden needs to be lifted. There is something of a tradition in social policy of finding reasons why people should not be helped directly, particularly when it comes to poverty. Imagine that someone is drowning in a lake. On the right, there are some who feel that it is a very nice lake which would look much nicer if people didn't make silly decisions about falling in. On the left, there are some others who want the lake to be drained. Somewhere in the middle is a social worker, who will not physically intervene but can offer swimming lessons over the megaphone. Poor relief is about dragging people out. Perhaps there are better answers, but it needs no apology.

If poverty consists of deprivations which resources are inadequate to meet, it can be relieved either by addressing the problem of deprivation or by increasing a person's resources. These tend to overlap, if only because it is difficult to meet deprivation without increasing a person's resources in one sense or another, and increasing resources in response to deprivation is likely to reduce the level of deprivation experienced. The distinction is fairly arbitrary, then, but it is still useful in helping to identify some of the elements of policy.

RESPONSES TO NEED

One option is to identify the nature of the deprivation in isolation from other issues – a 'symptom-centred' approach – and to make provisions which can reduce that deprivation directly. This, on the face of the matter, is the most direct form of poor relief. If people are homeless, they can be provided with housing, or the means to obtain it; if they are without food, they can be given food. Symptom-centred approaches are often dismissed in serious analyses, because they are almost invariably inadequate: some items will be missed, leaving gaps in coverage; they fail to address causes, or to prevent a recurrence of the problem. In the particular context of poverty, the scope of symptom-centred approaches is limited. It is in the nature of poverty that people experience, not isolated forms of deprivation, but a cluster of problems; and a person who lacks resources for one thing may have to balance that need against others. Housing benefits, as a result, are not spent only on housing; they act as a general form of income support.[1] Food stamps do not simply increase people's food intake; they also release resources for other items. Even if a measure is adequate to meet a particular problem, it is unlikely to be adequate to meet the other kinds of need which are associated with it.

One should not underestimate the importance of symptom-centred responses, however; they may not be sufficient, but that does not mean that they are not necessary or desirable. Homelessness, malnutrition, ill health or educational deprivation are all serious problems in their own right; a direct response to such problems is, even at its worst, better than nothing, and at best it can make a major contribution to the alleviation of deprivation.

The second approach is individualistic. In order to respond to the needs of people who are poor, it is necessary to identify who they are; this implies the introduction of some kind of means-test, either as a special procedure or as part of a general system of income assessment (like that undertaken for taxation). The problems of means-testing, which will be examined in more detail later, have made this an unpopular alternative. It is often presented as a more efficient way of relieving poverty, because resources go precisely to those intended. However, there are problems, not only because it is difficult successfully to identify individuals, but also because people's circumstances change, which implies that benefits should be withdrawn.

A third set of responses to deprivation can be made by responding to the general circumstances in which people have become deprived. This may relate, for example, to interruptions of earnings, through unemployment or sickness; to cases in which people have withdrawn from the labour market, as in retirement, disability and single parenthood; and to circumstances in which people's income is otherwise inadequate for their needs, as in the case of low earners. In other words, a response is made to the contingencies in which people become poor, as much as to the problems of poverty in themselves. This is very much the basis on which social security systems have been organised, and it will be returned to in that context later. In some cases, the assessments are easier than financial assessments – it is not usually difficult to identify old people or large families – but this is not true of all, and the problems are not necessarily less than those of an individualistic approach.

Interpreted more broadly, there is scope for directing responses not only to those who are identified as poor, but also to problems associated with poverty. This may include characteristics such as gender, race, age or locality. This kind of approach, the fourth, is controversial, because people in such circumstances, even if they are more vulnerable to poverty, are not necessarily poor – and many, even most, may not be poor. The World Bank refers to this approach as 'indicator targeting' – directing resources to the correlates of poverty, rather than to the problem itself – and defends it on the pragmatic basis that it is less costly administratively than directing resources to individuals.[2] Indicator targeting is sometimes used in relation to problems related to poverty, like community development, and in some cases for the purposes of income maintenance (for example, universal benefits for old people or children). The central argument for such an approach is that it allows a fairly effective response to be made to poverty with little of the administrative complications which accompany individualised approaches. There is a case, too, to suggest that indicator targeting may be less stigmatising, because it is less individualistic – though it is still possible to stigmatise a school, an area or a region no less than a family or a street. The main objections are, first, that it may not be efficient – many resources are used for people who are not necessarily poor – and, second, that it may fail to reach many poor people who are not reached by the special programmes. After some initial indicators have been identified, the marginal benefits of further programmes reduce, with some measures reaching many of the same people while at the same time leaving others without effective aid. This suggests that although an element of indicator targeting may be helpful as part of a broad strategy against poverty, it is unlikely to be sufficiently effective in its own right.

Lastly, one can seek to prevent deprivation from arising. Much depends, here, on the causes to which the different forms of disadvantage are attributed. Policies aimed at preventing poverty are often directed either to the perceived causes of poverty – for example, through the development of educational opportunities – or to effects which, like bad housing or malnutrition, might be seen as perpetuating the problems of poverty in the future. Poor relief has been accorded only a limited role in the prevention of poverty, not least because of the criticism (usually made on the right) that poor relief creates an incentive to people to accept low incomes.[3] The proposition is very questionable (it will be returned to in Chapter 8) but it has certainly been influential. There is an argument which says that meeting present needs is also an important way of protecting against future needs.

The shortage of cash in the short term is likely to create other problems in the long term, including the inability to obtain certain items, debt, and the sacrificing of some items in order to obtain others (for example, a failure to replace clothing in order to obtain food, or eating less to pay for heat). Poor relief can, then, be seen as an important preventative measure in itself.

THE LACK OF RESOURCES

There are three basic approaches to poverty which concentrate on the lack of resources.[4] One is to increase resources overall, on the principle that a general increase in the living conditions of the whole population will improve the conditions of all, including the poorest. Margaret Thatcher, a former Prime Minister of Britain, once suggested that the Good Samaritan would not have been able to have helped if he had not had the wealth to do so. The position is consistent with the kind of poor relief exercised in Victorian times. Although inequalities may remain, there is some evidence that inequalities are effectively reduced in richer countries, because of the greater levels of involvement in the economic process, the shared benefits of a common infrastructure, and a greater dispersion of resources (the main reservation that has to be made about this is the extremely disadvantaged position of poor people in middle-income countries, like Brazil, in contrast with the more equal distribution found in some poor countries, like Sri Lanka). However, there are important limitations to such a strategy. An increase in resources does not guarantee that the circumstances of poor people will be improved, or even maintained; there has to be one mechanism through which the poorest can obtain a share of extra resources. For one thing, there tends to be an implicit assumption that the main mechanism through which this will be brought about is participation in the labour market, but it is in the nature of poverty that many poor people are not participating in the labour market. For another, poverty consists not only in a lack of certain quantities of material goods but also an element of positional goods, and so the lack of positional goods cannot be redressed by an increase in national resources alone.

The second main strategy is to spend money on the social services, the 'strategy of equality' favoured by the Fabians. Public spending, by providing a range of goods and services available to all, has the effect of establishing a floor of resources below which no one needs to fall. The effect is similar, as a result, to the strategy of establishing a floor of income (see page 54). It has much the same advantages, coupled with the additional merit of achieving, through the judicious use of public funds, major economies of scale and the achievement of particular social objectives. Equally, though, it has an important limitation, which is that it does not directly address the problems of positional goods related to inequality; and one of the main criticisms of this strategy has been that it fails adequately to redress social inequalities.[5]

The third main option is to redistribute resources from rich to poor, either by establishing a minimum level of resources, or by changing the relative proportions of rich and poor. Social security consists of a direct redistribution of resources, in the sense that those who pay are not necessarily those who receive. Redistribution is described as 'vertical' when there is a transfer of income between people on higher and low incomes; it is 'progressive' when the direction of redistribution is from rich to poor; and it is 'regressive' when the direction is from poor to rich. Necessarily, redistribution must be progressive to some degree if it is to relieve poverty, and on the face of the matter the most effective means of dealing with poverty through the mechanism of social security should be one in which resources are redistributed directly to those who are worse off. But this proposition is disputed, because there are those who believe that the process of redistribution and the methods which are used to identify poor people (mainly means-testing) can have a negative effect on people who receive social security.

UNIVERSALITY AND SELECTIVITY

The objection to the identification of poor people as a specific target for direct redistribution is best explained by reference to the ideological divide between residual and institutional welfare. Redistribution is generally interpreted in terms of two opposing models of welfare, residual and institutional. Redistribution which is directed exclusively at people who are poor is residual in form. Residual welfare creates a social division between donors and recipients, which many believe to be inherently stigmatising. Townsend believes that this results in inadequate benefits, because the identification of a dependent population is likely to be seen as a public burden. It is important to recognise that the test of effectiveness in the relief of poverty is not whether money is used solely for the poor, but rather what level of resources is achieved in the process. Even if redistribution to those who are poorest is the primary intention of assistance, it may be necessary to disguise the recipient group, and to approach the issues obliquely in order to offer redistribution without stigma.

The model of institutional welfare, by contrast, presupposes a degree of acceptance of the circumstances of people who are poor, because it is based on a view that needs are a normal part of social life. Redistribution which is consistent with institutional welfare is therefore directed towards the kinds of contingency in which people experience needs – contingencies which would include childhood, sickness, unemployment and old age. In so far as poverty is largely accounted for within this kind of contingency, provision for poverty can be made effectively through provision to meet such needs.

I suggested in Chapter 1 that there was a degree of irrationality in the association of different principles and policies in terms of these models. The attempt to avoid stigma indirectly reinforces its worst effects, by failing to make resources available for those in need. Institutional benefits, and those which are based on social protection, are not necessarily progressive in form; some relate to contingencies in which people are also very likely to be poor, like the circumstances of elderly people, but others (particularly benefits relating to child care) relate far less to poverty and (because parents of older children are likely to be involved in the labour market) may even have a regressive effect. The institutional and residual models seem to relate to intention and purpose as much as they do to specific methods; even if residual benefits are subject to social disapproval, it is far from clear that benefits based on contingencies like unemployment or single parenthood would be more acceptable. The avoidance of direct redistribution because of its association with residual welfare also avoids the benefits of direct redistribution.

The difference between types of benefit is sometimes referred to on the basis of 'universality' and 'selectivity'. I am reluctant to go too far into the topic, because the debate is moribund and has been for years, but the terms have had such an impact in shaping the way in which people judge policies that it seems impossible to avoid the subject. 'Universality' and 'selectivity' are often used ambiguously. Selectivity is where people receive benefits according to need. Reddin[6] treats this as if it only meant means-testing, but this is not what selectivists argue; selectivity implies a test of means or need. Some writers, then, see benefits for mobility, for which the test is whether a person is able to walk, as selective; others do not.

Universality implies benefits which are given to all as a right. Jones, Brown and Bradshaw write that 'a universal social service is . . . one to which all citizens contribute equally, and from which all are entitled to draw equal benefits'.[7] The first part of this is wrong. No one expects everyone to contribute equally. Beveridge thought that his contributory scheme was 'universal', but this was because he believed rights had to be earned, not given by the state. If insurance is universal, it is because everyone gains rights on the same basis. The best example of a universal benefit is Child Benefit – everyone is a child at some time.

The basic argument against universality is the cost. One of the reasons why benefits are low, it has been argued, is that the jam is already spread too thinly,[8] though this is disputed by those who believe, like Townsend, that universality prepares people to accept a higher commitment to welfare services. The arguments against selectivity are, first, that it is complex, both because the identification of needs requires complex assessments and because the identification of different groups of need requires a complex, differentiated system of support. Second, any test of need has to exclude people at some point; there is invariably a problem of equity at the margins, between those people who qualify and those who do not. (There is also the problem known as the 'poverty trap', because benefits have to be withdrawn if people's circumstances improve.) Third, it is argued that people who receive selective benefits are likely to be stigmatised. The importance of the issue is disputable, because often the people who are selected as being in need are stigmatised before they receive services; a refusal to allocate benefits or services on that basis can reinforce the problems they experience.[9]

The arguments about universality and selectivity have been given a great deal of prominence, not because they are decisive in themselves, but because people associate them with institutional and residual models of welfare. Universality is linked with institutional welfare because the idea that everyone is in need at some time is linked with the idea that everyone should benefit. Selectivity is linked with residual welfare because the idea of a 'safety net' implies a concentration on those in need.

The political association of left- and right-wing views with universal and selective benefits stems from the association of these methods with the models of institutional and residual welfare. But universality and selectivity are methods; institutional and residual models represent principles. One might use the different methods for different purposes. It is possible to favour institutional welfare and selectivity – like Marx's 'to each according to his needs' – or residual welfare and universality, because one believes a universal approach is a more effective way than means-testing to provide a safety net against poverty. When it comes to practice, a host of considerations affect the choices made. The influences on different policies are complex, and it is rare to find that one simple, overarching explanation in terms of ideology can account for the adoption of one policy rather than another.

SOCIAL SECURITY AS A RESPONSE TO POVERTY

Social security is a term used for financial assistance, in whatever form it may take. Financial assistance compensates, principally, for a lack of financial resources, and if poverty is a wider concept than lack of money alone, social security can relate to it only to a limited extent. The nature of social security is that it provides not goods but money with which people can purchase goods. This assumes that people will meet their needs by spending the money – and so, that the distribution of goods takes place through an economic market.

Economic liberals argue that the private market is the best method of arranging the distribution of resources. Arthur Seldon argues that a price mechanism leads to choice for the consumer; a service led by the consumer rather than by the professions; a more efficient service at lower costs (because this increases profitability); responsiveness to need (because payment depends on it); and education of people as to the implications of their choices. He believes that collective provision is, conversely, inefficient and paternalistic. Seldon extends his case well beyond issues like food and clothing, which are ordinarily dealt with through social security, to other spheres of activity like health and education. The issue is not, he argues, that poor people might not be able to afford services. If this was the problem, then we could give them the money to decide for themselves – in other words, increase social security; there does not have to be a publicly provided service.[10]

The arguments against this position are both moral and economic. Some are concerned with the impact of decisions in the market on society as a whole. This might be understood in terms of 'externalities'. Education is worth something to society and to industry, not just to the person who receives it. Ill health affects more than the person who is ill, whether as part of an issue of public health or more generally from the fact that society needs healthy workers. This, in turn, implies that certain social needs have to be recognised. Welfare services are not only provided for the benefit of the consumer, they also perform important social functions, for example, acting as a 'handmaiden' to industry, or maintaining social morality – as they do in the case of probation or social work with child abuse. It is not clear that the choices exercised by individuals are necessarily the most appropriate form of distribution.

Equally, the effect of aggregating independent decisions made by individuals may not be socially desirable; the decisions which individuals make may not add up, collectively, into the best choices for a group of individuals. It may be reasonable for individuals to take risks, but it is much less reasonable when a large number of individuals are involved. It may be acceptable for individuals to take a serious risk of one in a thousand (people who ride motorcycles, smoke or even become pregnant accept risks which are far higher), but a risk of one in a thousand could affect 56 000 people in the UK.

Some call into question the effectiveness of the market as a means of distribution. First, the market tends to be selective rather than comprehensive. Insurance services commonly exclude 'bad risks' – for example, people with multiple sclerosis, chronic schizophrenics and elderly people – who will make their service uneconomic. There is also a problem in covering people for contingencies which they might be able to control – like pregnancy or unemployment. Second, the market may be less efficient than public provision. It may be cheaper to organise a large national service than it is to have smaller competing services. The National Health Service has been able substantially to reduce the costs of health care, by closing surplus resources and using its monopoly power to buy materials more cheaply. The private sector can be argued to duplicate facilities unnecessarily. Equally, the market may lead to a less efficient distribution of services. In the private market, services are distributed to reduce service costs and gain the largest access to the market – often next to other similar services. This often leads to a concentration of services in one place. Areas with limited demand (because of many poor people or limited populations) may not be served at all. Third, it is unclear that consumer choice is a desirable objective. There are commodities – like health, and possibly education – which people are not well placed to choose, because they have no criteria on which to base their choice. Health care is not like Kentucky Fried Chicken (despite the assertion of a former managing director of that company selling health care in Britain). It is in the nature of the commodity that it is difficult, if not impossible, for a consumer to judge the quality and value of what is being provided. People actually have to buy insurance, not health care *per se*, which is, in effect, the purchase of private social security.

The relief of poverty does not, then, have to be seen in terms of the distribution of cash benefits; it might equally be seen in terms of the distribution of goods or services. But in one important respect, social security provides a uniquely distinctive response to poverty – one which cannot be substituted by the supply of goods. One of the problems which is identifiably part of poverty is the lack of a personal disposable income. Social security can be used, as no other system can, to provide the options to obtain a number of 'inessential' items at the discretion of the consumer – items like alcohol, entertainments or other items which are so often disapproved of when people in receipt of benefits manage to obtain them. (In certain cantons in Switzerland, people in receipt of public assistance have not been allowed to enter bars.)[11] Paradoxically, the area in which the case for cash benefits rather than kind can be made most strongly – the right to use one's money on luxuries – is the kind of ground which is least likely to appeal to those who argue most strongly for the private market.

The distinction between public and private provision plays a major role in distinguishing 'left' from 'right' in welfare terms. This distinction is reinforced by the association of residual and institutional welfare with different parts of the political spectrum. A person who believes in the institutional model, and takes the view that needs are developed and experienced socially, is likely to favour collective social provision to meet them; equally, someone who opposes the private market is likely to find some justification for this opposition in the view that there are collective social responsibilities that the private market cannot meet. Someone on the right is more likely to favour provision by the state only when a person is unable to meet their needs in other ways, and the private market represents an important means of meeting needs at a minimal level, without recourse to public provision.

Social security, however, cuts across this divide. The very idea of financial assistance implicitly favours the private market as a means of distribution. One may reasonably argue for a National Health Service rather than Medicare, or for public heating schemes rather than heating allowances on social security. Social security benefits have been introduced to make up for the withdrawal of more general provision: examples in the UK are free prescriptions (introduced because prescription charges were introduced) and Housing Benefit (which followed a major withdrawal of subsidy to council housing). On the face of it, then, social security should be favoured most by those who support the private market, and opposed by those who prefer public provision; but in most cases, the exact reverse is true. It is usually thought of as left wing to favour an increase in benefits, and right wing to oppose it. It is left wing to give people money to spend on food, and right wing to insist that they should have vouchers or food stamps (usually because of the view that people might otherwise spend their money on other items).

The association of apparently contradictory ideas stems not from the issues of the public or private sector but from the links of different kinds of benefit with residual or institutional welfare. Provision on a general basis, whether in cash or in kind, is associated with the institutional model; provision only as a safety net is residual in form. Food stamps, Medicare, Housing Benefit or free prescriptions are residual forms of welfare; a National Health Service, Child Benefit or general subsidy for housing are institutional. A person may believe in institutional welfare and believe that the private market is still a better way than the state to distribute certain resources, like food, if only people are given the money. On the other hand, a person who believes that welfare should only be given to those in need may favour giving people the goods rather than money.

SOCIAL SECURITY AS POOR RELIEF

Poor relief can be achieved in other ways besides giving people money, and the close association of social security with poor relief requires some explanation. The main reason for the association is historical. Although not all social security provision has been developed in response to the problems of poverty – there is, in many countries, a tradition of mutual aid for social protection which runs concurrently with provision relating to poverty – the response to poverty has been a significant element, which has permeated not only the benefits specifically designed to address poverty and low incomes (like Income Support, Aide Sociale or Sozialhilfe) but also many of the arrangements made for pensions, unemployment benefits and single parents. Arguments about the nature of poverty have been fuelled by concern about the levels of social security and the coverage of benefits. Arguments about social security, conversely, have often centred on poverty, even when the benefits themselves have not been principally aimed at, or focused on, poor people.

The association of benefits with the relief of poverty is long standing. The development of poor relief can be seen as an outgrowth of the medieval dispensation of charity. This was not particularly associated with the distribution of alms in cash, at least in Christian cultures. On the contrary, the traditional works of charity included feeding the hungry, giving water to the thirsty and clothing the naked. (The Jewish and Islamic traditions, by contrast, emphasised the development of systematic provision and distribution of charity through tithes or taxation.) A significant by-product of the Reformation was that the monasteries, which had been a focal point for the distribution of charity, ceased to perform the function to the same extent, although it might equally be argued that the distribution of alms, which was seen to succour vagrants and to enable people to move off the land, was one of the political reasons behind the desire to reform the monasteries in the first place.

In Europe, the growth of vagrancy was linked with war and disease; vagrants were feared, with some reason, because wandering, they spread illness, and dispossessed, they threatened the possessions of others. The reorganisation of charity in city-states, of a type commended by Luther,[12] was intended to include those within the walls – the citizens – while excluding those beyond it. The systematic organisation of charity took two main forms. One was the model of the lazar-house, or hospital, which was later to be developed into alternatively hospitals or the poorhouse (in Britain, the two usually existed side by side.)[13] The other was the organisation of charitable donations through a community chest and ultimately through the levying of city rates. Already by the sixteenth century, Zwingli (one of the leading figures in the Reformation) was referring not only to the giving of alms but to the receipt of poor relief.[14]

The English Poor Law of 1601 made provision for a poor rate to be levied across the country, tied to a system of relief under 'overseers' of the poor, and for 'setting the poor on work'. It is easy to overemphasise the importance of the old Poor Law, because although it was national in its presentation it fell somewhat short of this in practice, with little indication that any national standards were applied. Despite the move to workhouses and poorhouses in the eighteenth century, out-relief – the principle of giving cash donations outside the poorhouse – was widespread; the Speenhamland system of 1795 is famous for regularising a system to low-paid workers, but out-relief was already important for other groups, including in particular old people and illegitimate children. When the 1834 Poor Law Amendment Act changed the rules, with the intention that there should be no relief outside the workhouse, this was effectively disregarded in many places, where various groups (and in particular old people) continued to receive out-relief. Charles Booth was to comment that old people had come, by the time of his research, to view the provision of cash benefits as 'a matter of course';[15] and Booth's research was distinguished by the strong case he made for the establishment of pensions as a response to the poverty of old people.

It is not possible to state with any confidence at what point cash benefits became centrally linked with the relief of poverty, but the indications are that the two developed hand in hand. Cash provision has to be seen as only one model of the relief of poverty, one which developed in competition with two others – the model of the poorhouse, which depends on provision in kind rather than in cash, and the principle of requiring work for support, which although it can be compounded with punitive measures might also be seen as developing alternative routes towards independence. But the reason why social security policies have been dominant in responses to poverty is clear enough: within a very restricted set of alternatives, social security developed as the principal means of alleviating poverty in the community, and the reaction against the Poor Law, and similar policies, guaranteed it a significant place. Cash benefits are a simple, direct response to one major part of the problem of poverty – the lack of resources. They were largely consistent with the moral principles associated with charity and the custom of giving alms. And the distribution of money has been a practical response – one which governments were able to implement even when communications were poor and the structure of civil government was restricted.

When the reaction against traditional poor relief led to a search for alternative methods of distributing welfare, it was largely through cash benefits that this was developed – in Britain, through Old Age Pensions (1908) and National Insurance (1911), in France through family policy and les mutualités, in the US through Social Security (1935). There are at least two different kinds of response represented here. One was the development of benefits as a right of citizenship; the other is the establishment of co-operative subscription as a basis for cash support. Social security policies developed, not only from the traditions of poor relief, but from the co-operative practices of the guilds. Social insurance was developed through solidaristic arrangements and by the nineteenth century it was principally the province of trades unions and friendly societies.[16]

Despite the importance of such benefits as a response to poverty, they were not exclusively addressed to the issues of poverty – insurance is as much concerned with social protection in the event of temporary interruption of income.

INCOME MAINTENANCE

Social security has not invariably been considered as the central response to poverty. Poverty was certainly an important issue in the development of the social security system in the UK, but the concern with poverty was reflected more widely in the foundation of the 'welfare state': cash benefits had to be seen as part of a comprehensive range of provisions designed to deal with the main forms of need which arose in society. The Beveridge plan was based on 'assumptions' which included a health service and full employment; contemporary writers argued for a broadly based welfare strategy which emphasised, among other things, the role of housing and education in dealing with poverty.[17] In other countries, by contrast, policies for poverty and social security were often developed quite distinctly. In France, the social security system was developed more in terms of family policy and 'social solidarity' than as a response to poverty, and 'poverty' itself was not a serious political issue till the 1980s. In the US, the benefits system continued to rely primarily on social insurance; when 'poverty' came to the fore, in the 1960s, the issue was presented and interpreted primarily in terms of urban and racial issues. Social security and the relief of poverty are not necessarily equivalent.

The Laroque report argues that 'social security' should be seen as:

> . . . the response to an aspiration for security in its widest sense. Its fundamental purpose is to give individuals and families the confidence that their level of living and quality of life will not, in so far as is possible, be greatly eroded by any social or economic eventuality. This involves not just meeting needs as and when they arise but also preventing risks from arising in the first place. . . . Thus social security requires not only cash but also a wide range of health and social services. . . .[18]

The first part of this identifies the role of social security as 'income maintenance' – the process of guaranteeing incomes – rather than 'poor relief'. The second part goes further, to identify social security with the wider aims of welfare states. The role of financial assistance has to be seen as part of a general strategy to improve people's lives.

Barry suggests, with some reason, that 'in a well-ordered welfare state almost all the job of relieving poverty will be done by policies whose objective and rationale are quite different'.[19] Part of this is because welfare states seek to prevent poverty to forestall the necessity of having to relieve it; part, too, it is because the relief of poverty is likely to be superseded by income maintenance. If poverty is to be understood in terms of a relationship between needs and resources, and welfare states seek to produce a comprehensive, institutional response to needs, then the situation in which people do not have the resources to meet their needs should not substantially arise. The role of social security provision within the welfare state is not only to provide a minimum income, but to maintain income and to protect people against the effects of a sudden decline in resources.

In many ways, however, the concept of universal income maintenance seems far too limited. The failure of British governments to address issues of poverty in the 1950s and early 1960s has been attributed to complacency, eventually to be punctured by the 'rediscovery of poverty'; but the problem was not simply that people had been lulled into a false sense of security. The welfare state of the post-war period relied on a strategy for dealing with poverty which would not be focused on poor relief, but which rested instead on a series of measures aimed at commonly occurring needs. The problems with this kind of strategy proved to be not simply that there were holes in the welfare net – holes which led to increasingly complex provisions as attempts were made to fill the gaps – but that it did not address the structured disadvantage arising from the labour market and the relationship of poor people to the economic system. Ultimately, the social security system has become more concerned with poor relief by default, because the more broadly based strategy of the 'welfare state' did not directly enough engage the kinds of problem presented by poverty.

8 The aims of social security

Financial relief is given for a wide range of reasons: the relief of poverty constitutes only a part of the functions of social security, and not all the purposes that social security is applied to can be treated as directly related to the provision of social security in itself. Social security is not only a form of income maintenance; it also constitutes a major element of the provision of welfare within many countries, and, no less important, a significant aspect of their economic structure.

All the social services can be viewed as fulfilling a range of objectives. Titmuss argued that social services are indeed defined by their common aims, rather than by the means which they employ to achieve them.[1] The idea that services follow 'aims' suggests that the policies are intended by someone, but the kinds of intention which can be attributed to the social services are varied and complex, as are the processes by which intentions can be translated into action. Another useful term, because it is neutral as to intentions, might be the 'functions' of social services – the uses that services seem to serve. Some relate to the welfare of individuals: they include altruistic or humanitarian concerns, and curative, protective and developmental functions. Others relate to the welfare of society as a whole: collective concerns include redistribution, solidarity, social control and economic development. It is difficult to represent these schematically, because the distinctions between many of the concepts are blurred, but I have made the attempt in Table 8.1.

If the functions attributed to social services seem very widely applicable, it is not least because social services are directed to social welfare. Any attempt to improve welfare can be seen as meeting needs or remedying disadvantage; any attempt to intervene in society to do so can be represented as maintaining or changing social circumstances or behaviour; and any measures which have a negative effect can be interpreted as producing disadvantage. The table is not exhaustive; these are not the only ways in which social services can be represented, or the methods through

Table 8.1 Functions commonly attributed to social services

	Focus	
Functions	*Individual*	*Collective*
Provision for needs	Humanitarian	Social welfare; economic development
Remedying disadvantage	Compensation; cure	Equality; social justice
Maintenance of social circumstances	Protection	Reproduction
The production of disadvantage	Punishment	Social division
Changing behaviour	Rewards; incentives; treatment	Social control
Development of potential	Development of individual capacities	Solidarity; integration

which the measures might be expressed. That welfare serves many different kinds of purpose is fairly firmly established in the study of social policy, and the functions I have referred to can be applied to any of the social services.[2] Each can, equally, be related to social security provision.

SOCIAL SECURITY AS PART OF THE WELFARE STATE

The first, and probably the most obvious, way in which welfare might be thought to help individuals is by meeting their needs. In the context of social security, this is most closely identified with the relief of poverty. It is probably the most obvious function of the social security system, because historically it has been a guiding principle in the development of benefits, and because it tends to dominate current debates about benefits. Some benefits are specifically geared to people on low incomes; others, like pensions or unemployment insurance, are not only available to people who are poor, but cover circumstances in which people might otherwise be likely to be poor.

At the same time, there are other needs which are met, which are not necessarily confined to the problems of poverty, or even the problems of low income. The special needs of disabled people are responded to through a range of benefits; pensioners receive health benefits. Benefits for survivors, like widows and orphans, have more to do with the provision of social protection than with the avoidance of poverty. Some benefits are designed to provide temporary stopgap relief. (This point will be returned to in a later chapter when provisions for various contingencies are discussed.)

In collective terms, meeting needs has to be seen not so much in the sense of dealing with the most common contingencies – like unemployment, disability or old age – as in the effect that social security has on the welfare of the whole society. Social security for unemployment is important not only for the effect it has on unemployed people but because it acts as an economic regulator, increasing expenditure at times of reduced economic activity and so bolstering demand (an effect not universally agreed upon). Equally, the development of a range of benefits covering the principal circumstances in which people are likely to become poor fosters a pattern of economic relationships. There are other ways, of course, in which social security provision can be seen to support the economic system; Titmuss described these as the 'handmaiden' functions of welfare.[3]

Remedying disadvantage

Disadvantaged people might receive some sort of compensation. For example, a disabled person may receive financial assistance, not because of financial need, but because the process of becoming disabled itself is undesirable. This is most clearly seen in systems of compensation for industrial disability (extended, in New Zealand and Sweden, to other forms of disability).

At the social level, remedying disadvantage is often represented in terms of equality or social justice. Social security is clearly an important element in the redistribution of income, both vertically and horizontally. Social assistance, or benefit for the poor, goes to people who are not working and on inadequate incomes at the expense of people who are working and paying tax, and is progressive. Benefits for children, by contrast, are mainly a form of horizontal redistribution, going from people without children to people with children, and from men and single women to mothers.

Maintaining circumstances

In order to maintain the circumstances of individuals, social services may seek to offer social protection. The idea of 'social security' itself implies that people ought to be able to feel secure. This involves, not only that people are protected against poverty, but also that they are protected against the hardships which are likely to arise through a sudden change in circumstances. If people become sick, or unemployed, they should not, the argument goes, have to lose their possessions or deprive themselves as a result. One sometimes hears the comment that 'people on benefit have cars and television sets', as if this was somehow reprehensible. The question is whether they should be forced to sell their car or television set before they can receive benefit. If the intention is to offer security, they should not.

The maintenance of social relationships takes us again back to the 'handmaiden' functions, but these have to be understood in this context in a sense which is wider than the relationship to the economic system alone. Each society, in order to survive, has to reproduce itself. This implies, not the maintenance of society as an unchanging network, but the birth and socialisation of new generations, the maintenance of relationships and the integration of different social elements. The clearest example of this in relation to social security is the way in which social security systems enforce solidarity between generations: people who are working pay both for children, through family benefits, and for old people, through pensions schemes.

The production of disadvantage

Social services are often represented not only as remedying disadvantage but as producing it, either through the maintenance of repressive social norms or through policies which are regressive in their distributive effects. Clearly, if social services have the power to produce changes which are positive, they must also have the potential to produce changes which are negative. The negative aspects of social services are important; if they are not taken into account, an increase in benefits would be relevant to social services whereas a reduction in benefit would not.[4]

Much of the production of disadvantage can be explained in terms of the application of other criteria, like the desire to maintain circumstances or to further the industrial process. If, for example, one believes (despite all evidence to the contrary) that industrial progress depends on developing incentives to the better off, the policies which are pursued will probably increase inequality. In relation to individuals, welfare provisions have been linked with punitive sanctions designed to ensure that they conform to dominant norms. Social security is probably most vulnerable to this criticism in its emphasis on work and participation in the labour market,[5] and in its reinforcement of familial norms.[6] In collective terms, there are criticisms of welfare systems for the preservation of social divisions on the basis of gender and race.[7]

Unfortunately, the literature on this topic is often muddled. In the first place, there is a widespread confusion of intention and effect; in an unequal society, one does not need to look to deliberate policy to explain the reproduction of inequality.[8] Second, policies which are restrictive – like attempts to reinforce a particular view of the family – are often referred grandiosely to the industrial structure or the distribution of power in society,[9] when the issues may equally relate to the enforcement of social norms. Third, supposedly 'critical' accounts often fail to distinguish between policies which do not engage disadvantage and those which actually bring the disadvantage about. Dominelli, to take an extreme example, claims that the Beveridge report is racist, presumably because immigrants have less opportunity to contribute,[10] and that tax relief is sexist because men have higher wages and gain more from it.[11] One might as well argue that pensions are racist because the ethnic minority population is relatively young, that child benefit is sexist because it favours better off families over older women, and that public transport is racist and sexist because it is mainly used by better off people in employment. This is codswallop, of the kind which gives anti-racist and anti-sexist literature a bad name, and it trivialises a serious set of issues.

What the muddle conceals is that there are, and have been, welfare policies, and indeed welfare systems, designed to produce social division as an end in itself. There are some clear examples of repressive welfare régimes. 'The base of Nazi politics', Furniss and Tilton comment, 'was the politics of the welfare state';[12] Nazi Germany sought to encourage breeding among 'Aryans' by forbidding abortion, encouraging birth and subsidising children; racial inter-marriage was forbidden; and mentally handicapped people were unable to marry at all. South Africa developed distinct welfare services, on different terms, for 'whites', 'Asians', 'coloured' and 'black' populations. The intentional production of disadvantage in most welfare systems is limited by comparison, but there are cases where policies are discriminatory, like the explicit exclusion of married women in the UK from entitlement to certain benefits (now largely struck out by the European Community), or restrictions preventing immigrants from claiming.[13] There are real grounds for complaint.

Changing behaviour

Benefits can be used to change people's circumstances and the way they behave. One example might be where benefits provide an incentive to rehabilitation – as in the allowance formerly given to disabled people to meet the expenses of travelling to work. Another is where benefits are tied to a programme in which people's behaviour is supervised. This aspect of the welfare state is less closely associated with the provision of social security in the UK, where there was a very deliberate separation of benefits and welfare after the abolition of the Poor Law, than in other countries like the US or France, where social work and welfare may still be part of the same administration. Despite the negative overtones of such a service, Piliavin and Gross, comparing circumstances in the US in which social workers administer benefits with those where they do not, suggest that the social workers who offered financial assistance were perceived more favourably by their clients, and more likely to achieve positive results.[14]

Collectively, this kind of change is often referred to as 'social control'. The term is highly ambiguous, tending to be used not only in cases of moral intervention but also in the use of power by elites, and not only for cases in which people are required to act differently, but for aspects of socialisation and reproduction. If social control is taken to mean the encouragement or enforcement of particular patterns of behaviour, then there are clear examples in the history of social security – not only in the Poor Laws, which sought to deter people from dependency, but in a range of policies designed to ensure that people are discouraged from indolence and vice (I use Victorian words to reflect the nineteenth-century tone). These include the inclusion of penalties for people who have not taken advantage of the opportunity to work, like the suspension of benefits or the prospect of prosecution; the development of incentives to work, often by holding down the level of benefits; the linking of benefits to training opportunities; and, in 'workfare' in the US, the use of work itself as a deterrent.

Developing potential

Social security may be used to foster individual development (an objective referred to in France as 'l'épanouissement', literally 'blooming'). Social security is often seen as a response to the rights of the individual, but this means more than the protection of individuals from undesired consequences; it can include the expansion of a range of opportunities, or at the very least some protection against reduction in opportunities. There have been benefits concerned, for example, with creating educational opportunities: one, the Educational Maintenance Allowance, was intended to assist people in low-income families to stay on at school. Another example might be the rehabilitation of disabled people: disabled people received taxi fares to go to work. The past tense is indicative of a particular trend. These benefits were limited in scope, and in the reforms of social security in the UK they have been largely removed. That does not invalidate the objective.

The development of collective units is usually referred to as 'solidarity'. The term is rarely used in Britain but is frequently found in texts on social security in France and Belgium, and increasingly in the European Community. Although there is considerable ambiguity in the use of the term,[15] solidarity can be represented as a form of mutual co-operation leading to group cohesion. Alfarandi describes the concept in terms of a series of social networks:

> Solidarity supposes the interdependence of individuals within a defined group. One can imagine a system of concentric circles of solidarity, wider and wider, which go from the nuclear family up to the international community.[16]

Social security is believed to foster solidarity partly through its development of systems of mutual responsibility, like friendly societies or 'les mutualités', and partly through the broader acceptance of responsibility, which a commitment to income transfer and social protection entails.

The placing of individuals within the framework of collective social networks is described as 'integration' (or, in France, 'insertion'). Boulding describes integration as an attempt 'to build the identity of a person around some community with which he is associated',[17] and the Commission of the European Community has argued for solidarity for unemployed people in the following terms:

> New kinds of social solidarity must be forged, comprising income transfer and also help with professional and social integration, the establishment of training establishments, support for employment creation.[18]

Both 'solidarity' and 'integration' refer to a process of social cohesion; people are integrated into society through a network of solidaristic relations.

SOCIAL SECURITY IN ITS OWN RIGHT

Up to this point, I have considered only general objectives relating to many forms of welfare provision. Although there are senses in which social security seems unusual among other kinds of social services, it is not usually because similar functions cannot be exercised through the medium of those services. Social security is truly distinctive in only one important respect: it gives people, not a service, but money with which they can meet needs. Although some benefits are tied to particular needs, like housing benefits, the evidence from the US is that these benefits act as a general income supplement,[19] as one might expect. The issue which distinguishes social security from other forms of social support is precisely that people have money to spend as they choose, rather than goods and services.

However, this does not mean that there is nothing distinctive which can be said about social security, because the service is not necessarily thought of in the same way as other services. Social security payments are often made, for example, as a form of compensation for a change of state, as they are in the case of industrial disability or war pensions. It would be wrong to say that no other service could perform a similar function, but in general health housing or social work do not, and 'compensatory education' refers to something quite different. In order to understand the specific purposes to which social security is put, then, it is helpful to consider it not only as a means to a general set of ends, but in terms of the kinds of justification which are made for specific types of payment.

Brian Barry distinguishes five categories of payment of this type.[20] They are:

1 Payments made in anticipation or reimbursement of special expenses. (This includes benefits for disability, sickness and medical care.)
2 Payments made to compensate for some loss other than, or over and above, impairment of earning capacity. (This includes benefits for impairments as a result of industrial accidents or diseases.)
3 Payments made to those whose status entails that they are not expected or permitted to work full time. (Examples are benefits for retired people, single parents and disabled people.)
4 Payments made without regard to means or income to those whose earnings fall short of some norm. (This is intended to refer primarily to the replacement of earnings, as opposed to the supplementing of general income. Contributory unemployment benefits are an example.)
5 Payments made to those whose means or income are insufficient to get them above some minimum income. (This refers to basic social assistance benefits, but the category seems too restrictive. There are benefits which relate to deficiencies in income but which are not determined by reference to a minimum income: Housing Benefit is an example.)

Other categories might include:

6 Payments made to protect the position of people in contingencies where the total household income is likely to be interrupted (such as sickness benefits, maternity allowances and payments for widows).
7 Payments made in recognition of some service or contribution (such as war pensions).
8 Solidaristic payments made on the basis of generalised reciprocity (such as occupational pensions, or those paid within professional societies).

Doubtless the list can be further expanded. It indicates, as Barry intends, that the kinds of aims which might be associated with social security are very much more complex than those which might be identified with the relief of poverty alone. 'Social security' is a blunt instrument, which can be turned to many different purposes.

ECONOMIC ASPECTS OF SOCIAL SECURITY

The importance of social security for economic policy stems not so much from the kinds of end that it serves, as in the implications of paying for and delivering benefits. The largest proportion of expenditure is accounted for, not by people in special or unusual need (like unemployment or disability), but by contingencies which are entirely normal and predictable – old age, childhood and (in systems where it is dealt with through social security) medical care. When European states have expressed concern about the 'crisis' of the welfare state, the problems refer principally to the pressure on expenditure from demographic trends, and especially from the growing numbers of pensioners relative to the working population. But the 'dependency ratio' – the number of people who do not work, as opposed to those who do – has fewer direct implications for the economy than short-term fluctuations in benefits. This is because the size of social security budgets is so great that even minor fluctuations can upset the balance of the economy, and in particular control over important elements of the economy like demand or public expenditure.

The monetarist view, which has become progressively more familiar since the mid-1970s, is that public spending has a number of pernicious effects. It reduces the total amount of saving in the economy; this reduces investment, and so undermines the basis for further growth. It 'crowds out' private spending, reducing the capacity of the economy to function. And it is parasitic on the economy, diverting resources from productive to non-productive activities. This view is hotly disputed. The International Labour Office argues that social security is a scapegoat for the weakness of Western economies:

> In so far as there is a crisis in social security, it is a crisis not of the structure of social security but of the erosion of the economic base for its operation. Social security is neither the cause of the crisis nor the cause of the recession. To a considerable extent, social security has moderated both the economic and the social effects of the latter.[21]

This squares with the Keynesian view, in which increased public expenditure can act as an economic regulator. The worse the condition of the economy, the more money is injected into the economy by the state. This spending will reinforce the demand for goods, reducing the extent to which they are affected by an industrial slump. In some cases, it may even stimulate economic activity to turn the economy around. Conversely, as economic activity increases, the need to spend money on social security for unemployed people falls, and the amount spent on social security decreases. These arguments played a large part in the foundation of social security in the US during the 1930s.

It is difficult, however, to maintain a view of social security as a form of pure expenditure. It can happen that social security entails expenditure – for example, where it is paid for by external borrowing which then has to be repaid. However, in many cases, if not most, the money which is being spent on social security is paid for directly from taxation or contributions. It is a transfer payment rather than an item of expenditure as such; it represents a transfer of resources from one person to another. The only 'spending' is represented by the costs of administration, or the 'production' of social security, and even that is principally accounted for as a labour cost, which is another transfer. Transfer payments are, at least at first sight, neutral in their consequences; the amount of money which is in the economy is the same before and after the transfer. The only real difference is in the people spending it.

Changes in the distribution of income can affect the economy in two main ways. First, the patterns of expenditure and saving of poor people may differ from those of richer people. If richer people spend more money on consumer goods, and poorer people more on food, then the transfer payment has implications for the producers and distributors of consumer goods (and, in the UK, for exports) and for food production and agriculture. It can be argued that this might have large-scale macro-economic effects: if the amount of saving is greater among richer people, then saving at a national level will be reduced by extensive transfer payments for the purposes of social security. Second, and in economic terms the more important, the way in which the money is collected, and the way in which it is distributed, make a difference to the way that people collectively behave. For example, social security is often represented as a form of compulsory saving, or redistribution over time. Barr describes one of its functions as 'income smoothing', reallocating a contributor's consumption over a lifetime.[22] Taxation, equally, can change people's behaviour if some kinds of activity are taxed more heavily than others, and some of the important consequences of insurance contributions by employers is that they make labour relatively more expensive, add to the costs of taking on extra staff, and lead to labour-intensive industry being relatively more expensive to the consumer than capital-intensive produce. Insurance-based pension arrangements have had a significant effect not only on personal saving but also, through the accumulation of large capital funds, on the development of financial markets.

One of the most important effects of social security policy concerns its effect on the labour market. In broad terms, the structure of benefits clearly does affect participation in the labour market: 'imagine', Hill writes, 'how different our labour market would be in the absence of state pensions. Bear in mind that British benefit policies for single parent families reduce labour market participation by the heads of those families.'[23] The point here is not to suggest that pensioners or single parents make their decisions solely in terms of the availability of benefits. Their participation in the labour market depends on other factors besides financial incentives; and the introduction of financial spurs to work (which could, of course, include positive incentives as well as negative ones) would still not mean that all pensioners and all single parents would, or could, subsequently move into employment. But the institution of retirement, or expectations about child care (and, perhaps, even the possibility of divorce for many people), have been shaped in conditions which have included the development of systems of financial support.

Debates about the impact of social security on the labour market have centred, in practice, on the circumstances of unemployed people. The labour market is seen, in classical theory, in relation to the simple terms of supply and demand. When the price of labour increases – that is, when wages go up – the supply increases (more people are willing to work) and the demand for labour falls (fewer employers wish to take people on). This causes unemployment. Conversely, when the price of labour falls, the demand for labour increases and the supply falls. When there is unemployment, the argument runs, the market can be brought back into balance by reducing wages, which will diminish the supply of labour and increase the demand for it. Social security affects the labour market by defining the wage at which people are willing to work. If people can be paid more on the dole, they will not choose to work. This is not directly equivalent to saying that everyone will choose not to work, though the case is often put individualistically, in terms of 'incentives'.

This is a simple argument, and it seems a powerful one – though it is not really the kind of argument one finds made by professional economists; it is fairly representative of what has been called 'do-it-yourself' economics, in which 'common sense' views are tempered with a smattering of economic theory gleaned from popular sources. It actually runs counter to much of the economic theory of the last 60 years. One of the central insights of Keynesian economics was the recognition that unemployment is not based on a simple relationship between wages, the demand for labour and its supply, but that it reflected the level of activity in the economy as a whole. Reductions in wages cut the demand for items, and so reduce the amount of economic activity; reduced wages tend to lead, therefore, to higher unemployment, and, conversely, higher wages can lead to greater employment (Sweden and Germany are high-wage economies, with low unemployment; Spain and Ireland have lower wages and much higher unemployment).

These two arguments are not directly incompatible. The theory of a labour market which can be described in terms of the supply and demand for labour depends on certain key assumptions. The relationship between supply and demand is not fixed; it can be affected directly by factors like the relative costs of other methods of production and the availability of finance, but also indirectly by broader issues like the level of economic activity. According to the Keynesian analysis, these parameters are likely to change as a result of various factors, including the very changes in the supply and demand for labour on which the simple model depends. The 'do-it-yourself' analysis may still be right, but that does not mean that it is right in every case, or even in most.

In practice, the effects of this argument are most keenly felt in the recurring debate about whether people are 'better off on the dole', which has also been called the 'unemployment trap'. The problem is greatly exaggerated: people are hardly ever better off on the dole,[24] and even in the rare cases where they are, many continue to work anyway. There are, for example, women who carry on working for low wages whose husbands receive benefits which are reduced in line with their wives' earnings, which means that the women are working almost for nothing.[25]

The real issue here has very little to do with the 'incentive to work'. The financial incentive for any individual to work depends on that individual's earning power, not on the lowest wage paid anywhere; and there are, of course, other incentives besides financial ones. The comparison of benefits with the lowest possible wage any labourer might receive is an historical survival – it stems from the principle of 'less eligibility' under the Poor Law[26] – and has much to do with the economic theory of the nineteenth century.[27] But the reasons for its survival are best understood in moral terms. The reason why the dependency of pensioners is accepted, while younger people have to work, relates to social expectations; and attempts to limit the amounts which unemployed people receive in benefit reflect both a popular sense of equity – that people who are working should not feel that others who are not working are receiving more than they are – and a desire to make the condition of unemployment still more unpleasant than it already is.

THE IMPOSITION OF EXTRANEOUS VALUES – WORK, FAMILY, NATIONALITY

Social values are often justified in economic terms – like the incentive to work – but most have little or nothing to do with economics. The essential reason why people are penalised for not working is that many people – and not only those on the political right – think that it is immoral not to work. Work represents, to many, a contribution to society: a person who is not working is considered not to be contributing. In the former USSR, laws against 'parasites, tramps and beggars' were intended to penalise people who do not contribute; Lenin was prone to quote St Paul's statement that 'he who does not work shall not eat'.[28] (By the way, Mrs Thatcher once quoted the same text, though I doubt that this reflects an interest in Marxist–Leninism.) The arguments for 'workfare' in the US – arguments which have been echoed in Britain by politicians of the right – are based partly in a desire to punish those who are unemployed, and partly to ensure that whatever their circumstances they do work. The difference between left- and right-wing views is not in general that people should be free to be unemployed: it is that the right wing consider that unemployment is best dealt with through individual efforts, which can be encouraged by a system of incentives and punishments, whereas the left wing tend to the view that one cannot sensibly impose individual sanctions unless there is employment within the economy for unemployed people to go to.

Work is not the only way in which people might make a contribution to society. A second major value is that of 'the family', which has been an important part of policy in France, as it has in other European nations with strong parties of the Christian right. Policy has reflected, in part, the desire to support childbearing; in part, it has assumed a dependent role for women, and a marginal status in relation to the labour market.

Despite the desire to foster family relationships, there can be strange and perverse effects arising out of the implementation of different rules.[29] Single parents are distinguished from two-parent families by the absence of one partner, usually the male; if there is to be any difference between the position of a single parent and a couple in which one person is not working, there has to be a 'cohabitation rule', so that a couple living together as man and wife are not treated more favourably than a couple who are married. Bizarrely, this means that people in stable relationships are penalised when people who are promiscuous are not; that homosexual couples are treated more favourably than heterosexual couples; and that people are deterred from developing relationships which may lead to marriage. If the intention is to reinforce the traditional family, the rule could hardly be less appropriate.

Third, there is the nation. Nationality clauses are used to exclude people from a wide range of different benefits. In the UK, the problem relates not to the rules under which social security operates, but rather the terms on which foreign nationals are permitted to enter the UK. Immigrants are required to state that they will not become dependent on 'public funds'. This is taken to exclude insurance benefits – on the basis that people who have paid insurance contributions should not be considered dependent – but not means-tested benefits, including Income Support and Housing Benefit, and not the non-contributory benefits. The non-contributory benefits also have residence requirements attached; for example, in order to claim Severe Disablement Allowance, a benefit for people who are 80 per cent disabled and who are not entitled to the contributory Invalidity Benefit, people must have lived in Britain for 10 out of the last 20 years and for most of the last six months. The benefit would be barred, in any case, to most immigrants from outside the European Community, and the prospect of thousands of disabled Germans and Italians flocking to Britain to claim about £30 a week seems so improbable that one has to ask what the basis of such an exclusion could possibly be. One answer, I suppose, might be reciprocity – that the people to whom we feel a responsibility are those who might have some responsibility towards us – but, then, there will always be some who are dependent and unable to make a contribution, and they would not be excluded on these grounds. A second answer might be 'solidarity', the identification of a group within which responsibilities are recognised; but the basic problem with the definition of solidarity is that the same process which implies the inclusion of certain people necessarily excludes others. Disillusionment with the concept of solidarity in France has stemmed not least from the realisation that it can justify the exclusion of those who are most disadvantaged. The third answer is racism, a motivation which seems all too prevalent in the operation of the benefits system.[30]

Irrespective of the explicit justifications for benefits, or of the methods according to which benefits are supposed to operate, social security – like other services within 'welfare states' – is conditioned by its social and political context. The values of work, family and nation reflect the climate of social norms within which social security systems operate.

POOR RELIEF AND THE FUNCTIONS OF SOCIAL SECURITY

Although the relief of poverty can be seen as part of the functions undertaken by social security systems, this role has to be understood within a much broader context. Social security is not 'about' the relief of poverty, and it is difficult even to claim that the relief of poverty is the primary objective; in some countries, the relief of poverty has had a relatively minor role (for example, in France, where concern with the family has been the dominant element in policy),[31] and in general the claims of social protection, compensation and provision for special needs seem at least as strong.

If poverty remains a major concern for social security systems, it is not least that many of the kinds of objective associated with social security systems are obstructed by its persistence. It is not really possible to foster personal development, to preserve the values of family life, to integrate people into society, or to achieve social justice while people lack the means to lead a decent independent life. Conversely, this means that poverty can be tackled indirectly; policies for social protection, inclusion, solidarity or the removal of disadvantage should subsume the aims of poor relief, and should in principle be able to do so without the risk of divisiveness or moral condemnation which has blighted poor relief in the past.

9 Patterns of social security provision

A review of social security policies is not the same thing as a review of responses to poverty. Strategies for dealing with poverty are broader in concept than poor relief, which is the main focus of this book; on the other hand, for historical reasons the idea of poor relief is largely subsumed in the provision of social security. The identification of social security with poor relief may be defective, but the extent to which such systems provide for poor people, and their effectiveness in doing so, is still one of the most important tests which can be applied.

The study of social security is a drier subject than the consideration of poverty alone; it has (or should have) less human interest. Clearly, the way people are treated, and the way they feel, are a very important part of why social security policies matter, and why I became interested in this area in the first place. It is true, too, that much of the literature on social security is concerned with these issues – the cases in which people fail to receive benefits, or receive them only on terms of stress, the negotiation of unnecessary obstacles, humiliation or degrading treatment. But the way people feel about social security benefits, the experiences they have and their reactions to them are not what the discussion of the subject should mainly be about. These issues concern the failures of social security; where social security is working well, this kind of problem should not arise. Although it sounds odd to say it, a successful system will not be one which people feel good about. People should not be expected to have 'positive' feelings about social security benefits – the idea reeks of an expectation of gratitude – any more than they should have 'positive' feelings about roads, electricity supplies or drains. The ideal situation of social security is one in which it is taken for granted. To achieve this, social security systems have to be accessible, adequate, efficiently run and as nearly automatic as possible. It is debatable whether this can be achieved by concentrating solely on the problems of poverty (though that point will be returned to later, in considering different patterns of benefit provision). One of the central arguments for universality, or the 'institutional' model of welfare, has been that with an adequate system of income maintenance – the protection of people's income in a variety of circumstances – much poor relief becomes unnecessary.

There is no simple way into understanding how social security policies work, because the experience of claimants often depends on a number of benefits of different kinds, payable in a range of circumstances. As a first step, this chapter considers the benefit systems in six different countries, giving some background for the later material on benefits and contingencies. The consideration is brief; the aim is to provide enough information to make comparisons possible, without covering so much ground that one loses sight of the general principles. The following chapters review the types of benefit in operation, the range of contingencies and the workings of social security systems overall.

SOCIAL SECURITY IN THE UNITED KINGDOM

The ideal of the 'welfare state' in Britain is, for many observers, the distinctive characteristic of the British system. The welfare state, founded in the 1940s, promised a comprehensive set of measures, provided at the best level possible, as a right of citizenship. The social security system in the UK is best understood as the product, directly or indirectly, of the kind of insurance system envisaged by the Beveridge report.[1] Beveridge's scheme depended on a pattern of insurance provision which had developed through friendly societies and industrial organisations. But he attempted to develop insurance into a system which would be comprehensive, covering people, in the words of the popular phrase, 'from the cradle to the grave'.

For a number of reasons, Beveridge's scheme failed to perform as it was intended. Part of this relates to the deficiencies of any insurance scheme; insurance cannot cover the full range of needs, because the beneficiaries have to have been able initially to contribute. The gaps included coverage for disability, unmarried mothers and long-term unemployment. Other criticisms might be made of some of the particular assumptions which Beveridge made – for example, he assumed that women, despite evidence that they were increasingly involved in the labour market, were likely to be dependent on male breadwinners, which meant that in cases of single parenthood or divorce (a contingency he considered 'uninsurable') the coverage of the insurance scheme was to prove grossly inadequate. In assessing the level of benefits, Beveridge adopted Rowntree's basic measures, without allowing adequately for inflation. He excluded housing costs, which have remained a vexed issue in the provision of benefits in the UK ever since. The scheme was not set up to be adequate. Further, when the scheme was introduced, economies were made. The exchequer contribution was very limited – 18 per cent of the cost instead of the 50 per cent recommended by Beveridge. The scheme introduced in 1948 also had lower benefits for children than Beveridge recommended because, the government said, of free school meals.

Insurance was firmly established as the basis for the social security system, but the failures of the scheme made it necessary to devise other kinds of benefit to plug the gaps. The main benefits which fulfilled this function were means-tested benefits and non-contributory benefits. The basic means-tested benefit was clearly aimed at people on low incomes, though the definition of a minimum income differed for pensioners and disabled people from the allowance for unemployed people and their families. The 'rediscovery of poverty' in the 1960s prompted concern about the inadequacy of this benefit – at the time, called 'National Assistance' – and the problems associated with means-testing. This, in turn, prompted a search for other kinds of benefit. Non-contributory benefits for disabled people were developed not least in reaction to, on one hand, the failure of National Insurance and, on the other hand, the perceived problems of means-testing.

Much of the policy for social security which has ensued has been built around the tension between universality and selectivity. In general, Labour has become associated with an institutional model of welfare and a resistance to means-testing; the Conservatives have tended to favour a residual model with means-tests that 'target' resources on those who are poorest.[2] Since 1970, Conservative governments have been responsible for Family Income Supplement and Family Credit (for people on low earnings), Housing Benefit and two major reforms of the basic means-tested benefit (Supplementary Benefit/Income Support); Labour has introduced non-contributory benefits for disabled people, and Child Benefit. However, the issue is not quite so simple: there are measures which do not fit the convenient political mould. The Conservative Tax Credit Scheme[3] of 1972 seems to be based on an institutional model of welfare. The 1975 pensions scheme, in which Labour replaced a Conservative plan with its own, greatly increased subsidies to private occupational pensions schemes. The reform of Supplementary Benefit introduced under the Conservatives in 1980 began life under a Labour government.[4] This reflects the kinds of constraint which the parties work under, as well as a process of compromise and balancing of conflicting principles. The Conservative Tax Credit Scheme was guided by the belief that more rationally ordered rules make financial control more effective; the scheme was dropped when practical difficulties were emphasised. The primary justification for Labour's support of private pension schemes, in 1975, was the government's determination to ensure adequate pensions in the future. No single set of principles is dominant.

SOCIAL SECURITY IN FRANCE

Welfare provision in France is not based on the kind of comprehensive, all-embracing principle identified with the British system. The most important justification for welfare has been the development of 'solidarity', an idea which developed from the turn of the century – at one point, it was the focus of a political movement, 'solidarism'.[5] The first article of the Code of Social Security declares that 'the organisation of social security is founded on the principle of national solidarity'.[6] This is understood partly in terms of the development of mutual aid and assistance, and partly in terms of social integration.[7]

The social security system in France has developed from a range of diverse insurance arrangements developed by friendly societies and professional associations (les mutualités). The system of insurance which has developed has two principal constituents: the *régime générale*, administered by the state, and the various *régimes spéciaux*, which are administered by, or for, different groups. There are also several non-contributory additions, such as the *allocation de solidarité spécifique* for long-term unemployed people. As in Britain, the insurance system can be seen as the core of the social security system overall, but the kinds of provision which are on offer are varied.

Despite attempts to extend the concept of solidarity to the nation as a whole, it is in the nature of a concept which depends on mutual aid that it relates to definable groups of people. Spitaels *et al.* argue that:

> . . . the lack of unity is at the same time the consequence and the cause of the break in the spirit of solidarity which ought to characterise every system of social security. At first, it was because they did not feel solidarity with other insured people that certain socio-professional groups claimed and obtained a special régime. Subsequently, this feeling was strengthened, and it was in the name of these special interests that the beneficiaries of these régimes refused every real reform of the structure.[8]

In contrast to Britain, poverty has not been a major element in the development of French social security; references to poverty in recent political debates depend more on cultural diffusion (from Britain and the US) than on a home-grown concept. The main issue has been family policy.[9] The French concern with family policy can be justified in terms of solidarity, which implies the acceptance of social responsibility for child care; but it also reflects 'natalism', or a concern with the birth rate. The development of family benefits in France has, bizarrely, attracted political support from both left and right; the unlikely alliance in the 1930s of feminists and the Catholic parties served to establish family benefits firmly.[10] The plethora of benefits which has developed since covers both universal family allowances (the *allocations familiales* and *allocation au jeune enfant initiale*) and means-tested benefits (the *complément familial*, the *allocation au jeune enfant*, the *supplément du revenu familial* and the *allocation rentrée scolaire*). For those who remain, there are residual benefits, of which the most important until recently was *aide sociale*. This linked discretionary assistance with personal support on a model related to social work.[11] However, the coverage of aide sociale has been restricted, and it has been suggested that half a million unemployed people were not being covered.[12]

Concern with poverty in its own right has been a fairly recent development. The socialist government under Mitterrand has referred to the idea of poverty with increasing frequency, though there has been a tendency to translate the consideration of poverty very widely into terms of 'exclusion' and 'inclusion' – which might be seen as a concern with solidarity in different ways. Young offenders, by this argument, enter a consideration of 'poverty' because they are socially excluded.[13] The principal response has been the development of the *Revenu Minimum d'Insertion* or RMI – 'l'insertion' representing here a concept similar to 'integration' – which seeks to address marginality, or social exclusion, as well as the economic position of the poor. The RMI has a wide remit, and the estimated number of people who should be able to benefit is about one and a half million, but if so the RMI has not reached all the groups intended, possibly because the emphasis on integration implies a set of conditions for entitlement.[14]

The French system is remarkably complex; it has made a virtue of diversity. This sits badly with attempts to develop a more comprehensive framework of services, and it is fair to say that there has been some disillusion with the concept of 'solidarity' as a result, not least because it is as capable of justifying the exclusion of disadvantaged groups as it is of including them.

SOCIAL SECURITY IN THE UNITED STATES

The US is sometimes characterised as the centre of free enterprise, competition and an individualistic, residual concept of welfare. But this gives an incomplete picture of a diverse, complex system, and it would be difficult to explain some major policies – like those of the 'War on Poverty' – on that ground alone. The cornerstone of the US system is that it is pluralistic, though it is pluralistic in a different sense to France; French social policy emphasises solidarity and group action, whereas the dominant ideology in the US stresses individual choice and limitations on government. In justifying the constitution, Madison argued for a system of government at different levels, in which people would be able to form coalitions of interests with others.[15] The principle that people should be able to make their own arrangements is seen as the core of 'American democracy'. Pluralism in welfare implies that many bodies are involved in the provision of services. The role of government in the US is often residual, particularly in relation to unemployment, but there are other examples – like those of health and disability – where government seems to be far more active. At the same time, the involvement of government even in these areas is patchy and ill-defined. The development of social welfare provisions in the US is described by Klass in terms of 'decentralised social altruism'.[16] The picture which emerges is of a patchwork of provision, with some fairly gaping holes, which is strongly dependent on location, administrative structure and the perceived locus of responsibility for people's circumstances.

Social security developed belatedly in the US and it has never gained the level of institutional acceptance that it enjoys in Europe. The US is a federal system, where issues like social security would fall into the remit of the states rather than that of the central (Federal) government. The introduction of a national insurance scheme in 1935, as part of Roosevelt's second 'hundred days', has been supplemented subsequently only in the most limited fashion. Federal interventions have often been resisted by the states, under the banner of 'states' rights', and the strategy which has been pursued by the federal government has been complex. Some issues, like a residual benefit for people without incomes – 'public assistance' or 'general assistance' – fall within the remit of the states. Some issues, like the Social Security programmes for old age, survivors, health and disability (OASDHI), Medicare (medical benefits for old people) or Food Stamps are controlled by the Federal government. But many measures straddle administrative boundaries. The Federal programme for Supplemental Security Income (SSI), which provides a minimum income for old, blind and disabled people, is generally supplemented by the states. For Medicaid, which offers health benefits to people on low income, the eligibility levels and standards are set by the states.[17] Federal measures which fall into the remit of the states can be proposed but have to be accepted by those states; Aid to Families with Dependent Children (AFDC), the main means-tested benefit aimed at single parents, is generally implemented, but the limited AFDC programme for unemployed people with families (AFDC-UP) was not accepted by many states – it applied in only 25 states in 1985, two less than ten years before,[18] and only underwent a general extension in October 1990.[19]

The states are able to vary the terms on which welfare is delivered, which has led to a certain amount of experimentation and variation. Once the measure has been accepted by the states, the continuation of the programme can be subject to federal regulation. So, for example, in the early 1950s, the 'Jenner amendment' made it obligatory for AFDC authorities to publish the rolls of people receiving welfare,[20] and most recently, 'workfare', a condition that people in receipt of AFDC must work in order to qualify for it, has been fairly generally imposed, albeit in a somewhat haphazard way.[21]

It is probably fair to say that social security, or at least that element of it described as 'welfare', is primarily directed towards poor people. Glazer comments, with a little exaggeration:

> The United States is not unique in having a division between the main national insurance programs (Social Security, unemployment insurance, Medicare) and the residual programs based on need (AFDC, Food Stamps, Medicaid). But the United States is unique in possessing so large a population of working age that is supported, along with their children, by residual programs, because it is not eligible for assistance by insurance programs.[22]

The emphasis on residual benefits has been an important political issue in the US; the issue is not that other people do not receive government support and services, but that these services – like the Veterans' Administration or Agricultural Relief – are not seen as welfare provision. By the same token, those benefits which are available for the poor are often available on only the most restrictive terms.

One of the peculiarities of a pluralistic, fragmented system is that it is likely to be expensive: the combination of extensive administrative conditions, the emphasis on personal supervision and professional intervention, overlaps between services, and gaps in provision mean that the US system offers staggeringly bad value for money. Gilbert comments that if public expenditure on welfare 'were directly distributed to the entire population in the form of cash grants, nobody would have fallen below the established poverty line of $6000 in 1978'.[23] The extent of welfare spending, and the number of programmes, sometimes gives critics the mistaken impression that the Federal government distributes largesse on an unparalleled scale. Charles Murray's book, *Losing Ground*, is based on the proposition that, despite everything which has been done for the poor since the 1960s, the numbers of poor people seem to be increasing. He proposes:

> . . . scrapping the entire federal welfare and income support structure for working-aged persons, inclusing AFDC, Medicaid, Food Stamps, Unemployment Insurance, Workmen's Compensation, subsidized housing, disability insurance, and the rest [24]

as if this demonstrated the extent of federal extravagance, rather an incomplete, inadequate, even desultory set of responses.

SOCIAL SECURITY IN ISRAEL

Israel was a society founded on utopian ideals. First, it was to be a Jewish homeland. Israel is Zionist and largely Jewish: over four-fifths of its population are Jews. It was founded in large part as a refuge against persecution, and all Jews (and first generation descendants) are deemed to have a 'right of return'; the absorption of immigrants has been a major focus of policy. However, as the balance of the population has shifted increasingly towards a settled population, the relative importance of immigrants has declined, and with this change there has been a shift away from the concentration on basic needs which providing for immigrants implied.

Another dimension of the religious nature of the state is that the principles of Judaism have played an important part in the development of welfare. But religion and state intervention are not always at one: orthodox Jews initially opposed Zionism, and in Me'a Sharim, the ultra orthodox quarter of Jerusalem, there is a prominent graffito on a wall: 'Zionism and Judaism are diametrically opposed'. The ultra orthodox do not accept the services of the Israeli state: their housing is dilapidated, and they live as far as possible by charity and mutual aid rather than by state welfare. However, religious influences are strong in the organisation of welfare. Because of the way the Israeli political system works, the religious parties have always played an important part in government. Generally, they have been the only people really interested in social welfare, an issue which other parties have been ready to concede to them, and have been in control of central government provision for over 30 years.

The influence of Judaism is evident in a number of ways. There is a central assumption that needs are in the first place going to be met by the family. For example, it is assumed that children will support their aged parents, and children whose aged parents go into residential institutions are required by law to pay towards the cost of keeping their parents, and may be prosecuted for not doing so. Charity is emphasised as a religious duty, and voluntary work is a compulsory part of the school curriculum. It should not be assumed, however, that the influence of religion is inevitably to push welfare into an individualistic or residual mould; Judaism has always fostered organised efforts to provide welfare. Most distinctively, burials are largely treated as the responsibility of the state – the acceptance of communal responsibility in this area being a long-standing element of the Jewish tradition.

The second aspect of the utopian aspirations was that Israel was to be socialist, and it would organise on principles of mutual aid. The emphasis on socialism was derived in large part from the ideal of the early pioneers in the kibbutz movement. Much of the reference to socialism is rhetorical;

the quote which follows comes from a propaganda film I saw at the Histadrut, the Israeli general federation of labour:

> The young men and women who arrived in Palestine in the early years of this century found their future home bleak and inhospitable. . . . Faced with the antagonism of veteran farmers hostile to their socialist ideals the newcomers were forced to share what little work there was. . . . Some of them realised their socialist ideals in collective farming. They contributed to a common fund to provide medical care. They formed a co-operative to supply food.

The Histadrut is substantially institutionalised within the system of government, providing many of the principal social services itself. The health service is substantially paid for by union subscription and run by the Histadrut; mutual aid schemes cover financial assistance, and residential care for children and old people. I was struck by the repeated reference to socialist ideals during the presentation of their material, and asked one of the trades unionists there about it. He was at pains to correct me. 'Social democratic', he said. 'Let's get it right.' But the influence of utopian socialism is still important for welfare, not least because it implies a very different approach from that concerned with the relief of poverty in other industrial societies. Eisenstadt emphasises that the activities of the Histadrut

> . . . were not defined as welfare activities but as part of the pioneering activities aiming at the construction by the settlers of a modern economy. Welfare in the sense of dealing with social problems was not acceptable, the assumption being that in the socialist society envisioned there would not develop special, distinct social problems.[25]

Thirdly, Israel was to be democratic, and it would have equal citizens in a pluralist society. This ideal owes much to the influence of the US, a position which sits uneasily with the socialist rhetoric. The organisation of welfare in Israel is diffused between central government, local government, the voluntary sector and the trades unions; Doron and Kramer suggest that one effect of the involvement of the labour movement, in practice, has been to force government into a residual role.[26] There is no national sickness benefit, for example, because that falls within the remit of the Histadrut. The National Insurance scheme, such as it is, is limited in both its contributory base and its benefits, and those who have to rely on the nominally universal pensions (currently under threat of abolition) need supplementary provision to achieve a tolerable standard.

Pluralistic systems are likely to have deficiencies at the best of times; the more complex the system is, the more likely it is that someone somewhere is going to fall through the net. But it would be unwise to pass over this observation without considering to some extent the divisions in

Israeli society. These divisions can be used to justify a pluralist ethic, but they also imply very different patterns of provision for different groups. Israel, Cnaan writes, 'is a stratified society wherein ethnic origin and religion are the best explaining factors of this stratification'.[27] There are three principal issues in the structure of social disadvantage. One is between European and North African Jews – Ashkenazi and Sefardi; 94 per cent of Israeli youths in poverty are Sefardi. Second, there is the division between Jew and Arab within Israeli citizenship.[28] Third, there is the distinction between citizens and non-citizens, which applies to most Arabs in the 'administered' or occupied territories. Welfare services have been maintained in these territories (and, Macarov argues, improved)[29] but there is an evident discrepancy in the standards which apply there and within Israel itself. The tension between the concern for defence security and the advancement of welfare permeates much of the social services. It affects not only the resources available for welfare provision but also the kind of ethos under which certain services, particularly those to Arabs, are delivered.

Cnaan suggests that by now 'there are no expectations that the welfare state will create an egalitarian society. The resources are simply not available. However, as a means for social integration, middle and upper classes are often included in universal social welfare programmes.'[30] At first sight, this might be reminiscent of much of what is written about the British welfare state. But the impact of the social divisions and economic crisis in Israel is not only to undermine claims for equality, but also in many ways to undermine the extent to which welfare is capable of acting as a force for integration. In recent years, welfare in Israel has suffered substantial retrenchments. The massive expenditure on defence, the parlous state of the economy and the experience of hyper-inflation have led to serious reductions in the coverage of state benefits. Child allowances have been abolished for smaller families; the scope of support for unemployed people has been reduced; and there are plans to reduce the scope of National Insurance still further. If Israel had acquired the characteristics of a welfare state, as Doron once claimed,[31] it is in the process of losing them. 'Five years ago', he has written recently, 'I presented the thesis that the Israeli welfare state was at crossroads. . . . Today it seems that Israel has made its choice.'[32]

SOCIAL SECURITY IN GERMANY

It is difficult, for a country in a state of flux, to give an accurate picture of the operation of its social security, but the philosophy, approach and methods of West Germany dominate the new German state so fully that it should be possible to use that as the basis for comment.

'The Federal Republic', Zapf suggests, 'has maintained to an astonishing degree the social politics tradition that dates back to the German Empire.'[33] Germany was the first nation to introduce a national scheme of social insurance, under Bismarck, covering sickness, industrial injuries and pensions. When, after the Second World War, Germany was being reconstructed, the tradition was maintained: a proposal for a different kind of scheme, modelled after the Beveridge report, met with:

> . . . intense opposition from bureaucrats and insurance fund officials, who had helped their programmes survive the political turmoil of previous decades, from self-employed and higher-paid workers, who insisted on a separate identity for their social insurance funds, and from leading politicians of the new Federal Republic, who discounted any need to rely on foreign models of a policy technique that the Germans themselves had invented.[34]

The German system has something of the diversity of the French, but benefits have developed within a different kind of framework, more directly related to the needs of industry. At a time when Britain was concerned with the 'welfare state', the reconstruction of the German welfare system was being justified in terms of a 'social state' (*Sozialstaat*), perhaps better understood as a 'social market economy'[35] rather than a 'welfare state'. The interests of economic development were largely put before social policy; and Chancellor Erhard argued that 'the best social policy is an effective economic policy'.[36]

In many ways, the social policy which has emerged seems to be residual in its implications. This has been reinforced by the influence of Catholic social teaching, which emphasises both solidarity and 'subsidiarity' – the principle that services should be organised and delivered at the lowest level possible.[37] Although this is not directly equivalent to residualism, it is often expressed in that form.[38] Residualism has been coupled with a strong commitment to the economic needs of society and a heavy dependence on the role of industry in providing occupational benefits. The focus falls on achievement in the market,[39] and welfare provision is strongly linked to the occupational status and employment record of the recipient.

Social security in Germany depends, as in many other places, on a combination of insurance-based benefits, largely geared to the occupational structure, and a supplementary set of safety-net provisions (mainly *Sozialhilfe*, or social assistance, and *Wohngeld*, a means-tested housing benefit). The German Basic Law (*Grundgesetz*) provides that adequate public assistance should be available as of right. The adequacy of social assistance is limited, based on a restricted 'basket of goods', and take-up is limited.[40] Importantly, these policies are backed up by an infrastructure geared to economic development and the prevention of unemployment, through job creation, employment training and fostering reductions in working hours.[41]

The heavy reliance of the German system on social insurance is an indication that poverty is less important as a justification for welfare than some other considerations, in particular social protection. The level of benefits depends strongly on past work record; those without such a record rely on social assistance, which is mainly provided through regional governments, and which is generally represented, like Income Support in the UK, as a stigmatised benefit. But the coverage of this safety net is uncertain. Mitton *et al.* comment, on the basis of a survey of the conditions of unemployed people, that:

> Protection of living standards was the main purpose of the German system and it had great success in this. In preventing poverty, however, it was not so good. The minority with little or no pension under social insurance could apply for means tested help from Social Aid (Sozialhilfe) but few did so. . . . There remained . . . an appreciable minority – slightly over one in ten – who were not being supported either by a pension or by social aid.[42]

The economic success of Germany suggests that there are few working poor in the West,[43] and the people who have not claimed social assistance are seen as the main group in poverty[44] – though one wonders how, if all this is true, the problems of poor areas, unemployment and homelessness described in the European Poverty Programme[45] could have arisen. There has been an increasing awareness of such poverty;[46] and since 1980, the number of people dependent on social assistance in West Germany has risen by more than half.[47] The general proposition that people in work are not poor needs to be qualified, too. Evidence from the 1970s suggested that women were substantially disadvantaged. Germany had an unusually high proportion of single-earner households – 61 per cent in comparison with Britain's 42 per cent[48] – which meant, in practice, that women had very much more limited opportunities for participation in the labour market. Leibfried and Ostner believe that this is still the case.[49] By contrast, Hauser and Semerau claim (on the basis of an individualised analysis of income by age and sex) that the gap between male and female has closed; they argue, surprisingly, that there is no feminisation of poverty in Germany.[50]

Social security is primarily directed at the circumstances of people outside the labour market – pensioners, unemployed, disabled and single parents. For the most part, it is the success of the German economic system which has relieved the necessity for social security to be tested; the adequacy of occupational pensions has meant that the success or failure of the residual benefits to reach their targets has not been such a serious political issue as it might otherwise have been. The economic pressures which result from the reabsorption of the East may well put this to the test.

SOCIAL SECURITY IN SWEDEN

Sweden is often presented as a model 'welfare state', with a considerable emphasis on comprehensive social provision. This comprehensiveness is expressed, Allardt suggests, in three ways: the direction of welfare programmes to the entire population rather than specific problem groups, the development of legal rights to welfare, and a broad coverage of welfare in relation to many different aspects of people's lives.[51] At first sight, Sweden appears to have a set of institutions very similar to the welfare state in Britain, with the difference that its relative generosity, efficiency and political support have enabled Sweden to realise the ideal of the welfare state rather more effectively. Heclo emphasises the similarities between the two countries, and plays down the relative importance of ideology. Policies on social security have been put forward, not by the organised political parties – which have at best a superficial grasp of the issues – and not through the electoral process; 'much of what has been specifically accomplished in state provision for old age and unemployment', he writes, 'has depended on calculations of what the public would stomach rather than what it demanded'.[52] The development of policies in both countries, he argues, has depended more on the lobby and the dynamics of the bureaucracy. But there are important differences in principle between Sweden and the UK, which are marked by the relative involvement of the labour movement in policy formation. In the UK, the labour movement has left social policy to the Labour Party; in Sweden, by contrast, the unions have played a more active role, often including the administration of unemployment benefits.[53]

The emphasis has fallen, in consequence, on attempts to tie in welfare systems to the occupational structure – a system that Mishra refers to as 'social corporatism'.[54] This is expressed through substantial use of occupational and earnings-related benefits, and an emphasis on incorporation into the labour market through education, training and equal opportunities. The stress on the occupational base does, however, lead to a degree of differentiation in the kinds of support that people can expect. Ringen describes the Swedish system as 'selective by occupational experience'.[55] On the face of the matter, this should mean that those who are left out of the occupational structure are likely to suffer, but Mishra argues that the effect of full employment policies is precisely to include those who would in other cases be marginalised.[56]

If there is a dominant theme within social security provision, it is not the relief of poverty. Probably more important is the principle of solidarity. The 1982 Social Services Act, which governs municipal welfare (including social assistance), is justified in the following terms:

> . . . on the basis of democracy and solidarity, the public social service should further people's economic and social wellbeing; equally in living conditions; active participation in the life of the community.[57]

'Solidarity', however, is understood in a different sense to its use in France. It is interpreted, not only as mutual aid and integration, but also to imply a degree of egalitarianism. Myrdal writes:

> In a society which claims solidarity as a basic principle, is demanded organised co-operation and strengthened influence in society in order to strengthen the position of the weak and in order that a redistribution of the unevenly distributed resources and opportunities can occur.[58]

The 'solidaristic wage policy' advocated by the unions is intended to pursue united action for an improvement of living and working conditions, the limitation of differentials, and a degree of income transfer.[59] Effectively, Sweden has become the model for what Titmuss called the 'institutional–redistributive' model of the welfare state,[60] in which the aim is not only to protect people against certain social contingencies, but also to produce a more equal society.

Olsson emphasises the extent to which the Swedish system has become universalised;[61] it offers a mix of universal minimum benefits – including pensions for old people, disabled and handicapped people, and child allowances – with earnings-related insurance benefits for unemployed people and pensioners. The system is not wholly universal, however; there are means-tested benefits for single parents, children in education and housing needs; social assistance, administered by local authorities, provides a safety net for each group. If there is an element of social rejection associated with this kind of arrangement, it is not evident from the literature; Wilson believes that Sweden does not have the problems of stigma and low take-up which bedevil benefits in the UK.[62] It is difficult to be certain to what extent this is true; Gould suggests that the mechanisms of public assistance, which treat claimants at an individual level and rely strongly on discretionary procedures, act as a barrier to claiming.[63] Under the constraints of industrial recession, there have been some attempts in recent years to curtail the level of expenditure committed to social security, of which one of the most important is de-indexation, which means that benefits might be eroded by inflation.[64] However, these changes do not seem to have changed the basis of the system.

SOCIAL SECURITY SYSTEMS IN OUTLINE

The sketches of social security systems presented here are sufficiently distinct for it to be possible to outline some of the dominant features of different systems, and the types of issue which distinguish their approaches to poverty.

There are many different classifications which might be made. Titmuss distinguished three main models of social welfare:[65] residual, institutional–redistributive, and the 'industrial achievement-performance' or 'handmaiden' model, which views welfare provision as the servant of the economic structure. On that basis, Sweden might be considered institutional, the US residual, and Germany devoted to 'industrial achievement'. It is difficult to classify the UK, France or Israel: the UK is institutional without being markedly redistributive; France has elements both of institutional welfare and of the orientation to work; and Israel has strong elements both of institutional and residual models at the same time, even if it is now lurching in the direction of the latter. These difficulties reflect some general problems with Titmuss's approach. Institutional welfare is not necessarily committed to progressive redistribution; it may also be mainly concerned with social protection, which covers people at different levels. And the 'handmaiden' model does not exclude the possibility of residual or institutional principles being applied at the same time.

Palme modifies Titmuss's approach by making a fourfold distinction between different kinds of system: confusingly, he uses similar terms in a slightly different way. His classification includes systems which are 'institutional' (which entails both that basic needs are met and that there is a degree of redistribution), residual (concerned only with basic needs), 'citizenship', which is concerned with basic security for all, and 'work-merit', where benefits are related to occupational status. He classifies pensions in Sweden on this basis as 'institutional', Germany as an example of 'work-merit', and France, the UK and the USA as 'residual'. Australia, where pensions are based on a test of income, and Denmark, which has many similarities to Sweden, are classified as examples of the 'citizenship' model.[66] This is a fairly idiosyncratic interpretation – I think I would have classified France and the UK as examples of 'citizenship' – but it helps to illustrate the considerable ambiguities which can arise in the interpretation of systems. As with Titmuss's scheme, there are some conceptual problems with Palme's terms: 'work-merit', like the handmaiden model, does not exclude residual principles, and his definition of 'citizenship' confuses a safety net for people unable to provide for themselves, which is associated with a residual model, and the principle that everyone should be helped, which is more commonly associated with the institutional model.

If the trouble was just that the terms do not fit the cases very well, it should be possible to find others which fit better. Unfortunately, the issue is not so easy to resolve. Any broad classification is likely to gloss over significant differences. I do not think it would be very convincing to put Israel, which relies centrally on mutual support organised through the trades union movement, in the same category as the US, or France, which has a pluralistic, fragmented system of different solidarities, in the same category as the UK; but that is the consequence of relying on simplistic descriptions like 'residual' or 'institutional'. The central problem with classifications based on such 'models' is that they try to do too much at once. Welfare systems are multi-dimensional. Rather than trying to describe systems as a whole, it is probably better to identify some of the elements of systems. This still has some problems – it relies on some very broad generalisations – but it makes it possible at least to get a handle on the material.

The first distinction that might be made concerns the kinds of redistribution which different countries make. Some offer provision for basic needs; others provide much more generous benefits, which is not so much a means of redistributing from rich to poor as a way of protecting the living standards of people whose circumstances might otherwise suffer. The US, UK and Israel fall mainly into the former category; France, Germany and Sweden are mainly in the latter.

Second, there is a difference between countries which offer benefits oriented to work and the labour market, and those which offer rights on the basis of citizenship. Germany and Sweden are in the former category; the UK and (I think) the US are in the latter. France seems to be moving from the first category to the second; Israel is difficult to classify, but it may be moving in the other direction.

Third, it is possible to classify these systems as representing individualistic or solidaristic approaches to welfare. France, Israel and Sweden are solidaristic, although this does not mean quite the same thing in each country; what they have in common is that welfare is conceived and developed as a collective enterprise. By contrast, the US, Germany and the UK tend to be individualistic (or 'liberal'), putting the stress on personal rights and responsibilities.

Fourth, there is a distinction between residual and institutional systems. This is related to the previous distinction, because liberal ideology tends to imply a marginal role for the state, but it is not the same; policy in the UK, which often emphasises individual responsibility, also contrives to have institutional welfare by emphasising the right of each individual to welfare. Sweden is clearly institutional; I think, in view of the extension of its safety net, that France can now reasonably be placed in the same category. The US and Germany are, relatively speaking, residual. Israel is again the most difficult to classify. If one was to consider only the contribution of state provision, Israel would have to be counted as 'residual', but welfare in

Israel cannot be interpreted exclusively in terms of state activity; the element of collective solidarity through trades unionism is much closer to the institutional model.

This points to a fifth dimension. Provision by the state is not necessarily the most important form of welfare provision; the distinguishing principle of welfare in Japan, for example, is the extent to which it relies on support from its corporate occupational structure in place of the state. Some systems – Israel, the US and France – are pluralistic in form; irrespective of whether or not systems are oriented to welfare or the market, they feature a diversity of provision. Others – Germany, Sweden and the UK – have attempted to introduce a generally applicable, comprehensive system.

There is no regular pattern here; none of the countries I have considered has the same basic profile as another. Sweden and the US are different in respect of each of the five dimensions I have identified, and one could choose these two countries as models, or representatives of 'ideal types'; but it would be difficult to know what to do with the countries which are left, because each of them differs from the others in important respects. What this kind of analysis shows is, not simply that countries are different, but that the differences defy categorisation in terms of basic models.

The comments I have made still rest on some pretty broad generalisations, and there are major reservations to make about them. Each of the systems is complex, and of necessity the characterisation I have made of each does not do justice to them. Intentions and practice often differ, and each of the countries might legitimately be represented in different lights. For all that, the UK appears to have a comprehensive, universal approach, it is actually much more pluralistic in its provisions than the ideology of the welfare state would suggest; Israel, despite its historical tradition, is well removed from the model of collectivised redistribution that its socialist rhetoric implies; neither the US nor Germany is truly 'residual' in the sense of concentrating on safety-net provision; and Sweden shares with France and Germany a stress on occupational status which it is difficult to reconcile with the model of 'citizenship'.

At the best of times, then, classifications of this type need to be treated with a healthy degree of scepticism. But there are also some fairly fundamental reasons why this kind of broad-brush approach can never be very accurate. In the first place, the functions of social security policies are complex, and they are not exclusively – or even primarily – associated with a single objective, like the relief of poverty; the effect is that no system can adequately be described in such simple terms. Second, even when the aims of systems appear to be similar, different methods are employed, which can produce very different kinds of result. And third, poverty itself is not a simple issue, but one which covers a wide range of different kinds of problem and contingency, so that a system which appears to be comprehensive in one respect might fail to meet other needs altogether. Considering the ways in which social security systems actually work takes us a long way from the relative certainties of ideological analysis.

10 Social security benefits

Social security is not for the most part designed to offer people a minimum level of resources, or even a minimum level of income. It may serve these functions to a greater or lesser degree, but the characteristic pattern of most social security systems is not the dominance of 'safety net' benefits or benefits designed to offer a basic income, but the diversity of options within which a safety net plays only a limited role, covering those contingencies not otherwise provided for. Poverty is dealt with, not through a close concentration or 'targeting' of benefit, but through the development of a framework of income maintenance which provides for people who are poor among others.

There are three standard components within most social security systems. The first is social insurance, which is the most widely used form of provision for old people and survivors (like widows and orphans), and which also commonly extends to cases of unemployment and invalidity where the people affected have been able to make contributions. Secondly, there are means-tested benefits, which by their nature are reserved for people with low resources. Third, there are 'non-contributory' benefits, which have no test of contribution or of means, but which may have a test of need (like benefits for disabled people).

This categorisation is not really sufficient to understand the different patterns of benefit provision, because within the two later categories in particular there is a certain amount of variation. Residual benefits – that is, benefits for those not covered by other benefits – include not only means-tested benefits, but also commonly include some discretionary element. A common pattern of 'social assistance' is that people receive some kind of personal assessment of supervision on the social work model. Despite the overlap between them, these kinds of benefit are sufficiently distinct to be treated as separate categories here. 'Non-contributory' benefits, equally, include two very different types of provision. In the case of benefits for old people or children, the only test which is applied is that a person is the right age. I have referred to these as 'universal' benefits, though the term is not always confined to such cases. In the case of disability or unemployment, a 'non-contributory' benefit also requires some kind of test of eligibility; this creates a set of problems more commonly associated with means-tested benefits than with universal benefits, and for that reason I have treated this kind of benefit as a separate category.

SOCIAL INSURANCE

The dominant element within most systems of income maintenance is social insurance – 'dominant' both in the sense that it commands the greatest element of resources, and because it provides the structure or framework around which other benefits are organised. However, the nature of social insurance can be understood in different ways, and this is reflected in the scope and adequacy of the benefits. The first model, which is the original pattern of social insurance, was developed in Bismarck's Germany, where the provisions were concerned less to provide against poverty than to offer protection to workers in the event of contingencies which might interrupt their income. Bismarck's system is most usually presented as a veiled form of repression, not least because of his own justifications for this kind of measure; it was presented as an antidote to communism, and a means of mollifying the workers. One should beware, though, of taking explicit justifications for policy of this type too seriously; it is far from clear why we should be enjoined cynically to disregard political claims which claim to serve the interests of the population and yet believe with a perfect faith protestations of underhand motives. Bismarck equally described himself as a 'Kathedersozialist' – an armchair socialist – and argued for independent benefits as a way of maintaining the dignity and rights of the recipients.[1] In justifying his actions to his *Junker* society, he appealed to their fear of socialism and their self-interest, but that is hardly the same as proving that his actions were only motivated by such factors. In so far as there was an ideological motivation, it was probably neither capitalist nor socialist. The feudal tradition, one which was still important in Europe in the nineteenth century (and which, some might say, is still fairly important now), demanded that landlords undertook some responsibility for the welfare of their charges, according to their standing in life. And that is what the Bismarckian system of insurance, much to the scorn of more 'progressive' liberals, did. It is difficult to see the hand of Bismarck in the current German social security system, but the tradition that social insurance is both a form of social protection and a form of guaranteeing social stability has been important in shaping the understanding of social security in Germany – among critics of the left, such as Habermas and Offe,[2] as much as those who would defend the position on the right. This tradition was to influence most European nations, as well as many countries outside Europe.

However, social insurance suffers from a major defect in its ability to offer social protection. It relies on a basic test – a test of contributions, and so of work experience – which tends to exclude large numbers of people who may need protection but who have not met the basic conditions. The people who are left out tend to be those unable to work – long-term unemployed, school leavers, young mothers, and chronically sick and disabled people. As for guaranteeing stability, it is unclear how far social insurance can perform any such function. If payments are to be made on the basis of insurance, they must be financed on an actuarial basis from funds based on contributions, or from the revenue from contributions on a dynamised or 'pay as you go' basis. The former arrangement requires a level of economic stability – both in the sense that people have to be able to contribute (Beveridge demanded full employment as a condition of the success of National Insurance), and in the sense that funds have to be secure. The latter requires political stability, because future generations have to be prepared to pay benefits on a basis at least equivalent to that on which people contribute. In other words, insurance requires as a precondition the kind of stability it is supposed to guarantee.

The second main model is that represented by the Beveridge report. The Beveridge report is often taken as the model for other Western European countries – during the Second World War, it was parachuted into occupied territory – though it is probably more accurate to say that the report reflected widely held views and reinforced existing developments. The rhetoric associated with the Beveridge scheme – not all of it Beveridge's – seemed to offer a broadly based response to poverty. The scheme was taken to promise coverage 'from the cradle to the grave'. Beveridge fuelled this impression with some ringing statements about the 'Giants' of 'Want', 'Idleness', 'Ignorance', 'Squalor' and 'Disease', and the claim that the scheme would be 'adequate' and 'universal' (by which he seems to have meant 'comprehensive'). Parts of the scheme proposed for social security were more concerned to reinforce the impression of comprehensiveness than to develop a sound basis for insurance – for example, Beveridge devised 'classes' for the insurance of children and old people, and 'credited' (or make-believe) contributions for some of those who were unable actually to pay their way. Beveridge stresed the importance of a basic minimal coverage, because, as he said, we need 'bread and health for all at all times before cake and circuses for anybody'.[3]

As an approach to poverty, however, there were important deficiencies in the Beveridge scheme. Some of them are peculiar to the scheme itself, and were considered in the preceding chapter. Some, however, are of general application. In the first place, universal coverage is hardly a realistic aspiration for an insurance scheme, because it is in the nature of insurance that it must be conditional to some extent on contributions, and many people are unable to contribute. Beveridge himself recognised that:

> However comprehensive an insurance scheme, some, through physical infirmity, can never contribute at all and some will fall through the meshes of any insurance.[4]

This, clearly, affects the ability of insurance schemes to respond to poverty, especially as those least able to contribute – those without regular patterns of employment – are often those most vulnerable to poverty.

The second problem was adherence to the contribution principle. Beveridge had the option of earnings-related or flat-rate benefits; he opted for flat-rate as the best way of ensuring adequacy at minimum cost. But this in turn had implications for contributions, because flat-rate benefits demanded flat-rate contributions – earnings-related contributions on flat-rate benefits would have been equivalent to a concealed tax. The contributions had to be set low, because too high a level of flat-rate contributions would have excluded large numbers of people from the scheme. In the words of a civil servant, contributions:

> . . . are not fixed on any particularly rational basis but on the basis that you want a reasonable test and do not want to make it too hard for people to get the benefits, because, after all, the contingencies are there. . . . None of us has ever paid, or ever will pay . . . the full value of our benefits.[5]

There are problems in developing universal coverage even for those in work at a level which can provide adequate benefits.

The third principal model of social insurance is represented by schemes which emphasise mutual aid. This is probably best represented by social insurance in France. The distinctiveness of the French system rests in the diversity which results from the application of the principle of solidarity to different groups. Solidarity applies not only at the national level but at other kinds of level – including local groups, professional associations, friendly societies. The French system is characterised, then, not by the uniformity of basic provision, but its diversity. In many ways, this reflects more faithfully the pattern of insurance cover which has become commonplace in industrialised countries – including Britain, where private and occupational pension schemes are an increasingly significant aspect of insurance provision.

The main advantages of social insurance in practice are that it is largely self-financing, politically well established and more likely to offer a higher rate of benefit where there is earnings-relation. But there are important disadvantages, particularly from the perspective of the poor. The work test associated with contributions means that low-paid workers (and women), people with marginal employment, or those who undergo spells of unemployment or sickness, are less likely to be able to contribute; where they can, they are less likely to be able to afford contributions. Where they cannot, of course, it is necessary to develop further tiers within a benefit system, and many people are in practice left out. The Child Poverty Action Group used to argue that the strengthening of insurance was the best strategy to protect the poor. In recent years, however, they have moved away from this position. Fimister and Lister acknowledge that the insurance principle:

> (a) . . . does not protect benefits against cuts . . .
> (b) . . . excludes some of the most vulnerable people from entitlement to benefit . . .
> (c) . . . creates complexities and administrative problems . . .
> (d) . . . is in any case a myth.[6]

MEANS-TESTED BENEFITS

The limitations of social insurance have meant that benefits have had to be developed to take over some of the roles which insurance fails to fulfil. The most important of the alternatives is means-testing – the award of benefit which is conditional on a test of resources, usually income, and sometimes capital. Although different means-tested benefits clearly act in very different ways, it is difficult to subclassify means-tested benefits in the same way as National Insurance. Much depends on the categories of people included or excluded, the relative generosity of the benefits, and on the type of benefit system in which the means-tested benefit is applied.

The inclusion or exclusion of different categories of people defines the function of particular means-tested benefits. Means-tests tend to be associated with 'safety-net' benefits, on the basis that most people do not require social protection and only those whose income falls below a certain level should qualify. In other words, means-tests tend to be residual in their nature. Within this broad category, though, there are important subdivisions. Some means-tested benefits are available very generally to people on low incomes, like Income Support in the UK, and can be seen as general safety-net benefits. Some relate only to a limited set of potential recipients, like AFDC in the US.

There are also some exceptions to the general description of means-tested benefits as residual. An alternative pattern of means-testing is directed not so much to the identification of people on low incomes as to the screening out of those on higher incomes, with a system designed to include most: examples are the Australian pensions scheme or the UK student grants scheme. (One might perhaps also include the upper limits on income used to determine the coverage of social insurance in Germany, though technically this does not fall into the category of a means-test.) If the former pattern is residual in principle, the latter is institutional.

The scope of means-tested benefits depends not only on the categories of people formally included or excluded but on the level at which benefits are set. The level of benefits matters in systems where either the benefit is used to determine a minimum level of income (like Income Support, or a number of French benefits for the family – the *supplément du revenu familial, allocation au jeune enfant* and *allocation de parent isolé*) or to establish a figure which is gradually withdrawn as other income increases (like Housing Benefit); both principles imply that higher levels of benefits make more people eligible for consideration. Effectively, the lower the level of benefits, the more residual they are likely to be; the higher they are, the more people will be included. If residual means-tested benefits are often linked with ungenerous provision – an accusation frequently levelled at them, for example by Townsend – it is not least because the level of means-tested benefits is one of the reasons they are described as 'residual'.

The functions which means-tested benefits perform depend, too, on the kind of system in which they have a place. In the UK, the central means-tested benefit is Income Support – formerly National Assistance (1948–66) and Supplementary Benefit (1966–88). The benefit is, in principle, a supplement to other benefits, bringing people up to a level of income (and therefore effectively acting as a guaranteed minimum income for a wide range of people entitled). Although the benefit has become increasingly important for a wide range of people, and has been adapted to a 'mass role', the central presumption behind the rules affecting the benefit is that people will receive it only when they do not have alternative sources of income through other benefits. This means that Income Support is genuinely a 'safety net', coming into force only when other benefits do not. In Australia, by contrast, the basic means-tested benefit performs a very different function, because there is no basic system of social insurance.[7] Effectively, then, the means-tested benefit is the only form of provision for important categories of beneficiary – particularly pensioners – and the role of the benefit is substantively different from that of Income Support in the UK, despite a number of factors in common. Mitton *et al.* write, on the basis of their work in the UK, France and Germany:

> That some means-tested benefits are extensively taken up while others are not suggests that it is not the means-testing itself that is the problem but rather the way in which the means-tested benefits are administered.[8]

The process of means-testing has been much vilified, on the somewhat questionable basis that means-tests are an intrinsically unsatisfactory method of distributing benefits. Much of this relates to an ideological view of means-tests as being uniquely closely linked with a residual model of welfare. But means-tests, like any other administrative process, have both advantages and disadvantages. The advantages of means-tests are, first, that they concentrate resources on those most in need and, second, that they are progressive, and redistribute resources vertically from rich to poor. Both of these factors would suggest that means-testing would be favoured by the left wing – but not a bit of it.

The first accusation levelled against means-tested benefits is that they are complex and difficult to administer. The French *allocation de parent isolé* has been criticised for taking up to six months to be delivered; benefits are often miscalculated, and if overpaid, reclaimed from the unfortunate recipient who is unlikely to have known there was an overpayment.[9] This is not difficult to cap. Housing Benefit in the UK has been described (in *The Times*) as 'the biggest administrative fiasco in the history of the welfare state';[10] in one case I encountered in my housing practice, the benefit authority (a London Borough) had taken eight years not to process the claims of a number of elderly women in sheltered housing, a claimant group whose circumstances were about as stable as the authority could have hoped to find.[11]

However, in fairness to means-tested benefits, they are not necessarily the most difficult benefits to administer; much depends on the rules which affect each benefit. Drawing on Treasury figures, Supplementary Benefit was expensive to administer, at about £2.85 per beneficiary each week, but so were many insurance benefits, like Unemployment Benefit at £2.50, Maternity Allowance at £2.40, or Sickness and Invalidity Benefits at £3.05.[12] Belorgey notes problems in claiming sickness and unemployment insurance in France, not least because of the demands for documentation.[13] The benefits which were cheaper to administer in the UK – retirement pensions at 45p, Family Income Supplement at 50p or Attendance Allowance at 80p – were cheaper because of the relative stability of individual circumstances and the use of postal claims, not because of the simplicity of the benefits.

The second objection to means-tested benefits is that they create a poverty trap. If benefits are given to people on low incomes, they must be taken away from people whose incomes go up. In combination with the tax system, the effect in Britain has been effectively to remove any advantage in an increase in income for people who receive such benefits. Getting out of poverty, Piachaud writes, is like getting out of a well; if you can't jump up far enough you simply slide back to the bottom again.[14]

Last, and most serious, means-tested benefits often fail to reach those in need. The reasons commonly given for low take-up are complex. Kerr suggests that there are a series of steps that a person has to take before claiming. Claimants have to feel a need. They have to know that a benefit exists, and that they are likely to be entitled. They have to feel that a benefit is worth claiming, which it may not be if the value of the benefit is too small. Next are the beliefs and feelings of the claimant, which might include issues of social acceptability, the desirability of 'managing', the person's role as a 'breadwinner', or general attitude towards benefit support. Finally, there is the perceived stability of the circumstances – people may not claim if they think their circumstances are likely to change.[15] He presents these as a number of hurdles which have to be surmounted consecutively, but they can equally be seen as interlocking; there is an interrelationship between lack of perceived need, knowledge of benefits and uncertainty about eligibility, and negative beliefs and feelings about the claiming process.[16]

There are other reasons, too, why people might fail to claim. Weisbrod suggests that people weight the costs of claiming, broadly understood, against the benefits.[17] Some people are afraid to claim, perhaps because of the consequences of asking landlords for evidence of rent, or employers about low wages. The reasons for not claiming include deterrence, degrading treatment and loss of rights; the history of means-testing, which is associated by many with repressive administration and the Poor Law; a feeling of being 'labelled'; and a dislike of 'charity', or pride.[18] These problems have led many critics to reject means-testing altogether. But the same criticisms could be levelled at benefits which are not means-tested, including both social insurance and the non-contributory benefits which have often been developed to avoid the stigma of means-testing.

NON-CONTRIBUTORY BENEFITS

Reactions to the failures of social insurance and the perceived limitations of means-testing have led to an increasing concern to develop alternative kinds of benefit. These benefits are usually referred to as 'non-contributory', though the defining characteristic of such benefits is not only that they are not based on contributions, but also that they have no test of means. Some still have a test of need. An example is the Disability Living Allowance, recently introduced as a replacement for Mobility Allowance and Attendance Allowance for people under 65. There are two components, one for 'care' and the other for 'mobility'. The general rules for the care component are that the disabled person must need attention for a significant part of the day, or be unable to prepare a cooked meal; the basic test for the mobility component is that claimants cannot walk outdoors without guidance or supervision. (The conditions are more stringent than this brief summary suggests. Claimants have to have suffered from the condition for at least three months before claiming, and the disability must be likely to last for at least six months more; this excludes most stroke victims, which is one of the main groups of people under 65 with mobility difficulties. And the allowance for mobility is only available for people who claim before they are 65, which excludes the vast majority of people in Britain who are unable to walk.)

The central arguments for non-contributory benefits seem to be based on criticisms of other kinds of benefit, but there is little reason to suppose that they are immune from similar kinds of complaint. If they are less complex, it is not immediately apparent; any test of need tends to create complexities of its own. Benefits for disabled people are not much less expensive to administer than others, and they are regularly the subject of complaint about administrative hurdles.[19] There is not much information on the time it takes to process claims, but before the reform of the system in 1988 Supplementary Benefit was being calculated in two days for a person coming into the office, and ten days for someone wanting a home visit. By contrast, a number of non-contributory claims took much longer: Attendance Allowance claims took an average 45 days to clear, Retirement Pension 47 days and Mobility Allowance 53 days.[20] Belorgey notes of the French system that in relation to the *allocation d'adulte handicapé*, where cases are contested, the process can drag on for years.[21]

Non-contributory benefits may avoid a 'poverty trap' in the strict sense of the word, but problems are still likely to occur at the points where people cease to be entitled to benefits. In the case of benefits for mobility, for example, a person who became able to walk again would lose benefit. It seems inappropriate to describe this as a 'disincentive' to rehabilitation, as there are very few people who would choose not to walk if they could, but it is an extra cost of rehabilitation during a stressful period. They are supposed to be free of stigma, but this stretches credibility – can it really be more stigmatising to declare that one's income is below a certain level than it is to have to declare that one is unable to use the toilet unaided?

The important distinguishing feature of non-contributory benefits is not that they are prima facie more universal, more generous or easier to administer; it is that by removing tests of qualification associated with work record or income, some of the worst obstacles to more comprehensive coverage can be removed. If their role has been limited, it is because their reliance on finance through taxation is difficult to justify in terms of redistribution (because the redistribution is not necessarily from rich to poor). Non-contributory benefits, where they have been used, have often been greatly restricted by qualifications on the basis of need, residence or category of claimant, largely because the cost of non-contributory provision is liable to exceed the willingness of governments to test the goodwill of the electorate.

UNIVERSAL BENEFITS

Non-contributory benefits are sometimes referred to as 'universal', but there is a distinction to be made between non-contributory benefits like Attendance Allowance, which depend on some kind of qualifying test, and those benefits which are available with no test of contribution, need or means. These are more legitimately described as 'universal'; another way of referring to them is as 'demogrants' (the term is, I think, Canadian, though it also featured in McGovern's 1972 election campaign in the US). It puts the situation too strongly to say that they go to 'everyone'; universal benefits are better considered as categorical benefits, relying on membership of a demographic category – like children or old people. This implies that social security is provided universally for certain classes of people, and it implies a minimum level of income for people in that class. The central advantages of such an arrangement are simplicity and stability – the benefits are simple to administer because people are old, or children, for an extended period of time. The same principle cannot be extendedeasily to unemployed people, single parents or sick people, because their circumstances change. Unemployment and disability, furthermore, would have to be defined – which implies the introduction of some kind of test.

Child Benefit is the principal demogrant in the UK system, and it attracts a wide range of support. Ostensibly, this is because it protects people against poverty – the principal pressure group which supports it is the Child Poverty Action Group – but in practice the support is for other reasons. Viewed as a benefit for those who are poorest, it is spectacularly unsuccessful. It is inefficient: three-quarters goes to people above the Income Support level. Poor families who are on Income Support do not benefit, because it is deducted directly from their benefit. The only families which gain from it when below the Income Support (IS) level, then, are those who are working for less than IS rates – a very small number of people. Among those who receive marginally more, very few are families with children. In redistributive terms, the intended effect of Child Benefit is horizontal – from people without children to people with children. Because people with more children tend to be older, and older families tend to be better off, the broad effect of Child Benefit is moderately regressive.

There are, however, other arguments for Child Benefit, which carry very much more conviction. First, Child Benefit works. Take-up is very high; it is simple to administer. It is difficult to generalise from this to other benefits; for example, the extra One Parent Benefit, which is paid as a supplement to Child Benefit, has a much lower rate of take-up (perhaps 70 per cent). Second, Child Benefit is expressive of solidarity. It represents an acknowledgement of social responsibility for childrearing. Third, it is paid to the mother. The view has been expressed that women in wealthy households who have no personal income should be considered to be 'poor',[22] which is unpersuasive. But there is a case of a different kind to be made for the redress of power between males and females; it is a means of protecting women's rights rather than of meeting their needs. The main objection to Child Benefit, on this argument, is that it is child related instead of being gender related, though this may be the only way in which benefits for women can be legitimised. Cass offers a depressing observation:

> Australia ranked with the United Kingdom, Denmark and Germany in providing relatively parsimonious child support; Belgium, France, Luxembourg and the Netherlands were the most generous in their level of support; Italy and Ireland were the least generous. What is significant about this listing is that in Belgium, France, Luxembourg and the Netherlands, family allowances are increased in line with an index, either on prices or earnings – *and* in all but Belgium, allowances are paid to the father. Of the less generous countries, allowances are not indexed and in all countries but Italy are paid to the mother.[23]

The principle of the demogrant is valuable, not least because it serves as a marker for a different type of social security system. It is perfectly feasible to envisage a system in which there are no special qualifying conditions, where every person receives an individual demogrant (as children do now), and the system is entirely tax financed. If the benefits are sufficiently generous, no other benefits should be necessary. This is the principle of the Social Dividend, or 'Basic Income' scheme.[24] The advantages of such a scheme are administrative simplicity, and the avoidance of problems like stigma, the poverty trap or low take-up. But there are also important disadvantages. The costs are viewed by some as prohibitive. The removal of conditions like availability for work are seen as a massive disincentive, particularly for those whose decision to work is currently marginal. The scheme cannot engage inequalities very fully – on the contrary, many of the beneficiaries would be non-working spouses in relatively wealthy households. And there is a risk of oversimplification – people's lives are complicated and some supplementary response for special needs would still have to be available.

DISCRETIONARY BENEFITS

Lastly, a range of benefits may be available for people in special circumstances on a discretionary basis. The advantages of discretionary benefits are that they can be adapted to the needs of individuals in a way in which formal regulations cannot. Where an individual's circumstances fall into a lacuna in the rules, nothing is likely to be done. The development of discretionary procedures can deal with exceptional circumstances. It can be argued that no scheme can hope to have truly universal coverage without having some provision for exceptional contingencies. Equally, they can be associated with other kinds of policy, like community care, which depend on assessment and responses being made for a particular set of needs, rather than on the basis of entitlement.

The term 'discretion' requires some clarification here. In the UK, the Supplementary Benefits Commission administered, until 1980, a range of payments under a 'discretionary basis', a term which was taken to mean that there was no formal entitlement to payment and that the issues fell within the decision of officers. But the judgement of officers in any individual case was limited by the creation of administrative rules which defined the limits of judgement no less strictly than a legal entitlement may have done. It is in the nature of discretion that it cannot be used consistently without being bound by rules, in which case it ceases to be 'discretion' in any meaningful sense. But decisions which are not consistent are not predictable, and uncertainty about the likelihood of receiving benefits, balanced against the costs, is a major element in the failure to take up benefits. Discretion on this model was largely (not wholly) abandoned in the period 1980–8. The government hoped at the time that this might limit the number of claims received, but it had the reverse effect, and by 1988 the government had decided to reintroduce a discretionary system, the Social Fund.

Discretion has only ever played a marginal role in benefit in the UK. In the US, a number of states have tied public assistance programmes to social work; and in France, discretionary elements linked to individual case work have played an important part within the system of public assistance. As part of *aide sociale*, provision was made to offer advice to recipients about budgeting, as well as counselling for personal problems; the assumption seems to have been that those who were on low incomes had some pathological problem. The new system, the *Revenu Minimum d'Insertion*, begins from the premise that poor people are 'excluded' from the course of society and have to be reintegrated – a position which is less reliant on the pathological elements but which still sees the problem in terms of patterns of behaviour rather than relative levels of resources.

If discretionary policies have not worked well, it is not least because, too often, the shortage of money induced by the inadequacy of existing systems generates problems which are not 'exceptional' in any sense – for example, the difficulty under the UK scheme of paying for the replacement of clothing or furniture – and implies a pathological reason for the lack of resources. In the US, Richard Nixon (one finds light in the most unexpected quarters) justified his proposals for reform in precisely these terms. He condemned

> . . . snoopy, patronising surveillance by social workers which made children and adults feel stigmatised and separate. The basic premise of the Family Assistance Plan was simple: what the poor need to help them rise out of poverty is money.[25]

Discretion is an inadequate response to the situation of people who are poor; rules need not to be bent, but to be changed.

BENEFITS IN COMBINATION

Benefits are not delivered in isolation; there is, in every system, a network of benefits, sometimes overlapping, sometimes alternative. On retirement, a claimant may receive either an insurance-based pension, a means-tested benefit or some combination of the two. On the face of it, the National Insurance Retirement Pension effectively brings about three-quarters of its recipients out of poverty. But if they did not receive the Retirement Pension, they would receive other benefits instead. Fry *et al.* detail the effects of reductions in the value of pensions on eligibility for other benefits. They suggest that over half of any marginal reduction in spending would be needed to pay for means-tested benefits.[26] (Atkinson, by contrast, puts the figure at 30 per cent.)[27]

Which is more effective – the Retirement Pension, which actually provides the bulk of the income, or Income Support, which would provide the income with less 'wastage' if there were no Retirement Pension? It is difficult, then, as a general proposition to attribute to any one class of benefit a greater or lesser degree of success in the relief of poverty. (The argument that any particular benefit should be increased is of a different kind – it assumes that there is already a context in which the benefits will have an identifiable effect.)

Many writers have represented social security benefits as institutional when they are based on categories, and 'residual' when they use the methods most commonly associated with residual welfare – in particular, means-testing and discretionary administration. However, the situation is more complicated than this implies. Most social security systems do not have benefits which fall exclusively into the category of institutional or residual welfare, but some mixture of both. The institutional benefits are those which are addressed to general contingencies, like old age or sickness.

Residual benefits are those provided for those who are unable to make provision in other ways. Benefits which are exclusively addressed to the issue of poverty might seem to be residual, but that is not the way that things work in practice; for any benefit which was addressed to the issue of poverty in a context where there were no other benefits would, of necessity, address the same issues as institutional benefits. In the UK, National Insurance represents the institutional aspect of benefits for pensioners, because National Insurance is sufficient in itself to deal with the circumstances of nearly three-quarters of all the pensioners; Income Support, the means-tested benefit which deals with about a fifth (though it should deal with rather more), is residual, because it is addressed to those who are left out. In Australia, by contrast, the means-tested pension applies to virtually the whole population of state pensioners; and, as such, it falls into the category of an institutional rather than a residual benefit. (Australians sometimes have difficulty, on this basis, recognising their benefits as 'means-tested'. The problem is not that there is not a means-test, but that it is difficult to identify in their system many of the kinds of issue associated with 'means-testing' in Europe.)

In order to identify the functions of different kinds of benefit, one has to examine the pattern of provision for each dependent group. The limited coverage of different types of insurance, or non-contributory benefits, and the limited adequacy of universal benefits means that there is often a complementary role for a residual benefit – whether means-tested or discretionary. The case of elderly people might be taken as an example. In the UK, the US, Germany, France or Israel, old people receive a basic pension which is dependent on insurance contributions. In Sweden, the basic pension is universal, though most pensioners also have a contributory supplement. The next question is what happens to those who are not covered, or are only covered inadequately, by these basic pensions. In most of these countries, there is a residual scheme of social assistance which meets the contingency; the main exception is the US, not because there is no such assistance but because it depends on the discretion of state governments as to what level and on what terms supplements are available.

There are, however, important differences in the pattern of provision for different client groups. Provision for elderly people may follow a fairly common pattern, but the pattern of provision for single parents varies enormously between countries: France and Sweden have universal family benefits backed up by means-tested additions (as does the UK, although the universal element is so small as not to count); the US has a means-tested benefit; and Germany and Israel have no special provision. An understanding of the way in which systems operate requires some examination of the provisions which are made for different kinds of contingency.

11 The principal contingencies

Most social security systems contain several kinds of provision for different contingencies. Where some contingencies are not adequately allowed for – like unemployment in the US, young single people in the UK, or part-time workers in France – there will be deficiencies in that respect, even though the system might be adequate in others. If one wishes to assess the adequacy of systems solely from the point of view of poor relief, then it seems clear that the number of contingencies covered, and the terms on which they are covered, becomes very important.

In Chapter 5, I described the situation of a number of groups vulnerable to low income or poverty. These included elderly people; chronically sick and disabled people; unemployed people; single parents; and people on low earnings. This does not define the same areas as those most commonly dealt with by social security systems. Although most developed social security systems address these problems to some degree, and make some provision for destitution (for example, benefits for people who are homeless, or disaster relief), there are often significant gaps, which are, admittedly, most easily identified when they become the subject of campaigns to remedy them. Disabled people, for example, received little specific help under the British system before 1970; gaps in provision for poor people in France have been responded to only recently by the RMI; and males suffering from long-term unemployment receive little help in the US. Equally, there are important issues often dealt with by social security which are not prominent in analyses of poverty. These include benefits for widows and orphans; short-term sickness and medical benefits; maternity benefits; and benefits for families with children. This is not an exhaustive list. A number of countries have special provision for ex-service personnel. In Britain, there are also benefits for students and (bizarrely enough) for people who cannot afford local taxes. In Greece and Italy, crop insurance for farmers has been seen as a form of social security.

The pattern of provision for each principal group tends to be different, not only because their needs are different, but because their relationship to the labour market is. Those who have been able to contribute towards insurance schemes – primarily pensioners – are in a different position from those who have not. Groups who have no reasonable prospect of entering the labour market – like many single parents or chronically sick people – are in a different position to those who have – like students, unemployed people or low earners. And women, because of their particular disadvantages in the labour market, are liable to have a different set of options and outcomes than men do – an issue which affects a range of benefits, including those affecting low earners, single parents, maternity and child care.

PROVISION FOR GROUPS IN NEED

Pensions

Because pensions are given at the end of a person's working life, it is usually possible to relate them successfully to the labour market, with fairly few exceptions. Pensions are commonly provided by means of social insurance, or at least contributory benefits – 'insurance' is something of a misnomer, as the issue is less one of protection against a contingency than of individual saving and collective provision to meet a predictable need.

The first issue concerns the question of whether pensions should be based on flat-rate or earnings-related benefits. Flat-rate benefits are egalitarian; they have the effect of levelling out the incomes of old people after retirement. Earnings-related benefits are solidaristic; they are justified mainly in terms of social protection, avoiding the situation in which individuals are required in retirement to take a substantial cut in income. At the same time, they are potentially inegalitarian, because they reflect the inequalities of the labour market – Titmuss's fear of 'two nations in old age'.

Closely related to this issue is the question of whether contributions should be flat rate or earnings related. If the scheme is to be a true insurance scheme, with benefits strictly tied to contributions, then flat-rate benefits demand flat-rate contributions – an earnings-related contribution would imply a concealed tax – and earnings-related benefits demand earnings-related contributions (flat-rate contributions would be regressive). If, on the other hand, the scheme is to involve some form of progressive redistribution, then earnings-related contributions or a tax subsidy are necessary, with the benefits being either flat rate or at least limited in the differentials they establish between different recipients.

Most countries have favoured an earnings-relation, and earnings-relation has probably proved to be the most effective way of guaranteeing adequacy – the best exemplar is Sweden. The UK moved substantially in that direction in the pension plan of 1975, though more recently there has been some retrenchment.[1]

Second, insurance of this kind may be funded or solidaristic. Funded schemes are based on a principle of saving – the benefits which a person receives are directly based on the contributions which that person has paid in. A solidaristic or 'pay-as-you-go' scheme is one in which pensions are paid for directly out of the contributions received at the time; the continuation of the arrangement rests on the commitment of each generation to pay for the pensions of the preceding generation. Although most occupational and mutual aid schemes rely on funding, it is unusual for a national scheme to do so; dynamisation, or allowance for inflation, is easier in the case of solidaristic pensions than of others, because adjustments to benefits can be paid for by adjustments to contributions.

The third dimension is between pensions which are publicly provided and those which are provided on an occupational or commercial basis. Although there is some scope for commercial schemes in areas other than old age – most notably for health insurance – it is difficult for such schemes to insure against unemployment or single parenthood. The problem is partly one of moral hazard (people can behave in ways which increase their liability of losing their incomes in this way) and partly a reflection of the length of the contribution period.

After insurance, the standard fall-back position is likely to be a means-tested benefit. Sweden is distinguished by a non-contributory minimum pension; in other cases, a minimum for pensioners is a residual benefit dependent on alternative sources of income. A widespread acceptance of the legitimacy of dependency in old age means that the terms on which old people receive benefits are less restrictive than others. However, the level of supplementary benefits varies. The figures from the Luxembourg Income Study seem to show that pensions in Sweden and West Germany are more successful in improving income than those in Britain or the US, although the British system does reach many people at a relatively low level of benefit. Superficially, the systems which are used are very similar. All have a core scheme run by the state (though that in Germany is not universal); all, with the exception of Sweden, are financed through the contributions of workers and employers rather than taxation (though the UK and France also have an exchequer contribution); and all of the systems can be supplemented by occupational schemes. The US and Germany have earnings-related benefits (in the case of the US subject to a means-test), whereas Sweden and Britain have a basic flat-rate benefit supplemented by a further earnings-related addition. If one wishes to explain the apparent differences in the successes of the different schemes, it probably rests, not in the mechanisms which are used to supply pensions, but in factors like the political and economic history of the systems, the levels at which they are set (and so the level of public expenditure) and the extent to which people have been able to participate in the labour market. Disappointingly, there is no existing mechanism of distribution which will automatically guarantee adequate benefits for the elderly population.

Disabled people

Unless disabled people are to receive the same benefits as everyone else, and on the same terms – which might include requirements to be available to work – benefits of this kind have to be subject to a test of need, because otherwise one cannot define people as 'disabled'. Of necessity, the assessment which is made will involve an element of judgement; it is possible to have a scheme for disabled people which limits the scope for administrative or expert discretion (the UK Industrial Injuries Scheme gives points for different parts of the anatomy lost), or benefits based on a particular kind of judgement (like ability to work), but only at the expense of sensitivity to individual need or the type of disability.

The level of definition which is needed depends on the purpose of the benefit. Benefits for disabled people have been founded on a range of principles besides financial need, including, for example, insurance, desert (e.g. war pensions), compensation for harm, and rehabilitation.[2] Historically, the most important of these have been insurance and compensation. The central problem with insurance-based benefits is that people who become disabled are not necessarily able to insure themselves through contributions or a work record. Those who have been able to do so can receive some kind of sickness or invalidity benefit, but those who have not – like people with disabilities from childhood, or those with incomplete work records – have to receive some kind of non-contributory benefit.

Systems of compensation for disability have provided a major alternative, most notably in the context of industrial injuries, or through the courts. The central limitation of such schemes has been the problem of attributing a cause to different kinds of disability. Most mental handicap, for example, has no attributable organic reason, but there have been controversies concerning the extent to which vaccinations or avoidable birth defects might cause mental handicap. The legal system, in such cases, offers a hard and difficult road, because of the problem of satisfactorily establishing causation. The deformations caused by thalidomide, which were pursued in different courts, are now clearly and universally identified, but the process of establishing compensation took many years. (The thalidomide scandal was also to play a major role internationally in highlighting the problems of disabled people.)[3]

The main alternative, developed in New Zealand, is the establishment of a no-fault system of compensation for disability.[4] The intention of this was to avoid the problems of establishing causation, concentrating solely on the level of impairment. The scheme has been less imitated than might be imagined – Sweden has introduced a similar scheme, but in the UK it applies only to those who are the victim of criminal injury. (The Pearson Commission, which considered the prospects of introducing a similar scheme in the UK, rejected the idea on the basis that it wished to maintain personal liability for compensation.[5] Lord Pearson defended the principle on the grounds that New Zealand was a smaller country than the UK and, besides, victims enjoyed having their day in court.) There are problems with such a scheme; there are inequities between those who have become disabled as the result of some identifiable event or accident, and those who have become progressively disabled through long-term sickness – like bronchitis – who are not eligible for compensation.

The development of non-contributory benefits has seemed to be the only equitable method of compensating people for disability without making invidious distinctions between groups. The problem has been that such benefits are liable to be expensive, because so many people are disabled; the initial generosity of Attendance Allowance (introduced in the UK in 1970) was not repeated in later benefits, like Mobility Allowance or Severe Disablement Allowance, introduced after economic crises. These were denied to elderly disabled people – who constitute the majority of disabled people.

The Disability Alliance argues for a universal Disability Allowance for all disabled people. The advantages of this are it will treat people more equitably, according to need rather than the cause of their disability; it should offer a basic minimum; and it will be simpler than the present system. The disadvantages are that it would be very costly if it was to be at all adequate; that there would be considerable resistance, as many disabled people, like war pensioners, have privileges they would not want to see eroded by a more rational system; that it will still require a test of need, with the accompanying problems of definition, barriers to access, and stigma; and that it will separate out the 'deserving poor'.

Unemployment

Unemployment is a complex set of issues rather than a single issue in itself, and people whose unemployment is casual, frictional, seasonal, short term or structural have different needs. Beveridge's analysis of unemployment, which was introduced in Chapter 5, may be unsatisfactory as a definition of the problem – because it mixes analysis of causation, presenting problems, and different patterns of work – but it offers a useful starting point for understanding the organisation of benefits. Beveridge's own scheme was principally concerned with casual, seasonal and short-term 'frictional' unemployment; for the rest, he had assumed full employment. The 'assumption' of full employment in his report meant, he wrote, 'that if there is mass unemployment, Social Security by income maintenance does not meet the needs; unemployment benefit is adequate treatment only for short interval unemployment'.[6] Many benefits are concerned with social protection, rather than with unemployment as a cause of long-term poverty.

The system of benefits for unemployment this produced was geared to short periods of unemployment. Within the detailed provisions of the National Insurance scheme, casual unemployment was accounted for by the calculation of unemployment benefits on a daily basis (a quirk of social insurance in the UK which has only recently been changed), and coverage for seasonal unemployment depended on the number of contributions made in a period between 9 and 21 months beforehand, rather than immediately before the period of unemployment – the relevant period has since been extended to up to 33 months. (There was an administrative rationale behind this, but the point is really rather too obscure to be worth pursuing in detail here.) Most important, entitlement to Unemployment Benefit was time limited, which meant that people who were unemployed for long periods of time ceased to be eligible for Unemployment Benefit, and then had to rely on means-tested benefits. In practice, this has meant that there are fewer long-term unemployed women than men, because women whose benefit entitlement is exhausted cannot claim and cease to be officially unemployed. In recent years, the numbers of people dependent on Unemployment Benefit while unemployed have been limited in comparison with those who receive Income Support, or those who are not entitled.

Despite the very different provenance of social security in other countries, there are some notable patterns in provision for unemployed people. In Sweden or Denmark, where unemployment insurance is administered through the trades unions, insurance-based benefits tend to be generous in comparison with the UK or US, where it falls to the state (though it would be dangerous to generalise – the same cannot be said for Israel). Even between similar schemes, there may be considerable variation, because much depends on the terms of the fund from which the benefit is administered. Unemployment benefits have to be tested by some kind of work criterion – if not, then people who withdraw from the labour market, or who opt to work part time, could claim. Insurance-based benefits effectively impose a test of a prior work record – this is, after all, how insurance is defined. Perhaps less predictably, for those who qualify, most schemes are time limited, which means not that all benefits subsequently stop (as they may in the US), but rather that the rate of benefit may be reduced (as in Denmark) or transferred to another benefit (as in France,

Germany and the UK). Effectively, then, virtually all systems of support for unemployment are stratified in two or more tiers.

Residual benefits have been important for those who fail to meet the requirements of an insurance programme, either because they lack an adequate contribution record or because their entitlement to insurance is exhausted. In conditions of mass unemployment – conditions which negate Beveridge's assumptions – both problems are likely to arise, because initial access to the labour market is affected along with re-entry. However, the level at which such benefits are provided is likely to be low, partly because they are residual, and partly because of moral judgements about unemployment or a belief that incentives to work may be undermined. There is no evidence to show that more generous unemployment benefits are likely to foster unemployment; on the contrary, countries with higher benefits (like Sweden and Austria) have been more resistant to unemployment, while those with more restrictive policies (like the UK and the US) have done relatively badly. This probably says more about the political agenda than it does about economic forces; the countries with more generous benefits also tend to be those committed to policies for full employment.[7]

Single parents

People become single parents through a variety of circumstances, and their benefit entitlements are likely to be different. The first case to consider is that of unmarried mothers. A number of circumstances are variable: whether the mother has a work record; whether the mother is able to work while responsible for a child; and whether there is financial support from the child's father.

The second main set of circumstances is divorce. The basic conditions which have to be dealt with are similar to those of unmarried mothers; the kinds of issue which are important are the relationship of the divorced parent to the labour market, and the extent to which the divorced parent is supported by the ex-spouse. It might also be possible to consider a spouse's work record in place of the responsible parent's. Beveridge thought that divorce was not an insurable risk, on the basis of moral hazard – people could control whether they became divorced or not; the reasoning behind this seems defective, because even if it were true it suggests a different standard is being applied to those who have self-inflicted sickness or injury. It is true, too, that large numbers of people divorce; but, then, large numbers of people become pensioners. The main distinction seems to be that divorce is disapproved of socially; effectively, a moral element seems to have intruded in the scheme. This seems, again, to be reflected fairly universally in different social security schemes.

Third, there is the position of survivors – widows and widowers. The issue of the claimant's relationship to the labour market remains; the spouse is (evidently) not able to offer regular maintenance, though it is possible to make provision through private schemes. Unlike the circumstances of divorced parents, widowhood is considered an insurable risk, and it is generally dealt with through insurance-based benefits. The adequacy of these benefits depends, like pensions, on a number of factors, including protection against inflation and whether the benefits are earnings related.

The main kinds of benefits introduced for single parents tend to be either universal or means-tested. On paper, the UK seems to have a core of universal benefits – an allowance for each child supplemented by a special addition for single parents – but this is not sufficient in practice to make a significant difference to the circumstances of single parents, and in many cases, because it is directly deducted from the value of other benefits, it yields no net value to single parents who claim. The French and Swedish systems appear to be more generous; the universal family allowances are supplemented by means-tested additions for single-parent families, though in the case of France the means-tested provisions are also subject to availability for work after the child reaches the age of three. In the US and, in practice, the UK, the main form of benefit for single parents is means-tested and residual.

Although single parents may receive benefits of different kinds, it is a necessary feature of any benefit which is intended for single parents that there must be a cohabitation rule. The difference between a single-parent family and a two-parent family is the absence of one partner. If single-parent benefits are not to be paid to everyone, there has to be a rule disqualifying couples. The problem can be avoided, in principle, by treating women and men within households independently for the purposes of benefit, but this has other implications: it would mean that all spouses who were not working would be entitled to benefit, and that the special income needs of single parents were not recognised. The attempt to introduce non-means-tested benefits for single parents, then, is probably unlikely to overcome the main disadvantages of benefits for this group. It is necessary to maintain a cohabitation rule, and it is very uncertain whether a benefit which picks out a stigmatised group can avoid being stigmatised itself.

Probably the most important difference in the rules between countries concerns the position of single parents in relation to the labour market. In the US, the rules for AFDC attempted, at one stage, to offer single mothers incentives to work (through the WIN programme); WIN had negative sanctions for mothers with children over six, and subsequent changes have pushed single mothers into 'workfare' on similarly punitive terms. The history of workfare has not, Brown comments, been particularly successful, which makes its extension hard to fathom; workfare offers low status jobs, few positive incentives, limited subsequent prospect of employment and creates potential problems in child care.[8] The atmosphere is punitive. In Germany and France, single parents are expected to be available for work once their children are over the age of three, and there are relatively high rates of participation in the labour force.[9] By contrast, the UK's residual scheme, which accepts that single parents with dependent children should not have to be available for work, seems almost liberal.

Provision for low earners

The problems of ensuring an adequate income for those in work go well beyond the scope of income maintenance; they have implications for the economic structure, and can probably be more effectively tackled through wage rates and regulation of industry. There is a strong case to argue that most provision for low earners is, or should be, largely unnecessary. A minimum wage should remove any necessity for special support of the incomes of employees through the benefit system. In conjunction with universal family benefits, a minimum wage provides a minimum level of income adjusted for family size. It is the dominant pattern in the European Community, with only two countries (Britain and Ireland) not having one. A minimum wage would not relieve all cases of working poverty, because there may be those who are self-employed (often, in practice, those in agriculture). This means that relief programmes for self-employed people might be represented as a form of social security (as they have been in Greece and Italy).

In the UK, the government reviewed the prospects for a minimum wage in 1969, but rejected it for two (or possibly three) main reasons. The first was that it was feared that increased wages would reduce the demand for labour and thereby increase unemployment (though there are reasons to doubt this in a Keynesian analysis). The second was that most of the beneficiaries would not be those who were poorest, but women earning a second wage for a household (an argument which can be seen to have aggravated the trend towards the feminisation of poverty). The third reason, which was not explicit, was probably that the public sector would be one of the employers principally affected by general minimum wage legislation, and the government was not prepared to pay increased wages.[10]

The main alternative is the introduction of benefits geared specifically to those on low incomes. In France, despite the existence of a minimum wage, there is also a means-tested supplement to family incomes, the *supplément du revenu familial*, for families with more than two children. In principle, the same effect could be achieved by relating minimum wage levels to the level of the universal family allowance (the *allocation familiale*). The existence of the supplement indicates an unwillingness to increase either the minimum wage or the family allowance to the level necessary.

The option selected in the UK was Family Income Supplement (FIS), introduced in 1971. It was based loosely on Friedman's proposals for a negative income tax (a related plan in the US, for a Family Assistance Plan, died at about the same time).[11] FIS was based on a bizarre calculation in which people received 50 per cent of the difference between their income and a set level. There were a number of problems with this approach. The calculation gave the unfortunate impression that the government was deliberately giving working families less than it thought they needed. It was capable of giving money to families on higher incomes which it was refusing to families on lower incomes. It relied on a statement from employers which they might be reluctant to give.[12] And in combination with the tax system – because people on very low incomes in the UK are still liable to tax – it created a major poverty trap, with those whose incomes increased losing, after the expiry of benefit, a substantial amount, often more than the increase in earnings. FIS was replaced in 1988 by Family Credit. Many of the problems were the same. It avoided the problem of giving people less than a set level by replacing the calculation with a different formula by which a maximum benefit is reduced as earnings increased – it comes to much the same thing – but suffered from a new problem: claimants could no longer determine at what point they were likely to become eligible for benefit. Recent research suggests further problems: people who are on low incomes are often on them for temporary periods, and there are doubts as to when to claim and problems when people are transferred between different categories of benefit.[13]

It is difficult to say to what extent this kind of complication is a necessary part of provision for low wages; there are few precedents, and those which there are scarcely unambiguous. (When the Nixon government was considering the introduction of the Family Assistance Plan in the US, they went back to 1795, to the Speenhamland system in England, for some kind of comparison.)[14] In theory, there is an incentive for employers to cut wages, and there is the problem of the poverty trap. In practice, the take-up of the benefits is poor, and there are administrative problems in assessing income and providing for a population whose circumstances often change. The obstacles seem overwhelming.

The main alternative, in theory, is the introduction of a social dividend scheme. By ensuring a basic income unrelated to the world of work, the issue of low earnings would become irrelevant to the subject of poverty. But this has not been practised anywhere, and it remains an option only in theory.

Provision for emergencies

Provision for emergencies looks very different from other kinds of benefit. It is in the nature of emergency relief that it has to be immediately available, and that it should not rely on an extensive set of conditions which have to be verified. Financial relief is not necessarily the most appropriate response in an emergency, both because it suggests that people should be able to make their own arrangements with the money, and because it assumes that the money can buy the kind of help which is necessary (which is not necessarily true after, for example, a town has been flooded). The kinds of cases in which people are most likely to need urgent payments are cases where they have been cut off from other resources – for example, some cases of fire, domestic violence, summary eviction or robbery – although, in practice, the 'urgent needs payments' which used to exist in the UK were often used where people were short of resources simply because of the inadequacy of the basic rate of benefits, and the system of 'crisis loans' which has replaced them is subject to the same criticism.

Emergency relief is probably the contingency which provides the strongest case for a personalised response. In many countries, including France, Germany and Sweden, because discretionary benefits are related to case work, the issue of additional provision for destitution does not arise; the main objection to this kind of provision is not that it does not exist, but that too often it is applied inappropriately to people whose poverty is of a more constant, less personal kind.

BENEFITS AS SOCIAL PROTECTION

Although the categories just discussed include people who are likely to become poor, they equally provide for many who are neither poor nor seem likely to become so. Benefits have many functions besides the relief of poverty. When this is related to principal categories of recipient, the most important seem to be benefits for sickness; survivors; and family benefits. These are not major categories in the consideration of poor relief, and in comparison with the previous sections I shall consider them only briefly.

Benefits for sickness

Benefits for sickness fall principally into the category of protection of earnings; they cover the circumstances where a person undergoes a temporary interruption in the capacity to earn. Such benefits should reduce the risks of poverty, though in practice their effects are limited; where people have a substantial household income, short-term sickness benefit offers some protection but is unlikely to be sufficient to be crucial, and where they do not, the protection is only partial because jobs are not necessarily secure.

Sickness benefit has other important functions, however. Beveridge recognised that sickness and unemployment benefits could not exist in isolation from each other. If a person became unemployed in a system where there was a sickness benefit but no unemployment benefit, that person would have to present as sick in order to receive a basic minimum income. Alternatively, if a person became sick in a system with no benefits to cover for it, that person might have to present as unemployed. If sickness benefits have a role in income maintenance, it is not least that for low paid workers in particular they bridge the periods of sickness and make continuity of employment possible. (By contrast, sick pay at the employer's expense creates an incentive for employers to discharge sick workers.)

Survivors: widows, widowers and orphans

Survivors' benefits have much less to do with poverty, or even earnings replacement, than with social protection; they are generally insurance based, and are sometimes earnings related (particularly in private schemes). Since they are often available to older people, who may have accumulated resources, the distributive implications are very similar to those of pensions.

Family benefits

Benefits for families with children are often represented as a counterbalance to poverty, but this is questionable. Although there may be some poor families, families do not necessarily represent a major category among people who are poor (if only because the parents tend to be of working age). The families with the greatest problems are those in which the woman in the family is unable to work because of child care responsibilities; this usually refers to families with young children. Large families may have difficulties where this means that the woman's earning capacity is interrupted for a long period of time, and one of the most common justifications for family benefits as a means of relieving poverty is that they compensate people with large families for their extra expenses and reduced incomes.

The principal justification for the institution of family benefits is solidarity, rather than the relief of poverty. The argument from solidarity is that children are the concern not only of the family into which they are born but of the whole society in which they are raised and to which they will subsequently be expected to contribute. But this does not necessarily imply that redistribution will be progressive; it is horizontal, going from households without children to those with, and many of those who are poor do not have children. Moreover, more money tends to be given to larger and older families, when the central problem is much more likely to be the position of the woman in the labour market, which is most affected by having very young children. It is questionable, as a result, whether family benefits can be generally seen as having a major impact on poverty.

PROVISION FOR CONTINGENCIES AS POOR RELIEF

Even if all the contingencies considered here are covered within a social security system, there may still be gaps, which have to be filled by some safety-net provision, if they are to be filled at all. It can be difficult to envisage the kinds of circumstances in which people would not be covered, but the experience of most social security systems is that even when the evident contingencies are provided for, there will be people whose circumstances are sufficiently unusual not to be covered adequately. Often, their situation is complex: what happens, for example, to the disabled child of a twice-divorced parent, the self-employed person on a low income who cannot afford to retire, the widow who is intermittently employed because of the demands of caring for an elderly relative, or the migrant worker who becomes a single parent? By the time Supplementary Benefit, the basic safety-net benefit in the UK, was abolished, it had accumulated more than 16 000 paragraphs of rules, trying to cover a huge range of different contingencies. One of the objections to a 'basic income' scheme is that, despite its considerable appeal, it cannot hope to deal with the complexities of real people's lives; it is in the nature of general schemes that there will be exceptions. The most effective schemes administratively tend to be those which generate fewest exceptions, but no system is immune.

There are three main strategies which are available to cover the circumstances of people who are poor. First, it is possible to increase the value of benefits and reduce the qualifications for entitlement, so that even if people have special circumstances which are missed, they are unlikely to be poor as a result. Sweden achieves this in the case of most old people, although not in its benefits system overall. A second option is to continue to multiply the number of different types of benefit, or at least of categories of people entitled, so that virtually every conceivable case is minimally covered which one would wish to have covered; there are many countries with a proliferation of different benefits, but if this strategy has succeeded in eliminating poverty for a group, I do not know where it has happened. Third, it is possible to provide a general safety net in addition to other provision. Unlike the other strategies, this approach requires a commitment specifically to the relief of poverty. The importance of a residual benefit of this type depends on the relative adequacy and coverage of other benefits.

12 Social security systems and the relief of poverty

CRITERIA OF SUCCESS

There is a strong case to argue that 'poverty' should not be the central concern of social security policy; claims for social protection, rights to welfare or the reduction of disadvantage are no less important than the relief of poverty, and to a large extent they can be taken to deal with poverty indirectly. If this is right, it seems unreasonable to judge policies on the basis only of the extent to which they succeed in alleviating the circumstances of the poorest. The problems of the poor remain an important test, because the persistence of poverty implies a negation of the other aims of welfare in respect of those people who remain poor; but the danger of focusing too closely on the poor is that one may lose sight of other objectives in the process.

In reviewing how successful a system is in relieving poverty, there are two main criteria which might be applied. One is coverage – the extent to which the benefits cover the range of contingencies in which people are likely to be poor. Second, there is adequacy – the level of benefits which are provided.

Coverage

It could be argued that in cases where coverage is restricted – for example where, as in the US, public assistance is not available to a wide range of people – the effective minimum is nothing, which implies that the system is necessarily inadequate. The comprehensiveness of a system depends crucially not on how many people are covered by the main form of benefit, but by how many people are picked up by the alternative provisions. The weakness of provision in the US, for example, reflects as much the absence of an adequate system of social assistance as it does the patchy and inconsistent coverage offered by the insurance benefits. In Germany, basic insurance cover extends only to a limited proportion of the population –

about 85 per cent of those in the West.[1] Many of those not included, however, are those whose incomes are above certain limits, who are expected to make alternative arrangements. It can be argued that this does indeed undermine the comprehensiveness of the system, because by excluding the better-off it undermines any concept of welfare as a right of citizenship or expression of solidarity; but if the test is to be the relief of poverty, then this kind of selection does not intrinsically threaten the scope of the social security system.

There is a difference between comprehensiveness on paper and in practice. Even where entitlement to benefit is established, many of those who are entitled do not, for one reason or another, receive the benefits they should. Atkinson argues that the preoccupation of the literature with take-up is in many ways a misidentification of the problem, because one cannot assume that all of those entitled are those whose poverty the benefit was intended to relieve, or conversely that all of those for whom the benefit is intended are actually entitled.[2]

The Luxembourg Income Study enables one to identify the extent to which those on the lowest incomes are receiving transfer payments to a sufficient extent to bring them above 50 per cent of median income, in most of the countries I have considered. This is not, I have suggested, equivalent to 'poverty', but one can at least establish how many of the people on the lowest incomes are being reached by social security benefits. Table 12.1 shows the results. It shows, fairly clearly, that the US is notably unsuccessful in bringing people above the level used as a measure; this does not necessarily demonstrate that the US is unsuccessful in addressing the problems of poverty (though there is plenty of other evidence to suggest that this is indeed the case), but it does show very clearly that the comprehensiveness and redistributive effects of the social security system are seriously deficient. From the figures, it emerges that provision for pensioners – an area in which the US has federal provision through Social Security – is comparable in its effects to many of the other countries; it is for the non-pensioners that problems are most evident. The French system is also particularly favourable to pensioners, and, by comparison with other countries, to couples with children. The German system, interestingly, seems to compare reasonably well with the UK, despite the less than universal remit of social insurance and what seems to be a less favourable ideological climate; this is not least because families with children are less likely to be poor in the first place. Overall, it is Sweden which seems to have the most comprehensive coverage.

Table 12.1 The effect of income transfers in reducing the numbers of people in poverty

	Percentage of households of different types receiving less than 50 per cent of median income						
Country	*Aged single*	*Aged couple*	*Single, no child*	*Couple, no child*	*Lone parent*	*Couple with children*	*Other*
France							
Pre-transfer	88	78	23	18	39	22	34
Post-transfer	1	3	11	8	19	9	13
% reduction	98	96	53	58	51	57	63
Germany							
Pre-transfer	86	71	25	12	23	5	25
Post-transfer	10	9	8	3	9	5	13
% reduction	88	88	67	70	59	–4	49
Sweden							
Pre-transfer	92	81	28	9	33	6	–
Post-transfer	0	0	9	1	5	2	–
% reduction	100	100	70	89	84	75	–
UK							
Pre-transfer	86	70	28	6	54	9	30
Post-transfer	16	18	9	2	19	5	3
% reduction	82	75	66	61	65	44	89
US							
Pre-transfer	73	57	22	8	53	12	35
Post-transfer	32	16	17	5	45	12	18
% reduction	56	71	20	33	14	–2	47
Israel							
Pre-transfer	57		–	–	53	26	–
Post-transfer	24		–	–	19	15	–
% reduction	58		–	–	78	43	–

Source: Adapted from D Mitchell, 1991, *Income Transfers in Ten Welfare States*, Aldershot: Avebury, p 68. The figures for Israel come from T Smeeding, M O'Higgins and L Rainwater (eds), 1990, *Poverty, Inequality and Income Distribution in Comparative Perspective*, New York: Harvester Wheatsheaf, p 67.

Adequacy

Traditionally, adequacy has been assessed in terms of a 'poverty line' – that is, a regular income. From the Luxembourg Income Study, it is possible to identify not only how many people fall below a certain income, but by what extent. They refer to this as the 'poverty gap'. Table 12.2, drawn from Deborah Mitchell's figures, shows the reduction in the poverty gap,

Table 12.2 The effect of income transfers on the 'poverty gap'

	For households of different types						
Country	*Aged single*	*Aged couple*	*Single, no child*	*Couple, no child*	*Lone parent*	*Couple with children*	*Other*
France							
% remaining below 60% level	11	23	63	60	67	69	57
Gap between income and 60% level	10	19	47	36	38	25	35
Germany							
% remaining below 60% level	27	24	41	54	40	48	47
Gap between income and 60% level	25	21	35	38	24	16	34
Sweden							
% remaining below 60% level	6	13	66	55	54	69	–
Gap between income and 60% level	5	10	43	31	30	24	–
UK							
% remaining below 60% level	17	21	32	36	28	59	20
Gap between income and 60% level	14	15	25	22	21	20	14
US							
% remaining below 60% level	39	46	74	70	61	74	65
Gap between income and 60% level	31	30	48	37	43	29	42

Source: Adapted from D Mitchell, 1991, *Income Transfers in Ten Welfare States*, Aldershot: Avebury, p 70.

considering both how many people remain below the level of 'poverty' – in this case, 60 per cent of median income – and how far they fall below this level. The differences which emerge from a consideration of coverage alone are important. Although the Swedish system has the greatest effect in reducing the numbers of people who are on very low incomes, those who are left still have a low relative income. Much the same is true for the French and German systems, particularly for non-pensioners; Mitchell comments of France that, despite relatively high spending on benefits, the high level of initial problems which the system has to address and the relatively inefficient pattern of redistribution leads to worse outcomes than one might reasonably expect.[3] By contrast, the UK system seems to do rather better in reducing the gaps. The same seems to be true of the Israeli system: Smeeding *et al.* note that both Israel and the UK 'are characterised by universal transfer systems that offer high coverage but fairly low benefit rates'.[4]

There are reasons to be cautious about this kind of approach. Although low income is a good indicator of poverty, it is not equivalent; it may mislead both in terms of command over resources and over the extent to which a person's needs are actually met. It seems clear that many of the kinds of problem associated with poverty – problems like homelessness, poor environments, a lack of security, or lack of positional goods – are not necessarily taken into account by this analysis. At best, the figures provide indicators of poverty in different countries.

THE DETERMINANTS OF EFFECTIVE POOR RELIEF

In Chapter 9, I outlined the systems of a number of countries in very broad theoretical terms. On the face of the matter, one might expect countries with more comprehensive coverage to perform better than countries with pluralistic aspirations; this is largely borne out. Then, one might expect egalitarian policies to be more generous to those with least than institutional ones, and institutional policies to offer more than residual. The case of Germany is the clearest exception, for it seems to do better in helping people on low incomes, despite its residual ethic, than the UK. This can be explained in several ways. One option is to seek to challenge the figures or the construction put on them, which it is not difficult to do; the UK does close 'poverty gaps' further. A second is to challenge the way in which the countries have been represented – which would be wholly reasonable, for in none of the countries do policies fit the simple characterisation I made of them. A third option is to search for other factors which may influence the results, of which there are only too many. Wilensky finds that the main determinants of expenditure on social security are the age of the system, the percentage of the population over the age of 65 and national income per capita.[5]

This casts some doubt on whether the ideology of a government makes much difference to the level of social security payments. Wilensky thinks it does not. Against this, Barnes and Srivenkataramana point out, by reworking Wilensky's figures, that the amount a country spends on social security is inversely proportional to its distance from Vienna. This, they suggest, shows evidence of cultural diffusion – countries draw ideas and practices from their neighbours – which, in turn, suggests that ideology does play a part.[6]

The kind of 'ideology' which is being considered, though, is far more complex than a simple distinction between 'left' and 'right' might identify. Much of what I have written should call into question the existence of a simple association between 'residual' and 'institutional' models with patterns of provision of differing adequacy. The level of resources which is committed relies, in so far as it depends on ideological influences, on a much more complex set of influences than a division between 'residual' and 'institutional' models; ideas like social protection, solidarity or a commitment to family support may cut across the divide. The economic context, and political interpretations of it, limit what is considered feasible or even desirable. Organisational arrangements, themselves owing much to historical developments within countries, play a major part; the influence of federalism in the US, or the involvement of the labour movement in Sweden or Israel, are examples. And the problems of poverty are understood differently in different countries: 'poverty' is a socially constructed concept, which has been taken to refer not only to a lack of resources but also to issues like inequality, social exclusion, problems within families and social exclusion. Responses to poverty are conceived within different contexts, for different purposes; unsurprisingly, policies differ.

By the same token, there is no reason to suppose that left-wing and right-wing policies, because they are linked with these differing views, should be more or less likely to provide poor relief at a level sufficient to mitigate the problems of poverty. Many of the associations are based not in irrefutable truths about the way in which social security operates but in a historical and political framework. The principles which distinguish 'right' and 'left' – issues like the interpretation of freedom, the role of the state, and the workings of the economy – are all of considerable importance to social security, but they are not the only principles which apply. Other conflicting principles, like values of solidarity, work, family or country, are liable to intrude, and they do not necessarily fall within the 'left–right' divide. In the development of pension policies in the UK, the uncertainty of the parties as to what weight to put on progressive redistribution, social protection, financial constraints and poor relief have led to a jockeying of different, sometimes contradictory, policies which cannot be simply explained in terms of 'left' or 'right' wing.[7] In France, the emphasis on the family has cut across the divide. In Italy, the Communist Party has opposed expanding unemployment benefits on the basis that an increase in productive employment is a greater priority. And in Belgium, a proposal by the Christian Democrats for a basic minimum benefit was opposed by socialists on the basis that the money would only benefit 'drunkards, whores and nuns'.[8]

COMPARING SOCIAL SECURITY SYSTEMS

The similarities between countries are in some ways more striking than their differences. Most developed countries have a similar set of problems to deal with – notably retirement and the dependency of older people, support for people who are long-term sick or disabled, unemployment and, in general, the inadequate incomes of people excluded from the labour market or marginal to it. They draw on a common range of responses, partly as a result of imitation, and partly as a result of common pressures. Although there are exceptions to every generalisation, most developed countries have the basic framework of an insurance system (the main exception is Australia), a supplementary framework of means-tested benefits to fill in the gaps (though the US still has notable deficiencies in its coverage), and a potential range of other non-contributory benefits for special needs groups. The similarities between policies have supported a view of modern industrial states as 'converging'.[9]

It should be possible, on this basis, to offer some insights into social security systems and their effectiveness in dealing with poverty. Insurance benefits work well in a wide range of conditions, but they leave gaps which have to be filled by other benefits; for example, research in Britain, France and Germany found, in each case, that insurance payments failed to protect people suffering from long periods of unemployment.[10] Universal benefits, an important part of provision for families in France, have major advantages, but the relief of poverty is not foremost among them. On the other hand, there is evidence that some common beliefs are misleading. Despite the claims made for universal benefits, there is no basis on which to believe that they become more generous because they represent an institutional ideal. The British experience seems to suggest that means-tested benefits suffer from intrinsic disadvantages; the cross-national comparison with France and Germany calls this into question, as well as casting doubt on the supposed advantages of insurance-based benefits. (The Australian system, though it does not show that all of the problems can be avoided, also seems to challenge some of the propositions which are made.)[11]

There are grounds for caution about such conclusions. Generalisations about the level and coverage of benefits can be seriously misleading. It is hardly possible to consider the relative strengths and weaknesses of a maternity benefit without considering the impact of maternity benefits in context. Maternity benefits are only part of a package of support available to mothers, which might include maternity pay, medical care and benefits for the child. The role of maternity benefits depends on their role as income replacement, and their duration, their relationship to other benefits (like unemployment and sickness benefits) and their adequacy in relation to wages have to be considered. The issue of wage replacement points to further issues which need to be considered – the wages which are being replaced, the role of women in the labour market, and the options which women have after childbirth.

The problems of comparison become significant whenever it is intended to adopt a measure from one country and apply it to another. The ideological gloss put on different kinds of policy cannot be expected to travel without alteration, because the interpretation of such policies depends on the context in which the benefits are set. Family benefits in the UK are strongly advocated by the 'left', most notably by the Child Poverty Action Group. In much of Europe, family benefits are the concern of the Christian parties of the right. Conversely, loans are identified as a 'right-wing' policy in Britain, because they have been used by a right-wing government to limit the availability of benefits to claimants with pressing needs, and because benefits are inadequate to permit payment without hardship. Loans in the Netherlands, by contrast, have sprung out of mutual aid societies – the nearest in Britain is the principle of the 'credit union' – which has more of a left-wing flavour, even if their practice tends to be conservative.[12]

If one was to begin the formation of policy with a blank sheet, it might be possible to describe the policy in idealised terms – the kinds of ringing phrase, like 'welfare state', 'solidarity' or the 'social market system', with which I introduced social security systems. But in real life, one is rarely, if ever, privileged to begin anew. The kinds of policy which are introduced are usually specific, introduced into a system in which other benefits exist, and – most important – into a well-established social and economic context. An understanding of the way in which different kinds of benefit work depends on a set of parameters which are liable to change. Benefits do not operate in isolation, but within a system of other benefits, in the context of different kinds of welfare provision, and within different economic and social settings. The most effective comparisons, then, depend on consideration of the overall pattern of provision in different countries. This is intrinsically difficult to do. Different administrative systems, different patterns of consumer response, the nuances of difference in eligibility and the purposes of benefit make comparison difficult. More seriously, the social and economic conditions in which the systems operate are so different that generalisations about different patterns of benefit cannot be extended easily from one country to another. A range of factors need to be treated as parameters for the purposes of making comparison possible. The efficiency of the administration, access to communications, or the existence of alternative services or sources of income might all affect the way in which a social security system operates within any particular country.

SOCIAL SECURITY IN PRACTICE

Whatever the appearance of a social security scheme on paper, the process of implementing the scheme is liable to lead to complications, and potentially even to change its character. The scheme must be administered, and administration takes time, manpower and resources. It must be received, which generally means that it must be claimed (though there is no obvious reason why the onus of initiating a claim must fall on the claimant), and there are a number of obstacles to overcome in order for claims to be made.

From the point of view of the claimant, the kinds of factor which affect their behaviour were referred to in the context of means-testing, though they extend no less to other types of benefit. Claimants have to identify whether or not a claim can and should be made; whether it is worth claiming; and then they must undergo the process. The first step implies that claimants have to know about the benefit, and have some idea that they might be entitled. In some cases, this will be related to the structure of the benefits; the more complex a system is, the less likely that the claimant will know about particular benefits, and the more important appropriate signposting becomes. Equally, the more complex an individual benefit is, the less chance claimants have of working out whether or not they are entitled. How people feel about benefits is no less important at this stage; if people do not think they are the sort to whom a benefit applies, they will not learn about it. The next step – whether a benefit is worth claiming – implies a calculation of costs against benefits. The value of a benefit relates primarily to the amount of money it yields and its duration. The costs include the direct costs of going through the claiming process (like travel and time), overcoming fear of landlords or employers where declarations have to be made, and the social costs of stigmatisation. Third, to complete a claim the claimant has to pass a number of obstacles, including access to offices, filling in forms, undergoing assessments (like income tests or medical examinations) and, if necessary (and possible), appealing.

The importance of the administrative process stems from the central requirement that benefits, in order to relieve poverty, have actually to be delivered. There is not in most systems only one type of benefit to deliver to one type of claimant, through one type of process. Rather, there are several different kinds of benefit for which the conditions differ. It is not difficult to say, for example, that non-contributory benefits should be easy to administer, because there are few preconditions to check; or that maintaining a record of contribution conditions should lead to benefits being delivered more rapidly than would be the case for means-testing, because the process of recording contributions is cumulative over time, whereas the process of means-testing demands a fresh assessment of the status quo. But this is not necessarily the case, because there are also conditions attached to non-means-tested benefits which have no less to be assessed.

The kinds of factors which distinguish the effectiveness with which a benefit can be administered are both internal and external. Internal factors include, first, the complexity of the benefit – like the number of steps required, the clarity of the rules, the length of the procedure required to process the benefit, and the scope for error. Second, they include the terms on which people qualify, and the extent to which the benefit deals with an identifiable and stable client group. Some conditions are relatively easy to identify, like childhood and old age – they are also, incidentally, the most stable; some require a test or assessment, like disability; and some may be ambiguous, like certain patterns of unemployment. It is also important to know to what extent there is an infrastructure of complementary agencies (like doctors) able to make assessments, which can substantially affect the operation of benefits for sickness, disability and housing. Third, there is the extent to which the benefit works to defined rules. As a broad proposition, rule-based systems should be easier to administer than those which rely on the exercise of judgement; they also have the advantage of relative consistency. But simpler systems are also easier to administer than more complex ones; the situation in the UK was that the rule-based system for single payments became so complex that administrators effectively began treating the scheme as discretionary in any case, because of their ignorance of the rules.[13]

External factors are more wide ranging. They include, for example, the number of claims and the number of cases which require special treatment (although this could also be seen as a reflection on the benefit's rules). Decisions on discretionary benefits should in principle be capable of being delivered within hours, but the larger the number of claims, the less feasible this becomes. This implies that the operation of a system may depend not just on the kinds of method which the system operates, but also the pressures on it – factors which are conditioned by the size and make-up of the population covered, and the economic background. Ultimately, the operation of a benefit – and so its practicality – depends on the social and economic context.

Information about the practical aspects of social security in different countries varies considerably in quality and quantity. Some countries, notably Britain and the US, have been looked at critically in some detail; some, like France, have hardly been touched on;[14] and for others, like Israel, although there may be such evidence, the problems of language make critical commentary difficult to find. Even once the issues are identified, it is difficult to put them into perspective. There may be some administrative problems, but do they vitiate the scheme's effects overall? On paper, for example, social security in Sweden seems easily the most effective of the various systems. But Gould suggests that there are a number of problems in receiving benefits; the political concern with dependency and self-improvement is associated with a number of barriers to claiming. Claimants do not receive assistance as of right: the model on which benefits are given is 'therapeutic', which justifies an insistence on the presence of claimants and spouses. They are subject to personal assessment and interrogation about their circumstances.[15] What is not clear from this account is how important the administrative problems are in relation to what the system achieves.

One important attempt made to overcome the difficulties is in the study by Mitton *et al.* of Britain, France and Germany.[16] This covered three samples, each including about 3000 people, and it provided insights which would have been difficult to establish from an examination of social security systems alone – for example, that large families in France were likely to be poorly off despite apparently generous benefits because of their weak relationship to the labour market.[17] The qualitative elements of the study serve to place information about the different schemes in a social and administrative context, which a purely statistical exercise cannot hope to do.

EFFECTIVE POOR RELIEF

The tests of coverage and adequacy can be applied in many ways: one of the simplest, for a policy-maker, is to consider who is left out within present provision, and to consider, among those who are included, who receives the least support from the available range of services. But this approach can, if applied repeatedly, produce undesirable results in itself, because a complex system devoted to covering contingencies as they arise is all too likely to leave further gaps. Inevitably, there has to be some residual provision for those who are not catered for in other ways, and this provision is likely itself to be complex, difficult to administer and stigmatised.

The problem stems from the attempt to consider benefits in isolation. Benefits have to be seen as part of a system. In the first place, benefits are necessarily interrelated: one cannot distinguish the impact of housing benefits or food stamps wholly from that of general income support. There may be alternatives: if there are no sickness benefits, people may have to claim unemployment benefits instead, or vice versa. Secondly, the benefits interact with other measures – like the provision of health care, employment or housing. Family benefits in conjunction with minimum wages have effects in maintaining household income which neither measure has in itself. In practice, it is usually the portfolio which matters, not the structure of individual benefits. The focus on certain benefits as 'residual' or 'institutional' in themselves fails to identify what role they play in relation to other benefits. Child Benefit may be an 'institutional' benefit, but it is not equivalent to institutional provision for children, because it is limited in its scope and its effects. Unemployment insurance cannot be considered without other provisions for unemployed people.

To the extent that benefits extend coverage and increase the adequacy of resources, they can be considered to be effective in relieving poverty. But if one is examining the relative performance of different benefits – like unemployment insurance and income support – in achieving the same ends, one cannot achieve greater effectiveness by opting for one benefit in preference to the other. (It is more efficient to select a benefit which targets a client group more selectively, but that is not the same thing. Efficiency implies a minimum of waste; effectiveness, the maximum achievement of goals.) Rather, one has to consider how the benefits work together.

It follows that if policy-makers wish to introduce an institutional system of poor relief, rather than a residual one, they must consider means by which the whole range of benefits might act on an institutional basis. This implies a comprehensive range of benefits backed up by the necessary safety-net provision. I think that is what Titmuss was driving at when he wrote:

> . . . the real challenge resides in the question: what particular infrastructure of universalist services is needed in order to provide a framework of values and opportunity bases within and around which can be developed acceptable selective services provided, as social rights, on criteria of the needs of specific categories, groups and territorial areas . . .?[18]

Effective poor relief – or the development of any effective welfare system – requires the development of a structured scheme in which the coverage is fully comprehensive, and the effect of different provisions, either in combination or as alternatives, is to increase the command over resources of those who are poorest to the greatest extent possible.

There are many ways in which this might be achieved. In practice, it seems most effectively to have been achieved in Sweden, in a very different way, and then only for one group (pensioners); it relies on social insurance, solidaristic financial arrangements, an orientation to the workplace, and a substantial element of progressive redistribution, backed by residual provision. It is difficult to see how this could be duplicated successfully in another country without having very similar economic and social arrangements in place. In principle, it might also be achieved by an extensive basic income or social dividend scheme, although the criticisms I have made of such schemes suggest that at least two other elements would be required – a progressive system of financing, and some kind of supplementary safety-net provision to provide for the inevitable complexities of people's lives.

Reforming systems takes time, and partial moves towards a different kind of system will not necessarily yield partial improvements in poor relief. It is unlikely that an expansion of the range of benefits would reduce either coverage or adequacy directly. But an expansion of the range which takes insufficient account of the context in which benefits are introduced can increase the complexity of a system overall, which can affect take-up; and it can create overlaps between benefits, which cause confusion and limit the marginal value of residual benefits. A non-contributory benefit which is inadequate – like One Parent Benefit – could still reduce entitlement to means-tested supplements, and the value of those benefits. At the same time, it changes the direction of resources, and the pattern of future claims of resources – increases in benefits for all old people necessarily cost far more than increases only for old people on low incomes. Worse, the limitation it implies on residual benefits can limit their coverage, their scope and their capacity to meet need. 'Second-best' solutions are not always preferable to an original position.

In the short term, then, probably the best way to relieve poverty is to concentrate not on the reform of systems but rather on the benefits which currently relieve poverty most effectively. In most cases, these benefits are residual, means-tested benefits, like Income Support or *Sozialhilfe*. Some people fear that, if this approach was extended indefinitely, it would lead to a residual system by default; but there is no reason to suppose that it will be extended indefinitely, and it is abundantly clear that the alternative strategy of trying to develop universal benefits incrementally does not deliver resources to poor people rapidly enough. In the long term, the expansion of coverage and increasing commitment of resources should make it possible to consider structural reform; but there is a long road to travel, and people who are poor now need help now.

The development of poor relief is not an 'answer' to the problem. Poverty is not one problem, and there is not one solution to it. But relief is a more limited, and more modest, aim. It is far from being impracticable; most developed countries have been doing it for some people, if not for most, for much of the last century. Poor people remain who are not reached by the existing systems, or who are helped only inadequately. By reviewing the aims and methods through which poor relief is undertaken, it should be possible to extend provision for them.

Notes

1 INTRODUCTION

1 OECD, 1976, *Public Expenditure on Income Maintenance Programmes*, Paris: OECD, p 63.
2 See P Spicker, 1990, 'Charles Booth: the examination of poverty', *Social Policy and Administration* **24**(1) pp 21–38; J Veit-Wilson, 1986, 'Paradigms of poverty: a rehabilitation of B S Rowntree', *Journal of Social Policy* **15**(1) pp 69–99.
3 J L Roach and J K Roach (eds), 1972, *Poverty: Selected Readings*, Harmondsworth: Penguin, p 23.
4 T M Smeeding, M O'Higgins and L Rainwater (eds), 1990, *Poverty, Inequality and Income Distribution in Comparative Perspective*, New York: Harvester Wheatsheaf.
5 P Townsend, 1979, *Poverty in the United Kingdom*, Harmondsworth: Penguin, p 915.
6 See P Spicker, 1988, *Principles of Social Welfare*, London: Routledge.
7 M Blaxter, 1974, 'Health "on the welfare"', *Journal of Social Policy* **3**(1) pp 39–51.
8 R M Titmuss, 1968, *Commitment to Welfare*, London: Allen and Unwin, p 26.
9 D Piachaud, 1979, *The Cost of a Child*, and 1980, *Children and Poverty*, both London: Child Poverty Action Group.
10 P Townsend, 1985, 'A sociological approach to the measurement of poverty – a rejoinder to Professor Amartya Sen', *Oxford Economic Papers* **37** pp 659–68.
11 B Deer and M Jones, 1989, 'Threadbare and feckless', *Sunday Times* 14 May p A13.
12 A Sen, 1985, 'A sociological approach to the measurement of poverty: a reply to Professor Peter Townsend', *Oxford Economic Papers* **37** p 673.
13 P Townsend, 1985, 'A sociological approach to the measurement of poverty – a rejoinder to Professor Amartya Sen', *Oxford Economic Papers* **37** p 664.
14 A Sen, 1985, 'A sociological approach to the measurement of poverty: a reply to Professor Peter Townsend', *Economic Papers* **37** p 673.
15 P Townsend, 1985, 'A sociological approach to the measurement of poverty – a rejoinder to Professor Amartya Sen', *Oxford Economic Papers* **37** p 664.

2 THE NATURE OF POVERTY

1 See, for example, K Joseph and J Sumption, 1979, *Equality*, London: John Murray.
2 D Piachaud, 1981, 'Peter Townsend and the Holy Grail', *New Society* 10 September p 421.
3 M S Baratz and W G Grigsby, 1971, 'Thoughts on poverty and its elimination', *Journal of Social Policy* **1**(2) pp 119–34.
4 P Spicker, 1990, *Poverty and Deprivation in Tayside*, Dundee: Tayside Regional Council Social Strategy Unit.
5 Cited M Brown and S Payne, 1989, *Introduction to Social Administration*, 7th edn, London: Unwin Hyman, p 53.
6 P Townsend, 1979, *Poverty in the United Kingdom*, Harmondsworth: Penguin.
7 See, for example, European Community, 1989, *Poverty*, ESC–89–013–EN Brussels: Economic and Social Consultative Assembly of the European Communities.
8 J Bradshaw, 1972, 'A taxonomy of social need', in G MacLachlan (ed.) *Problems and Progress in Medical Care* (7th series), Oxford: Oxford University Press.
9 The list comes from D Harvey, 1973, *Social Justice and the City*, London: Arnold, p 102; K Jones, J Brown and J Bradshaw, 1978, *Issues in Social Policy*, London: Routledge and Kegan Paul, p 28; and P Spicker, 1988, *Principles of Social Welfare*, London: Routledge, p 28.
10 M S Baratz and W G Grigsby, 1971, 'Thoughts on poverty and its elimination', *Journal of Social Policy* **1**(2) p 120.
11 See, for example, S Damer and R Madigan, 1974, 'The housing investigator', *New Society* 25 July; J Henderson and V Karn, 1986, *Race, Class and State Housing*, Aldershot: Gower.
12 Department of Health and Social Security, 1980, *Inequalities in Health*, London: HMSO .
13 V George, 1988, *Wealth, Poverty and Starvation*, Hemel Hempstead: Wheatsheaf Books, p 208.
14 K Marx, 1844, 'Economic and philosophical manuscripts', in D McLellan (ed.) *Karl Marx: Selected Writings*, Oxford: Oxford University Press, 1977. See also A Heller, 1976, *The Theory of Need in Marx*, Allison and Busby (her account is somewhat clearer than Marx's).
15 A McAuley, 1979, *Economic Welfare in the Soviet Union*, Hemel Hempstead: George Allen and Unwin.
16 A Sen, 1983, 'Poor, relatively speaking', *Oxford Economic Papers* **35** p 160.
17 P Townsend, 1979, *Poverty in the United Kingdom*, Harmondsworth: Penguin, pp 50–1.

3 OPERATIONALISATION OF THE CONCEPT

1 T M Smeeding, M O'Higgins and L Rainwater (eds), 1990, *Poverty, Inequality and Income Distribution in Comparative Perspective*, New York: Harvester Wheatsheaf.
2 *Ibid.* p 93.
3 J Bradshaw, D Mitchell and J Morgan, 1987, 'Evaluating adequacy: the potential of budget standards', *Journal of Social Policy* **16**(2) pp 165–81.
4 See, for example, Department of the Environment Inner Cities Directorate, 1983, *Urban Deprivation*, London: Department of the Environment; B Jarman, 1983,

'Identification of underprivileged areas', *British Medical Journal* **286** pp 1705–9; and P Townsend, 1987, 'Deprivation', *Journal of Social Policy* **16**(2) pp 125–46.

5 Fondation Nationale pour la Recherche Sociale, 1980, *Poverty and the Anti-poverty Policies*, Brussels: European Commission, pp 12–13.

6 *Ibid.* p 322.

7 See P Spicker, 1990, 'Charles Booth: the examination of poverty', *Social Policy and Administration* **24**(1) pp 21–38.

8 C Booth, 1902, *Life and Labour of the People in London, First Series: Poverty*, London: Macmillan, Vol 1, p 33.

9 K Williams, 1981, *From Pauperism to Poverty*, London: Routledge and Kegan Paul, p 325.

10 See, for example, T H Marshall, 1981, *The Right to Welfare*, London: Heinemann, p 37.

11 C Booth, 1902, *Life and Labour of the People in London, Second Series: Industry*, London: Macmillan, Vol 5, p 266.

12 T Simey and M B Simey, 1960, *Charles Booth: Social Scientist*, Oxford: Oxford University Press, p 279.

13 J Bradshaw and H Holmes, 1989, *Living on the Edge: A Study of the Living Standards of Families on Benefit in Tyne and Wear*, Tyneside: Child Poverty Action Group.

14 Cited G Bowpitt, 1985, *Secularisation and the Origins of Professional Social Work in Britain*, Ph.D.: University College of Swansea.

15 Cited *ibid.* p 379.

16 B S Rowntree, 1922, *Poverty: A Study of Town Life*, London: Longmans (new edn), Chapter 9.

17 *Ibid.* pp 133–4.

18 M Brown and S Payne, 1989, *Introduction to Social Administration*, 7th edn, London: Unwin Hyman, pp 15–16.

19 Cited J Veit-Wilson, 1986, 'Paradigms of poverty', *Journal of Social Policy* **15**(1) pp 69–99.

20 A Sen, 1981, *Poverty and Famines*, Oxford: Clarendon Press, p 22.

21 R Lawson, 1980, 'Poverty and inequality in West Germany', in V George and R Lawson (eds) *Poverty and Inequality in Common Market Countries*, London: Routledge and Kegan Paul; A McAuley, 1979, *Economic Welfare in the Soviet Union*, Hemel Hempstead: Allen and Unwin.

22 Council of Economic Advisers, 1966, 'What is poverty? Who are the poor?', in H Miller (ed.) *Poverty American Style*, Belmont, CA: Wadsworth, p 22.

23 Cited P Townsend, 1983, 'A theory of poverty and the role of social policy', in M Loney, D Boswell and J Clarke (eds) *Social Policy and Social Welfare*, Milton Keynes: Open University Press, p 66.

24 E Hunt, 1991, 'Families on benefit "too poor to buy food"', *Independent* 4 June p 4.

25 US Department of Health and Human Resources, cited V George, 1988, *Wealth, Poverty and Starvation*, Hemel Hempstead: Wheatsheaf Books, pp 89, 91.

26 B Abel-Smith and P Townsend, 1965, *The Poor and the Poorest*, London: Bell, p 17.

27 See, for example, H Miller (ed.), 1966, *Poverty American Style*, Belmont, CA: Wadsworth; E James, 1970, *America against Poverty*, London: Routledge and Kegan Paul; J Higgins, 1978, *The Poverty Business in Europe and America*, Oxford: Blackwell/Robertson.

28 R Layard, D Piachaud and M Stewart, 1978, *The Causes of Poverty* (Royal Commission on the Distribution of Income and Wealth background paper no 6), London: HMSO.
29 B Abel-Smith and P Townsend, 1965, *The Poor and the Poorest*, London: Bell, pp 69, 71.
30 D Piachaud, 1979, *The Cost of a Child*, London: Child Poverty Action Group.
31 J Mack and S Lansley, 1985, *Poor Britain*, London: Allen and Unwin.
32 Policy Studies Institute, 1984, *The Reform of Supplementary Benefit: Working Papers*, London: Policy Studies Institute.
33 P Townsend, 1979, *Poverty in the United Kingdom*, Harmondsworth: Penguin.
34 P Townsend and D Gordon, 1989, 'What is enough? New evidence on poverty allowing the definition of a minimum benefit', paper presented to the ISA Seminar on the Sociology of Social Security, Edinburgh 4–6 July.
35 See, for example, J Bradshaw, D Mitchell and J Morgan, 1987, 'Evaluating adequacy: the potential of budget standards', *Journal of Social Policy* **16**(2) pp 165–81; J Bradshaw and H Holmes, 1989, *Living on the Edge: A Study of the Living Standards of Families on Benefit in Tyne and Wear*, Tyneside: Child Poverty Action Group; or J Bradshaw, 1990, *Child Poverty and Deprivation in the UK*, London: National Children's Bureau; all use different kinds of definition and approach.
36 Cited J Bradshaw, D Mitchell and J Morgan, 1987, 'Evaluating adequacy: the potential of budget standards', *Journal of Social Policy* **16**(2) pp 170–1.

4 CONCEPTS OF POVERTY

1 C Booth, 1971, *Charles Booth's London*, A Fried and R Elman (eds), Harmondsworth: Penguin, p 55.
2 J Veit-Wilson, 1986, 'Paradigms of poverty: a rehabilitation of B S Rowntree', *Journal of Social Policy* **15**(1) pp 69–99.
3 S Ringen, 1988, 'Direct and indirect measures of poverty', *Journal of Social Policy* **17**(3), p 353.
4 P Townsend, 1979, *Poverty in the United Kingdom*, Harmondsworth: Penguin, p 57.
5 J L Roach and J K Roach (eds), 1972, *Poverty: Selected Readings*, Harmondsworth: Penguin, p 23; National Children's Bureau, 1987, *Investing in the Future*, London: National Children's Bureau.
6 B van Praag, A Hagenaars and H van Weeren, 1980, *Poverty in Europe*, Leyden: University of Leyden.
7 See, for example, R Hauser, H Cremer-Shaefer and U Nouvertné, 1980, *National Report on Poverty in the Federal Republic of Germany*, Frankfurt: University of Frankfurt; R Hauser and P Semerau, 1990, 'Trends in poverty and low income in the Federal Republic of Germany 1962/3–1987', in R Teekens and B van Praag (eds) *Analysing Poverty in the European Community* (Eurostat News Special Edition 1–1990), Luxembourg: European Communities.
8 R Walker and R Lawson, 1984, 'How Europe helps its poor', *New Society* 8 March pp 375–6.
9 Department of Social Security, 1990, *Households below Average Income: A Statistical Analysis 1981–1987*, London: Government Statistical Service.
10 T M Smeeding, M O'Higgins and L Rainwater (eds), 1990, *Poverty, Inequality*

and Income Distribution in Comparative Perspective, New York: Harvester Wheatsheaf. See also C Oppenheim, 1990 *Poverty: The Facts*, London: Child Poverty Action Group for a similar usage.

11 C B Leite, 1990, 'Brazil', in J Dixon and R Schewell, *Social Welfare in Latin America*, Beckenham: Croom Helm, p 42.

12 See R Teekens and B van Praag (eds), 1990, *Analysing Poverty in the European Community* (Eurostat News Special Edition 1-1990), Luxembourg: European Communities.

13 K Joseph and J Sumption, 1979, *Equality*, London: John Murray, p 27.

14 See, for example, J L Roach and J K Roach, 1972, *Poverty: Selected Readings*, Harmondsworth: Penguin; Department of Social Security, 1990, *Households below Average Income: A Statistical Analysis 1981–1987*, London: Government Statistical Service; T M Smeeding, M O'Higgins and L Rainwater (eds), 1990, *Poverty, Inequality and Income Distribution in Comparative Perspective*, New York: Harvester Wheatsheaf.

15 M O'Higgins and S Jenkins, 1990, 'Poverty in the EC: 1975, 1980, 1985', in R Teekens and B van Praag (eds) *Analysing Poverty in the European Community* (Eurostat News Special Edition 1-1990), Luxembourg: European Communities, p 207.

16 D Piachaud, 1980, *Children and Poverty*, London: Child Poverty Action Group.

17 W G Runciman, 1966, *Relative Deprivation and Social Justice*, London: Routledge and Kegan Paul.

18 The term is drawn from P Berger and T Luckmann, 1967, *The Social Construction of Reality*, New York: Anchor.

19 T Simey and M B Simey, 1960, *Charles Booth: Social Scientist*, Oxford: Oxford University Press, p 88.

20 See J Veit-Wilson, 1986, 'Paradigms of poverty: a rehabilitation of B S Rowntree', *Journal of Social Policy* **15**(1) pp 69–99.

21 A L Bowley, 1923, *The Nature and Purpose of the Measurement of Social Phenomena*, 2nd edn, London: P S King.

22 J Veit-Wilson, 1989, 'Memorandum . . .', in House of Commons Social Services Committee, *Minimum Income: Memoranda Laid before the Committee*, HC 579, London: HMSO.

23 C Booth, 1971, *Charles Booth's London*, Harmondsworth: Penguin, p 93.

24 *Ibid.* pp 54–5.

25 M Desai, 1986, 'Drawing the line: on defining the poverty threshold', in P Golding (ed.) *Excluding the Poor*, London: Child Poverty Action Group.

26 D Piachaud, 1987, 'Problems in the definitions and measurement of poverty', *Journal of Social Policy* **16**(2) pp 161–3 .

27 See M Wynn, 1970, *Family Policy*, Harmondsworth: Penguin.

28 H Land, 1983, 'Poverty and gender', in M Brown (ed.) *The Structure of Disadvantage*, London: Heinemann.

29 C Glendinning and S Baldwin, 1988, 'The costs of disability', in R Walker and G Parker (eds) *Money Matters*, London: Sage.

30 See H Parker, 1979, 'Why we should work out family budgets', *New Society* 24 May pp 450–1; D Piachaud, 1987, 'Problems in the definitions and measurement of poverty', *Journal of Social Policy* **16**(2) pp 161–3; K Cooke and S Baldwin, 1984, *How Much is Enough?*, London: Family Policy Studies Centre.

31 B van Praag, A Hagenaars and H van Weeren, 1980, *Poverty in Europe*, Leyden: University of Leyden; T M Smeeding, M O'Higgins and L Rainwater (eds), 1990, *Poverty, Inequality and Income Distribution in Comparative Perspective*, New York: Harvester Wheatsheaf.
32 D Rae, 1981, *Equalities*, Cambridge, MA: Harvard University Press.
33 R Walker, R Lawson and P Townsend (eds), 1984, *Responses to Poverty: Lessons from Europe*, London: Heinemann.
34 R Teekens and A Zaidi, 1990, 'Relative and absolute poverty in the European Community', in R Teekens and B van Praag (eds) *Analysing Poverty in the European Community* (Eurostat News Special Edition 1-1990), Luxembourg: European Communities.
35 World Bank, 1990, *World Development Report 1990*, Oxford: Oxford University Press. The figures are based on 1985.
36 R Teekens and A Zaidi, 1990, 'Relative and absolute poverty in the European Community', in R Teekens and B van Praag (eds) *Analysing Poverty in the European Community* (Eurostat News Special Edition 1-1990), Luxembourg: European Communities.
37 J Veit-Wilson, 1989, 'Memorandum . . .', in House of Commons Social Services Committee, *Minimum Income: Memoranda Laid before the Committee*, HC 579, London: HMSO, p 79.
38 This is apparently the means of establishing the poverty line in Canada: A B Atkinson, 1990, *Comparing Poverty Rates Internationally*, London: Suntory-Toyota International Centre for Economics and Related Disciplines, p 10.
39 A B Atkinson, 1990, 'Poverty, statistics and progress in Europe', in R Teekins and B van Praag (eds) *Analysing Poverty in the European Community* (Eurostat News Special Edition 1-1990), Luxembourg: European Communities.

5 UNDERSTANDING POVERTY: DESCRIBING THE CIRCUMSTANCES OF POOR PEOPLE

1 T M Smeeding, M O'Higgins and L Rainwater (eds), 1990, *Poverty, Inequality and Income Distribution in Comparative Perspective*, New York: Harvester Wheatsheaf, p 65.
2 Department of Social Security, 1990, *Households below Average Income: A Statistical Analysis 1981–1987*, London: Government Statistical Service; C Oppenheim, 1990, *Poverty: The Facts*, London: Child Poverty Action Group, pp 29–30.
3 C Oppenheim, 1990, *Poverty: The Facts*, London: Child Poverty Action Group, p 20.
4 Central Statistical Office, 1991, *Annual Abstract of Statistics 1991*, London: HMSO, p 61.
5 S Clayton, 1984, 'Elderly women and the challenge of inequality', in D B Bromley (ed.) *Gerontology: Social and Behavioural Perspectives*, London: Croom Helm.
6 J Martin, H Melzter and D Elliot, 1988, *The Prevalence of Disability among Adults*, London: Office of Population Censuses and Surveys/HMSO.
7 J Martin and A White, 1989, *The Financial Circumstances of Disabled Adults Living in Private Households*, London: Office of Population Censuses and Surveys/HMSO, Chapter 3.

8 *Ibid.* Chapter 4.
9 *Ibid.* , p xviii.
10 W Beveridge, 1944, *Full Employment in a Free Society*, London: Allen and Unwin, p 75.
11 *Ibid.* p 409.
12 *Ibid.* pp 408–9.
13 See J Millar, 1989, *Poverty and the Lone Parent Family*, Aldershot: Avebury.
14 See T Stark, 1988, *A New A–Z of Income and Wealth*, London: Fabian Society, p 18. More up-to-date information is available in Department of Employment's annual *New Earnings Survey* (London: Department of Employment) but it is difficult to interpret.
15 R Layard, D Piachaud and M Stewart, 1978, *The Causes of Poverty*, London: HMSO.
16 J Millar and C Glendinning, 1989, 'Gender and poverty', *Journal of Social Policy* **18**(3) pp 363–81.
17 H Land, 1983, 'Poverty and gender', in M Brown (ed.) *The Structure of Disadvantage*, London: Heinemann; J Millar and C Glendinning, 1987, 'Invisible women, invisible poverty', in C Glendinning and J Millar (eds) *Women and Poverty in Britain*, Brighton: Wheatsheaf.
18 I Garfinkel and S McLanahan, 1988, 'The feminisation of poverty', in D Tomaskovic-Devey (ed.) *Poverty and Social Welfare in the United States*, Boulder: Westview Press.
19 J Millar and C Glendinning, 1989, 'Gender and poverty', *Journal of Social Policy* **18**(3) pp 363–81.
20 V George, 1988, *Wealth, Poverty and Starvation*, Hemel Hempstead: Wheatsheaf Books, p 101.
21 I Garfinkel and S McLanahan, 1988, 'The feminisation of poverty', in D Tomaskovic-Devey (ed.) *Poverty and Social Welfare in the United States*, Boulder: Westview Press, p 10.
22 G Vaux and D Divine, 1988, 'Race and poverty', in S Becker and S Macpherson (eds) *Public Issues, Private Pain*, London: Insight, p 208.
23 C Brown, 1984, *Black and White Britain*, London: Heinemann, p 293.
24 Office of Population Censuses and Surveys, 1991, *General Household Survey 1989*, London: HMSO, p 42.
25 D J Smith, 1977, *Racial Disadvantage in Britain*, Harmondsworth: Penguin, p 234.
26 M Bayley, 1973, *Mental Handicap and Community Care*, London: Routledge and Kegan Paul.
27 C R Blacker (ed.), 1952, *Problem Families: Five Enquiries*, London: Eugenics Society.
28 D Clapham and K Kintrea, 1986, 'Rationing, choice and constraint', *Journal of Social Policy* **15**(1).
29 M Flynn, P Flynn and N Mellor, 1972, 'Social malaise research: a study in Liverpool', in Central Statistical Office *Social Trends* **3**, London: HMSO.
30 S Holtermann, 1975, 'Areas of deprivation in Great Britain', in Central Statistical Office *Social Trends* **6** pp 43–8, London: HMSO.
31 M Carley, 1981, *Social Measurement and Social Indicators*, London: Allen and Unwin, p 146.
32 J Floud, A H Halsey and F M Martin, 1956, *Social Class and Educational Opportunity*, London: Heinemann.
33 Central Advisory Committee for Education (England), 1954, *Early Leaving*,

London: HMSO; Central Advisory Committee for Education (England), 1959, *15 to 18*, London: HMSO.

34 Central Advisory Committee for Education (England), 1963, *Half Our Future* (the Newsom Report), London: HMSO.

35 See Office of Population Censuses and Surveys, 1990, *General Household Survey 1988*, London: HMSO, p 157.

36 J W B Douglas, 1964, *The Home and the School*, London: MacGibbon and Kee.

37 Department of Health and Social Security, 1980, *Inequalities in Health*, London: HMSO.

6 CAUSES AND RESPONSES

1 Although I have not followed his framework directly, I am indebted to R Holman, 1978, *Poverty: Explanations of Social Deprivation*, Oxford: Martin Robertson.

2 C Oppenheim, 1990, *Poverty: The Facts*, London: Child Poverty Action Group, p 124.

3 See, for example, D Anderson, 1990, 'Making up the numbers: a poor man's guide to the poverty game', *Sunday Times* 29 July.

4 J Bowlby, 1952, *Maternal Care and Mental Health*, Geneva: WHO.

5 Cmnd 2742, 1965, *The Child, the Family and the Young Offender*, London: HMSO.

6 Cited R Holman, 1978, *Poverty: Explanations of Social Deprivation*, Oxford: Martin Robertson, p 117.

7 M Brown and N Madge, 1982, *Despite the Welfare State*, London: Heinemann.

8 See I Kolvin, F J W Miller, D M Scott, S R M Gatzanis and M Fleeting, 1990, *Continuities of Deprivation?: The Newcastle 1000 Family Study*, Aldershot: Avebury.

9 O Lewis, 1964, *The Children of Sanchez*, Harmondsworth: Penguin; O Lewis, 1968, *La Vida*, London: Panther.

10 O Lewis, 1968, *La Vida*, London: Panther, p 53.

11 C Valentine, 1968, *Culture and Poverty*, Chicago: University of Chicago Press.

12 A Leeds, 1971, 'The concept of the "culture of poverty"', in E B Leacock (ed.) *The Culture of Poverty: A Critique*, New York: Simon and Schuster.

13 C Valentine, 1968, *Culture and Poverty*, Chicago: University of Chicago Press, p 144.

14 K Auletta, 1983, *The Underclass*, New York: Vintage Books; C Murray, 1989, 'Underclass', *Sunday Times Magazine* 26 November pp 26–46.

15 K Auletta, 1983, *The Underclass*, New York: Vintage Books, p 21.

16 C Murray, 1989, 'Underclass', *Sunday Times Magazine* 26 November, p 26.

17 J MacNicol, 1987, 'In pursuit of the underclass', *Journal of Social Policy* **16**(3) pp 293–318.

18 P Spicker, 1984, *Stigma and Social Welfare*, Beckenham: Croom Helm.

19 M Rokeach and S Parker, 1970, 'Values as social indicators of poverty and race relations in the United States', *The Annals* **388** pp 97–111 .

20 H Rodman, 1971, *Lower Class Families*, Oxford: Oxford University Press.

21 J Higgins, 1978, *The Poverty Business in Britain and America*, Oxford: Blackwell/Robertson.

22 R M Titmuss, 1968, *Commitment to Welfare*, London: Allen and Unwin, Chapter 11.

23 See R Holman, 1978, *Poverty: Explanations of Social Deprivation*, Oxford: Martin Robertson.
24 S Lukes, 1978, 'Power and authority', in T Bottomore and R Nisbet (eds) *A History of Sociological Analysis*, London: Heinemann.
25 P Spicker, 1988, *Principles of Social Welfare*, London: Routledge, Chapter 8.
26 European Community, 1989, *Poverty*, ESC–89–013–EN Brussels: Economic and Social Consultative Assembly of the European Communities, p 7.
27 R A Pinker, 1971, *Social Theory and Social Policy*, London: Heinemann.
28 P Spicker, 1984, *Stigma and Social Welfare*, Beckenham: Croom Helm.
29 R Lister, 1990, *The Exclusive Society*, London: Child Poverty Action Group.
30 P Spicker, 1984, *Stigma and Social Welfare*, Beckenham: Croom Helm, Chapter 5.
31 M Weber, 1967, 'The development of caste', in R Bendix and S M Lipset (eds) *Class, Status and Power*, 2nd edn, London: Routledge and Kegan Paul, pp 31–2.
32 R Lister, 1990, *The Exclusive Society*, London: Child Poverty Action Group; C Oppenheim, 1990, *Poverty: The Facts*, London: Child Poverty Action Group, p 15.
33 D Matza, 1967, 'The disreputable poor', in R Bendix and S M Lipset (eds), *Class, Status and Power*, 2nd edn, London: Routledge and Kegan Paul.
34 See, for example, D Marsden, 1973, *Mothers Alone*, Harmondsworth: Penguin, pp 136–8, 175–6; or Titmuss and Townsend, cited J MacNicol, 1987, 'In pursuit of the underclass', *Journal of Social Policy* **16**(3) p 300.
35 This is the sense in which the term is used in F Field, 1989, *Losing Out*, Oxford: Blackwell.
36 G Simmel, 1908, 'The poor', in *Social Problems* 1965 **13** pp 118–39.
37 D Matza and H Miller, 1976, 'Poverty and proletariat', in R K Merton and R Nisbet (eds) *Contemporary Social Problems*, 4th edn, New York: Harcourt Brace Jovanovich, pp 661–2.
38 W G Runciman, 1963, *Social Science and Political Theory*, Cambridge: Cambridge University Press.
39 M Loney, 1983, *Community against Government*, London: Heinemann.
40 P Spicker, 1988, *Principles of Social Welfare*, London: Routledge, Chapter 12.

7 STRATEGIES FOR THE RELIEF OF POVERTY

1 H Wolman, 1987, *Help with Housing Costs*, London: Policy Studies Institute.
2 World Bank, 1990, *World Development Report 1990*, Oxford: Oxford University Press, p 92.
3 See, for example, C Murray, 1984, *Losing Ground*, New York: Basic Books.
4 P Spicker, 1988, *Principles of Social Welfare*, London: Routledge, Chapter 9.
5 J Le Grand, 1982, *The Strategy of Equality*, London: Allen and Unwin.
6 M Reddin, 1970, 'Universality versus selectivity', in W A Robson and B Crick (eds) *The Future of the Social Services*, Harmondsworth: Penguin.
7 K Jones, J Brown and J Bradshaw, 1978, *Issues in Social Policy*, London: Routledge and Kegan Paul, p 44.
8 A W Dilnot, J Kay and C N Morris, 1984, *The Reform of Social Security*, Oxford: Clarendon Press, Chapter 2.
9 P Spicker, 1984, *Stigma and Social Welfare*, Beckenham: Croom Helm.
10 A Seldon, 1977, *Charge!*, London: Temple Smith.

11 International Council on Social Welfare, 1969, *Social Welfare and Human Rights*, New York: Columbia University Press, p 150.
12 M Luther, 1536, 'Ordinance for a common chest', in F R Salter (ed.) *Some Early Tracts on Poor Relief*, London: Methuen, 1926.
13 B Abel-Smith, 1964, *The Hospitals 1800–1948*, London: Heinemann.
14 U Zwingli, 1525, 'Ordinance and articles touching almsgiving', in F R Salter (ed.) *Some Early Tracts on Poor Relief*, London: Methuen, 1926.
15 Cited M Bruce, 1976, *The Rise of the Welfare State*, London: Weidenfeld and Nicolson, p 119.
16 H E Raynes, 1960, *Social Security in Britain*, Westport, CT: Greenwood Press.
17 *Picture Post*, 1941, 'A plan for Britain', 4 January.
18 International Labour Office, 1984, *Into the Twenty-first Century: The Development of Social Security*, Geneva: International Labour Office.
19 B Barry, 1990, 'The welfare state versus the relief of poverty', in A Ware and R E Goodin (eds) *Needs and Welfare*, London: Sage.

8 THE AIMS OF SOCIAL SECURITY

1 R M Titmuss, 1955, 'The social division of welfare', in *Essays on 'the Welfare State'*, 2nd edn, London: George Allen and Unwin.
2 I have, for example, applied most of them elsewhere to housing: P Spicker, 1989, *Social Housing and the Social Services*, London: Longmans.
3 R M Titmuss, 1974, *Social Policy: An Introduction*, London: Allen and Unwin.
4 J Baker, 1979, 'Social conscience and social policy', *Journal of Social Policy* **8**(2) pp 177–206.
5 P Squires, 1991, *Anti-social Policy*, Brighton: Harvester Wheatsheaf.
6 G Pascall, 1986, *Social Policy: A Feminist Analysis*, London: Tavistock.
7 See, for example, F Williams, 1989, *Social Policy: A Critical Introduction*, Cambridge: Polity Press.
8 P Spicker, 1988, *Principles of Social Welfare*, London: Routledge.
9 See, for example, P Corrigan and P Leonard, 1978, *Social Work under Capitalism*, London: Macmillan.
10 L Dominelli, 1990, *Women across Continents*, Brighton: Harvester Wheatsheaf, p 66.
11 *Ibid.* p 68.
12 N Furniss and T Tilton, 1979, *The Case for the Welfare State*, Bloomington: Indiana University Press, p 7.
13 P Gordon and A Newnham, 1985, *Passport to Benefits*, London: Child Poverty Action Group.
14 I Piliavin and A Gross, 1977, 'The effects of separation of services and income maintenance on AFDC recipients', *Social Service Review* **51**(3) pp 389–406.
15 See P Spicker, 1991, 'Solidarity', in G Room (ed.) *Towards a European Welfare State?*, Bristol: SAUS.
16 E Alfarandi, 1989, *Action et Aide Sociales*, 4th edn, Paris: Dalloz, p 73.
17 K Boulding, 1973, 'The boundaries of social policy', in W D Birrell, P A R Hillyard, A S Murie and D Roche (eds) *Social Administration*, Harmondsworth: Penguin, p 192.
18 *Social Europe, 1989, The Social Aspects of the Internal Market*, July, Brussels: European Commission, p 70.

19 H Wolman, 1987, *Help with Housing Costs*, London: Policy Studies Institute, Chapter 3.
20 B Barry, 1990, 'The welfare state versus the relief of poverty', in A Ware and R Goodin (eds) *Needs and Welfare*, London: Sage.
21 International Labour Office, 1984, *Into the Twenty-first Century: The Development of Social Security*, Geneva: International Labour Office, p 99.
22 N Barr, 1991, 'The objectives and attainments of pension schemes', in T Wilson and D Wilson (eds) *The State and Social Welfare*, London: Longmans, p 144.
23 M Hill, 1990, *Social Security in Britain*, London: Edward Elgar, p 143.
24 See, for example, L Burghes, 1980, *So Who's Better Off on the Dole?*, London: Child Poverty Action Group, which was written before the reforms to prevent the supposed problem.
25 A Dilnot and M Kell, 1989. 'Male unemployment and women's work', in A Dilnot and I Walker (eds) *The Economics of Social Security*, Oxford: Oxford University Press.
26 S G Checkland and E Checkland (eds), 1974, *The Poor Law Report of 1834*, Harmondsworth: Penguin .
27 J R Poynter, 1969, *Society and Pauperism*, London: Routledge and Kegan Paul.
28 A McAuley, 1979, *Economic Welfare in the Soviet Union*, Hemel Hempstead: George Allen and Unwin, pp 300–1, 316.
29 M Phillips, 1981, 'Favourable family impact as an object of means support policy', in P G Brown *et al.* (eds) *Income Support*, Totowa, NJ: Rowman and Littlefield.
30 See P Gordon and A Newnham, 1985, *Passport to Benefits*, London: Child Poverty Action Group.
31 J Baker, 1986, 'Comparing national priorities: family and population policy in Britain and France', *Journal of Social Policy* **15**(4) pp 421–42.

9 PATTERNS OF SOCIAL SECURITY PROVISION

1 W Beveridge, 1942, *Social Insurance and Allied Services* Cmnd 6404, London: HMSO.
2 See S MacGregor, 1981, *The Politics of Poverty*, London: Longmans.
3 Cmnd 5116, 1972, *Proposals for a Tax Credit System*, London: HMSO.
4 Department of Health and Social Security, 1978, *Social Assistance*, London: Department of Health and Social Security.
5 Associated with L Bourgeois, 1902, *Solidarité*, 2nd edn, Paris: Armand Colin.
6 J J Dupeyroux, 1989, *Droit de la Securité Sociale*, 4th edn, Paris: Dalloz, p 290.
7 P Spicker, 1991, 'Solidarity', in G Room (ed.) *Towards a European Welfare State?*, Bristol: SAUS.
8 G Spitaels, D Klaric, S Lambert and G Lefevere, 1971, *Le Salaire Indirect et la Couverture des Besoins Sociaux, Vol. III: La Comparaison Internationale*, Brussels: Université Libre de Bruxelles, p 45.
9 J Baker, 1986, 'Comparing national priorities: family and population policy in Britain and France', *Journal of Social Policy* **15**(4) pp 421–42.
10 R Talmy, 1962, *Histoire du Mouvement Familial en France 1896–1939*, Paris: Union Nationale des Caisses d'Allocations Familiales.
11 See E Alfarandi, 1989, *Action et Aide Sociales*, 4th edn, Paris: Dalloz.
12 C Flockton and E Kofman, 1989, *France*, London: Paul Chapman, p 40.

13 E Mossé, 1985, *Les Riches et les Pauvres*, Paris: Editions du Seuil.
14 M Collins, 1990, 'A guaranteed minimum income for France?', *Social Policy and Administration* **24**(2) pp 120–4.
15 *The Federalist Papers, 1787–8*, New York: New American Library, 1961.
16 G M Klass, 1985, 'Explaining America and the welfare state', *British Journal of Political Science* **15** pp 427–50.
17 P Smith and B Wolfe, 1990, 'Methodological issues in the international comparability of poverty: an analysis of the United States', in R Teekens and B van Praag (eds) *Analysing Poverty in the European Community*, Luxembourg: European Communities.
18 R Moffitt and A Rangarajan, 1989, 'The effect of transfer programmes on work effort and human capital formation', in A Dilnot and I Walker (eds) *The Economics of Social Security*, Oxford: Oxford University Press, p 117.
19 L Morris, 1991, *Social Security Provision for the Unemployed*, London: HMSO, p 108.
20 W S Cohen and J Berman, 1952, 'Safeguarding the disclosure of public assistance records', *Social Service Review* **26** pp 229–34.
21 K Ogborn, 1986, *Workfare in America*, Canberra: Social Security Review; J Handler and Y Hasenfeld, 1991, *The Moral Construction of Poverty*, London: Sage.
22 N Glazer, 1986, 'Welfare and "welfare" in America', in R Rose and R Shiratori (eds) *The Welfare State East and West*, Oxford: Oxford University Press, p 65.
23 Cited D Critchlow and E Hawley, 1989, *Poverty and Public Policy in Modern America*, Chicago: Dorsey, p 287.
24 C Murray, 1984, *Losing Ground*, New York: Basic Books, pp 228–9.
25 S Eisenstadt, 1986, 'The Israeli welfare system', in R Rose and R Shiratori (eds) *The Welfare State East and West*, Oxford: Oxford University Press, p 159.
26 A Doron and R Kramer, 1975, 'Ideology, programme and organisational factors in public assistance: the case of Israel', *Journal of Social Policy* **5**(2) pp 131–49.
27 R A Cnaan, 1987, 'The evolution of Israel's welfare state', in R Friedman, N Gilbert and M Sherer (eds) *Modern Welfare States*, Brighton: Wheatsheaf, p 201.
28 H J Karger and M Monnichendam, 1991, 'The radical right and social welfare in Israel', in H Glennerster and J Midgley (eds) *The Radical Right and the Welfare State*, Hemel Hempstead: Harvester Wheatsheaf.
29 D Macarov, 1987, 'Israel', in J Dixon (ed.) *Social Welfare in the Middle East*, Beckenham: Croom Helm, pp 46–50.
30 R A Cnaan, 1987, 'The evolution of Israel's welfare state', in R Friedman, N Gilbert and M Sherer (eds) *Modern Welfare States*, Brighton: Wheatsheaf, p 197.
31 A Doron, 1985, 'The Israeli welfare state at crossroads', *Journal of Social Policy* **14**(4) pp 513–25.
32 A Doron, 1991, 'Social security in Israel in transition', draft paper: personal communication.
33 W Zapf, 1986, 'Development, structure and prospects of the German Social State', in R Rose and R Shiratori (eds) *The Welfare State East and West*, Oxford: Oxford University Press, p 132.
34 A J Heidenheimer, H Heclo and C Adams, 1983, *Comparative Public Policy*, New York: St Martin's Press, p 215.
35 G V Rimlinger, 1971, *Welfare Policy and Industrialisation in Europe, America and Russia*, New York: John Wiley, Chapter 5.
36 Cited S Mangen, 1991, 'Social policy, the radical right and the German welfare

state', in H Glennerster and J Midgley (eds) *The Radical Right and the Welfare State*, Hemel Hempstead: Harvester Wheatsheaf.

37 D Jarré, 1991, 'Subsidiarity in social services in Germany', *Social Policy and Administration* **25**(3) pp 211–17.

38 See P Spicker, 1991, 'The principle of subsidiarity and the social policy of the European Community', *Journal of European Social Policy* **1**(1).

39 C Jones, 1986, *Patterns of Social Policy*, London: Tavistock, pp 32 ff.

40 R Lawson, 1980, 'Poverty and inequality in West Germany', in V George and R Lawson (eds) *Poverty and Inequality in Common Market Countries*, London: Routledge and Kegan Paul.

41 M Gordon, 1988, *Social Security in Industrial Countries*, Cambridge: Cambridge University Press, pp 257–9.

42 R Mitton, P Wilmott and P Wilmott, 1983, *Unemployment, Poverty and Social Policy in Europe*, London: Bedford Square Press, p 72.

43 K Furmaniak, 1984, 'West Germany', in R Walker, R Lawson and P Townsend (eds) *Responses to Poverty: Lessons from Europe*, London: Heinemann.

44 R Hauser and P Semerau, 1990, 'Trends in poverty and low income in the Federal Republic of Germany 1962/3–1987', in R Teekens and B van Praag (eds) *Analysing Poverty in the European Community*, Luxembourg: European Communities.

45 G Adam, U Becher and E Kern, 1980, *EEC Pilot Project Projecktverbund Obdachlosenarbeit Duisburg/Essen*, Duisburg: Institut für Sozialarbeit und Sozialpaedagogik.

46 G Room, 1990, *New Poverty in the European Community*, London: Macmillan, Chapters 1 and 2.

47 Working Group on Wealth and Poverty in Germany, Evangelische Fachhochschule Rheinland-Westfalen-Lippe: found by my colleague Richard Freeman in Frankfurter Rundschau, 25.5.90.

48 B van Praag, A Hagenaars and H van Weeren, 1980, *Poverty in Europe*, Leyden: University of Leyden, p 552.

49 S Leibfried and I Ostner, 1991, 'The particularism of West German welfare capitalism: the case of women's social security', in M Adler, C Bell, J Clasen and A Sinfield (eds) *The Sociology of Social Security*, Edinburgh: Edinburgh University Press.

50 R Hauser and P Semerau, 1990, 'Trends in poverty and low income in the Federal Republic of Germany 1962/3–1987', in R Teekens and B van Praag (eds) *Analysing Poverty in the European Community*, Luxembourg: European Communities, p 329.

51 E Allardt, 1986, 'The civic conception of the welfare state in Scandinavia', in R Rose and R Shiratori (eds) *The Welfare State East and West*, Oxford: Oxford University Press, p 108.

52 H Heclo, 1974, *Modern Social Politics in Britain and Sweden*, New Haven: Yale University Press, Chapter 6.

53 D Wilson, 1979, *The Welfare State in Sweden*, London: Heinemann.

54 R Mishra, 1990, *The Welfare State in Capitalist Society*, New York: Harvester Wheatsheaf, Chapter 3.

55 S Ringen, 1989, *The Possibility of Politics*, Oxford: Clarendon Press, p 13.

56 R Mishra, 1990, *The Welfare State in Capitalist Society*, New York: Harvester Wheatsheaf, p 58.

57 Cited M Chakrabarti, 1987, 'Social welfare provision in Sweden', in R Ford and M Chakrabarti (eds) *Welfare Abroad*, Edinburgh: Scottish Academic Press, p 145.

58 Cited K Kvist and G Agren, 1979, 'Social democracy in the seventies', in J Fry (ed.) *Limits of the Welfare State: Critical Views on Post-war Sweden*, Farnborough: Saxon House, p 34.
59 D Robinson, 1972, *Solidaristic Wage Policy in Sweden*, Paris: Organisation for Economic Co-operation and Development.
60 R M Titmuss, 1974, *Social Policy: An Introduction*, London: Allen and Unwin.
61 S Olsson, 1987, 'Towards a transformation of the Swedish Welfare State', in R Friedman, N Gilbert and M Sherer (eds) *Modern Welfare States*, Brighton: Wheatsheaf.
62 D Wilson, 1979, 'The Swedish dream grows tired', *New Society* 6 December pp 544–6.
63 A Gould, 1988, *Conflict and Control in Welfare Policy: The Swedish Experience*, London: Longmans, Chapter 6.
64 S Marklund, 1991, 'Lessons from the recession in Scandinavia 1975–85', in M Adler, C Bell, J Clasen and A Sinfield (eds) *The Sociology of Social Security*, Edinburgh: Edinburgh University Press.
65 R M Titmuss, 1974, *Social Policy: An Introduction*, London: Allen and Unwin.
66 J Palme, 1990, 'Models of old-age pensions', in A Ware and R E Goodin (eds) *Needs and Welfare*, London: Sage.

10 SOCIAL SECURITY BENEFITS

1 See G A Ritter, 1983, *Social Welfare in Germany and Britain*, Leamington Spa: Berg.
2 J Habermas, 1976, *Legitimation Crisis*, London: Heinemann; C Offe, 1984, *Contradictions of the Welfare State*, London: Hutchinson .
3 K Williams and R Williams, 1987, *A Beveridge Reader*, London: George Allen and Unwin, p 39.
4 W Beveridge, 1942, *Social Insurance and Allied Services*, Cmnd 6404, London: HMSO, para 23.
5 A W Dilnot, J Kay and C N Morris, 1984, *The Reform of Social Security*, Oxford: Clarendon Press, p 34.
6 G Fimister and R Lister, 1980, *Social Security: The Case against Contribution Tests*, London: Child Poverty Action Group.
7 M A Jones, 1980, *The Australian Welfare State*, Sydney: Allen and Unwin.
8 R Mitton, P Wilmott and P Wilmott, 1983, *Unemployment, Poverty and Social Policy in Europe*, London: Bedford Square Press, p 91.
9 J-M Belorgey, 1988, *La Gauche et les Pauvres*, Paris: Syros/Alternatives, p 52.
10 Cited R Walker, 1986, 'Aspects of administration', in P Kemp (ed.) *The Future of Housing Benefits*, Glasgow: Centre for Housing Research, p 39.
11 See also P Kemp, 1984, *The Cost of Chaos*, London: SHAC; R Walker and A Hedges, 1985, *Housing Benefit: The Experience of Implementation*, London: Housing Centre Trust.
12 Cmnd 9702, 1986, *The Government's Expenditure Plans 1986–7 to 1988–9*, Vol 2, London: HM Treasury, p 240.
13 J-M Belorgey, 1988, *La Gauche et les Pauvres*, Paris: Syros/Alternatives, pp 53–4.
14 D Piachaud, 1973, 'Taxation and poverty', in W Robson and B Crick (eds) *Taxation Policy*, Harmondsworth: Penguin.

15 S Kerr, 1983, *Making Ends Meet*, London: Bedford Square Press.

16 C Davies and J Ritchie, 1988, *Tipping the Balance: A Study of Non Take-up of Benefits in an Inner City Area*, London: HMSO.

17 B Weisbrod, 1970, *On the Stigma Effect and the Demand for Welfare Programmes*, Madison, WI: University of Wisconsin Institute for Research on Poverty.

18 See P Spicker, 1984, *Stigma and Social Welfare*, Beckenham: Croom Helm.

19 Cmnd 9519, 1985, *Reform of Social Security*, Vol 3, p 79.

20 Cmnd 9702–II, 1985, *Reform of Social Security*, Vol 3, p 242. Information released while the book was in press states that some claims for disability benefits, including Invalid Care Allowance, are seriously delayed: P Wynn-Davis, 'DSS taking two years to pay some war pensions', *Independent* 10.6. 92, p9.

21 J-M Belorgey, 1988, *La Gauche et les Pauvres*, Paris: Syros/Alternatives, p 53.

22 J Pahl, 1985, 'Who benefits from Child Benefit?', *New Society* 25 April pp 117–19.

23 B Cass, 1983, 'Redistribution to children and to mothers', in C Baldock and B Cass (eds) *Women, Social Welfare and the State*, Sydney: Allen and Unwin, p 84.

24 See, for example, A B Atkinson, 1969, *Poverty in Britain and the Reform of Social Security*, Cambridge: Cambridge University Press; B Jordan, 1984, 'The social wage: a right for all', *New Society* 26 April pp 143–4; P Esam, R Good and R Middleton, 1985, *Who's to Benefit?*, London: Verso; H Parker, 1988, *Instead of the* Dole, London: Routledge.

25 Cited D Critchlow and E Hawley, 1989, *Poverty and Public Policy in Modern America*, Chicago: Dorsey, p 93.

26 V Fry, S Smith and S White, 1990, *Pensioners and the Public Purse*, London: Institute for Fiscal Studies, p 64.

27 A B Atkinson, 1991, *The Development of State Pensions in the United Kingdom*, London: LSE Suntory-Toyota International Centre for Economics and Related Disciplines, p 34.

11 THE PRINCIPAL CONTINGENCIES

1 See J Creedy and R Disney, 1989, 'The new pension scheme in Britain', in A Dilnot and I Walker (eds) *The Economics of Social Security*, Oxford: Oxford University Press.

2 See P Spicker, 1988, *Principles of Social Welfare*, London: Routledge, Chapter 11.

3 See P Knightley, H Evans, E Potter and M Wallace, 1980, *Suffer the Children: The Story of Thalidomide*, London: Futura.

4 B Easton, 1980, *Social Policy and the Welfare State in New Zealand*, London: Allen and Unwin.

5 Cmnd 7054, 1978, *Report of the Royal Commission on Civil Liability for Personal Injury*, London: HMSO.

6 K Williams and R Williams, 1987, *A Beveridge Reader*, London: George Allen and Unwin, p 209.

7 See R Mishra, 1990, *The Welfare State in Capitalist Society*, New York: Harvester Wheatsheaf.

8 J C Brown, 1989, *Why Don't They Go To Work?: Mothers on Benefit*, London: HMSO, pp 64–72.
9 *Ibid.* pp 52–6.
10 Department of Employment and Productivity, 1969, *A National Minimum Wage*, London: HMSO; see also S Bazen, 1985, *Low Wages, Family Circum- stances and Minimum Wage Legislation*, London: Policy Studies Institute.
11 V J Burke and V Burke, 1974, *Nixon's Good Deed*, New York: Columbia University Press.
12 A Corden, 1987, *Disappointed Applicants*, Aldershot: Avebury.
13 A Corden and P Craig, 1991, *Perceptions of Family Credit*, London: HMSO.
14 V J Burke and V Burke, 1974, *Nixon's Good Deed*, New York: Columbia University Press.

12 SOCIAL SECURITY SYSTEMS AND THE RELIEF OF POVERTY

1 S Leibfried and I Ostner, 1989, 'The particularism of West German welfare capitalism: the case of women's social security', in M Adler, C Bell, J Clasen and A Sinfield (eds) *The Sociology of Social Security*, Edinburgh: Edinburgh University Press.
2 A B Atkinson, 1989, *Poverty and Social Security*, New York: Harvester Wheatsheaf, Chapter 11.
3 D Mitchell, 1991, *Income Transfers in Ten Welfare States*, Aldershot: Avebury, p 178.
4 T M Smeeding, M O'Higgins and L Rainwater (eds), 1990, *Poverty, Inequality and Income Distribution in Comparative Perspective: The Luxembourg Income Study*, New York: Harvester Wheatsheaf, p 72.
5 H Wilensky, 1975, *The Welfare State and Equality*, Berkeley: University of California Press, Chapter 2.
6 J Barnes and T Srivenkataramana, 1982, 'Ideology and the welfare state: an examination of Wilensky's conclusions', *Social Service Review* **56**(2).
7 P Spicker, 1991, 'Equality versus solidarity', paper presented to the Political Studies Association, April.
8 J Vranken, 1984, 'Anti-poverty policy in Belgium', in J C Brown (ed.) *Anti-poverty Policy in the European Community*, London: Policy Studies Institute.
9 H Wilensky, 1975, *The Welfare State and Equality*, Berkeley: University of California Press; R Mishra, 1981, *Society and Social Policy*, London: Macmillan.
10 R Mitton, P Wilmott and P Wilmott, 1983, *Unemployment, Poverty and Social Policy in Europe*, London: Bedford Square Press, p 55.
11 M A Jones, 1980, *The Australian Welfare State*, Sydney: Allen and Unwin. Saunders claims that the Australian system has subsequently become more 'selective', by which he means more restrictive: see P Saunders, 1991, 'Selectivity and targeting in income support: the Australian experience', *Journal of Social Policy* **20**(3) pp 299–326. By contrast, Mitchell comments that the take-up of benefits in Australia is over 95 per cent: see D Mitchell, 1991, *Income Transfers in Ten Welfare States*, Aldershot: Avebury, pp 190–1.
12 S Tester, 1987, *Social Loans in the Netherlands*, London: Policy Studies Institute.

13 J Allbeson and R Smith, 1984, *We Don't Give Clothing Grants any more*, London: Child Poverty Action Group; Policy Studies Institute, 1984, *The Reform of Supplementary Benefit: Working Papers*, London: Policy Studies Institute.
14 But see J-M Belorgey, 1988, *La Gauche et les Pauvres*, Paris: Syros/Alternatives.
15 A Gould, 1988, *Conflict and Control in Welfare Policy*, London: Longman.
16 R Mitton, P Wilmott and P Wilmott, 1983, *Unemployment, Poverty and Social Policy in Europe*, London: Bedford Square Press, p 55.
17 *Ibid.* pp 64 ff.
18 R M Titmuss, 1968, *Commitment to Welfare*, London: Allen and Unwin, p 122.

Name index

Subject index

THE
NORTHERN COLLEGE
LIBRARY
53686
BARNSLEY